TIKAL

AN ILLUSTRATED HISTORY

THE ANCIENT MAYA CAPITAL

ILLUSTRATED HISTORIES
FROM HIPPOCRENE

Published . . .

Arizona
Patrick Lavin

Celtic World
Patrick Lavin

China
Yong Ho

England
Henry Weisser

France
Lisa Neal

Greece
Tom Stone

Ireland
Henry Weisser

Israel
David C. Gross

Italy
Joseph F. Privitera

Korea
David Rees

Mexico
Michael Burke

Poland
Iwo Cyprian Pogonowski

Poland in World War II
Andrew Hempel

Russia
Joel Carmichael

Spain
Fred James Hill

Tikal
John Montgomery

Forthcoming . . .

Cracow
Zdzislaw Zygulski

Egypt
Fred James Hill

Gypsy World
Atanas Slavov

Jewish World
David Gross

London
Nick Awde & Robert Chester

Moscow
Kathy Murrell

Paris
Elaine Mokhtefi

Portugal
Lisa Neal

Romania
Nicholas Klepper

Sicily
Joseph F. Privitera

Venice
Lisa Neal

Vietnam
Shelton Woods

Wales
Henry Weisser

TIKAL

AN ILLUSTRATED HISTORY

THE ANCIENT MAYA CAPITAL

JOHN MONTGOMERY

HIPPOCRENE BOOKS, INC.
New York

Maps, Photographs, and Illustrations by the Author.

Additional photographs courtesy of Pictures of Record, Inc. and Peter Harrison.

ISBN 0-7818-0853-7

For information, address:
HIPPOCRENE BOOKS, INC.
171 Madison Avenue
New York, NY 10016
www.hippocrenebooks.com

Cataloging-in-Publication data available from the Library of Congress.

Printed in the United States of America.

In memory of

Patricia Solís

And for

Miguel-san, Luís, Clarence, Juanito,

and the guides of Tikal

1979 and 1980

ACKNOWLEDGMENTS

To preserve the narrative flow of the following pages, I have endeavored to keep footnotes and references to a minimum. As a result, much of the technical background and evidence for the history presented here will be found in the extensive bibliography. That being said, I would point out that I draw heavily on the "historical" approach and hypotheses pioneered by Tatiana Proskouriakoff, Clemency Coggins, and Joyce Marcus during the 1960s and 1970s. Much of this work grew out of a reevaluation of their ideas, and generally upholds, reaffirms, and updates many of their original conclusions.

At the same time, the present book incorporates more than forty years of archaeological research conducted by the Guatemalan government and the University Museum of the University of Pennsylvania. No work about Tikal can proceed longer than a few words without incorporating the vital and extensive material brought to light by these projects.

Above all, this work draws on the most recent decipherments in hieroglyphic writing advanced by many different scholars, the foremost of whom include the late Linda Schele, as well as Peter Mathews, David Stuart, and Stephen Houston. Epigraphic research that has shed light on the organization of the Maya state and the development of Classic Period political "alliance blocks" lies at the heart of the present historical reconstruction, a theoretical position advocated primarily by Simon Martin and Nikolai Grube. Their approach has revolutionized the way in which scholars think about Maya warfare, political organization, and the civilization's ultimate collapse. In fact, it remains fair to say that this book could not have gone forward without Simon and Nikolai's special insights.

Numerous individuals have given generously of their time and knowledge to help make this book possible, either directly or indirectly. I wish to thank Barbara MacLeod, Phil Wanyerka, Marc Zender, and Dicey Taylor for their kind and repeated assistance, often at short notice and at crucial moments. Peter Harrison very generously offered the use of his map of the Central Acropolis, his photograph of the North Terrace, and drawings of stucco sculpture from the Central Acropolis. I would especially like to thank Donald Hales for making available his extraordinary archive of photographs of rare and often unpublished artifacts, and for providing access to his notes. Similarly, Justin Kerr contributed invaluable photographs as the basis of some of the drawings to illustrate the text. In an identical spirit, Nancy Hammerslough allowed me to publish photographs of artifacts and key architectural monuments from the Pictures of Record slide sets.

Finally, my long-suffering wife, Mary, and my son and daughter, Robin and Helen, deserve thanks for their extended patience. Any mistakes or misrepresentations of the views of the above-mentioned scholars, or of any other data, remain entirely my own.

TABLE OF CONTENTS

ACKNOWLEDGMENTS   vii

LIST OF ILLUSTRATIONS AND PHOTOGRAPHS   xi

LIST OF MAPS   xiv

INTRODUCTION: Tikal and the Classic Maya   1

PART 1—The Preclassic Period (600 b.c.–a.d. 250)   5

    CHAPTER 1: Beneath the Trees, Beneath the Vines   7

    CHAPTER 2: The Dawn of History   17

PART 2—The Early Classic Period (a.d. 250–448)   29

    CHAPTER 3: Children of Yax Eb' Xook   31

    CHAPTER 4: The Rise of Tikal's Jaguar Dynasty   43

    CHAPTER 5: The Arrival of Strangers   55

    CHAPTER 6: Sky-Born "Ancestor"   79

PART 3—The Middle Classic Period (a.d. 448–682)   91

    CHAPTER 7: The Children of K'an Chitam   93

    CHAPTER 8: *Hubuy Mutul*: The "Downing of Tikal"   105

    CHAPTER 9: The Second Mutul   119

PART 4—THE LATE CLASSIC PERIOD (A.D. 682–909)   139

    CHAPTER 10: His Flint, His Shield: The Life of Jasaw Kaan K'awil   141

    CHAPTER 11: The Successors of Yax Eb' Xook   169

    CHAPTER 12: Enter the Sun: The Last Days of Tikal   195

    CHAPTER 13: Collapse and Abandonment   223

EPILOGUE: APOTHEOSIS   231

APPENDICES

    APPENDIX 1: Tikal's Dynastic Sequence   239

    APPENDIX 2: Chronology   247

REFERENCES   255

INDEX   265

LIST OF ILLUSTRATIONS
AND PHOTOGRAPHS

1. The Tikal Area, looking northwest from Temple IV   9
2. Thatched House   9
3. Interior of the Rain Forest   11
4. Olmec Colossal Head   19
5. Izapa Stela 1   22
6. Lost World Pyramid   26
7. Name Glyph of Foliated Jaguar   34
8. Stela 29, front   35
9. The Tikal Emblem Glyph   37
10. North Acropolis   39
11. Name Glyphs of Yax Eb' Xook   40
12. Name Glyph of Lady Une B'alam   44
13. Name Glyph of Muwan Jol   44
14. Stela 39, front   45
15. Name Glyphs of Chak Tok Ich'aak I   46
16. Portrait of Chak Tok Ich'aak I, from an unprovenanced
   cache vessel lid   47
17. The Palace of Chak Tok Ich'aak I (Structure 5D–46)   48
19. Name Glyph of Nuun Yax Ayin I   57
20. Old Fire God Figurine, Burial 10 *(Courtesy of Pictures
   of Record, Inc.)*   58
21. Pyramid of the Sun, Teotihuacan   61
22. Ring-Stand Bowl, with domed lid painted with the Mexican Rain
   God (Tlaloc), Burial 10 *(Courtesy of Pictures of Record, Inc.)*   64

23. Stela 4, front   65
24. Name Glyph of Siyaj K'ak'   66
25. Tikal Ball Court Marker, now in the National Museum,
        Guatemala City   67
26. Stela 31, right side   70
27. Name Glyph of Jatz'am Ku   71
28. *Lechuzas y Armas* Motif, from an unprovenanced mural
        from Teotihuacan   72
29. Stela 32   75
30. Stela 31, front and sides   78
31. Name Glyphs of Siyaj Kaan K'awil II   81
32. Cylinder Tripod, Burial 48 *(Courtesy of Pictures of Record, Inc.)*   87
33. Stela 1, front   89
34. Name Glyph of K'an Chitam   97
35. Stela 9   99
36. Stela 23, front   101
37. Stela 10, front   103
38. Stela 12, back and right side   104
39. Greenstone Mask, Burial 160   111
40. Name Glyphs of Wak Kaan K'awil   116
41. Name Glyph of E Te'   120
42. K'awil Effigy, Burial 195 *(Courtesy of Pictures of Record, Inc.)*   127
43. Name Glyph of Nuun U Jol Chaak   130
44. The original version of Structure 5D–33, North Acropolis   140
45. Name Glyphs of Jasaw Kaan K'awil   141
46. The "Reviewing Stand" (Structure 5D–43)   146
47. Temple I, Lintel 3   151
48. Temple II   153
49. Altar 5   156
50. Stela 16   157
51. Bound Prisoner (MT39b)   163
52. Canoe Scene (MT38a)   164
53. Chaaks Fishing (MT51b)   165
54. Temple I   167
55. Name Glyphs of Yik'in Kaan K'awil   169
56. Temple IV, Lintel 2   175
57. Temple IV, Lintel 3   176

58. North Facade of the Central Acropolis 178
59. Maler's Palace (Structure 5D–65), with Temple V in background 178
60. Interior of Maler's Palace (Structure 5D–65) 180
61. Five-Story Palace (Structure 5D–52) 182
62. Jade Jaguar, Burial 196 *(Courtesy of Pictures of Record, Inc.)* 185
63. Hummingbird Vase, Burial 196 *(Courtesy of Pictures of Record, Inc.)* 186
64. Temple IV *(Courtesy of Pictures of Record, Inc.)* 191
65. The view east from Temple IV 192
66. Name Glyph of Nuun Yax Ayin II 195
67. Twin Pyramid Complex Q 197
68. Stela 22 198
69. Name Glyph of Dark Sun 206
70. Name Glyphs of Nuun U Jol K'inich 206
71. Temple III, Lintel 2 207
72. The view west from Temple 1 209
73. Name Glyph of Jewel K'awil 215
74. Stela 11 219

LIST OF MAPS

1. Mesoamerica   xv
2. The Maya World   xvi
3. El Petén, Guatemala   xvii
4. Tikal   xviii
5. The Great Plaza and Adjacent Areas   xx

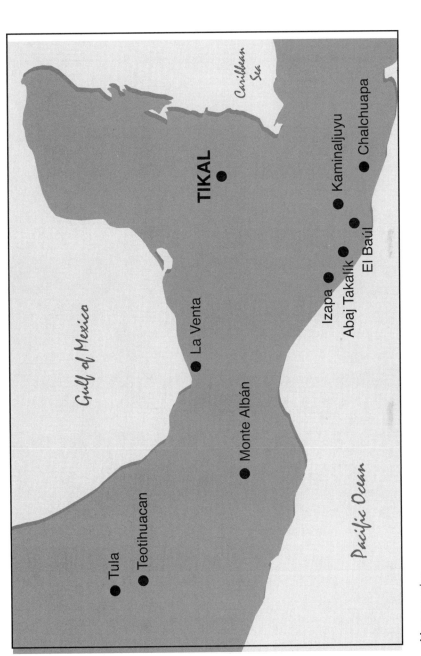

Mesoamerica.

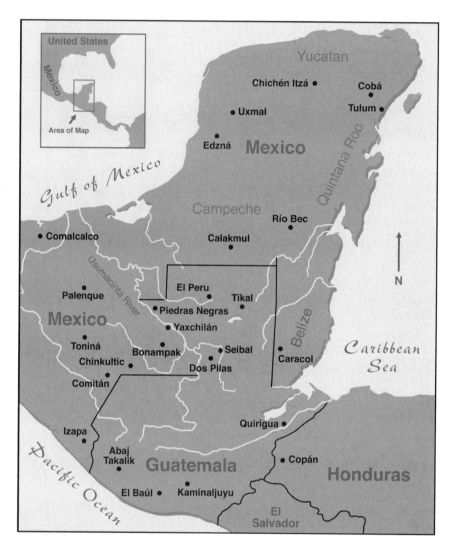

The Maya World.

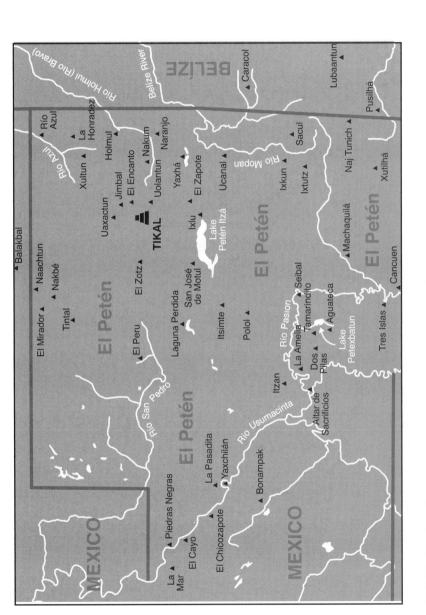

El Petén, Guatemala.

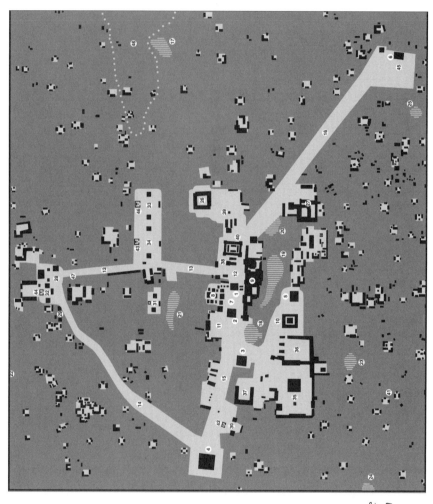

Tikal (based on a map drafted by the University Museum of the University of Pennsylvania).

KEY FOR MAP OF TIKAL

1. Temple I
2. Temple II
3. Temple III
4. Temple IV
5. Temple V
6. Temple VI (Temple of the Inscriptions)
7. Great Plaza
8. North Acropolis
9. Central Acropolis
10. South Acropolis
11. West Plaza
12. East Plaza
13. Maler Causeway
14. Maudslay Causeway
15. Tozzer Causeway
16. Mendez Causeway
17. Tikal Reservoir
18. Temple Reservoir
19. Palace Reservoir
20. Hidden Reservoir
21. Causeway Reservoir
22. Bejucal Reservoir
23. Madeira Reservoir
24. Perdido Reservoir
25. Inscriptions Reservoir
26. Group F
27. Group G
28. Group H (The North Zone)
29. Twin Pyramid Complex M
30. Twin Pyramid Complex N
31. Twin Pyramid Complex O
32. Twin Pyramid Complex P
33. Twin Pyramid Complex Q
34. Twin Pyramid Complex R
35. Lost World Plaza and Pyramid
36. Plaza of the Seven Temples
37. Bat Palace (Palace of the Windows)
38. East Plaza Ball Court
39. Sweat Bath
40. Marketplace
41. Mexican Suburb
42. Stela 16 and Altar 5
43. Stela 19
44. Stela 20 and Altar 8
45. Stela 21
46. Stela 22
47. Rock Sculpture
48. Area of Modern Village, Hotels, Restaurant, and Museums

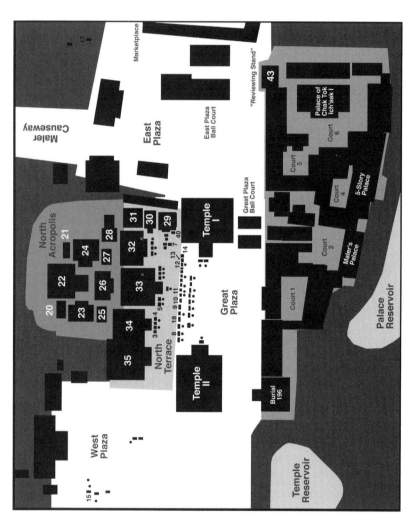

The Great Plaza and Adjacent Areas.

"The desire for political power is the motor which drives men to public action. And power tends to spread over ever larger areas . . . It is also the politically dominant, a small fraction at most times . . . who are largely responsible for the cultural qualities of an age."

—Denys Hay, *Europe in the Fourteenth and Fifteenth Centuries*, 1966

"We can hope, by just thinking in terms of the structure of history, to understand all those glyphs pertaining to history."

—Heinrich Berlin, *The Tablet of the 96 Glyphs*, 1968

INTRODUCTION:
TIKAL AND THE CLASSIC MAYA

The Maya of southeastern Mexico and Central America founded one of the world's great civilizations. Mathematicians, astronomers, and inventors of a hieroglyphic writing system, they came to blanket the land with hundreds of villages, towns, and cities. Prospering where today dense jungle prevails, they were an industrious, hard-working people who built their shrines and monuments without metal tools, without wheeled transport, and without beasts of burden.

Nowhere was this civilization—a culture of cloud-cresting pyramids and labyrinthine palaces, of arena-style ball courts and paved roadways—more spectacular and grandiose than at Tikal. Built continuously from the last centuries B.C. until the late ninth-century A.D. under dozens of great kings, Tikal's monumental towers rear from the jungle-shrouded Department of Petén, Guatemala, in the southern-most extension of the peninsula of Yucatan. Inhabited for at least thirteen hundred years, this mega-metropolis came to encompass some fifty square miles and thirty to one hundred thousand inhabitants—greater in both extent and population than London or Rome of the day.

Tikal embodies everything essential about the lost world of the ancient Maya. Originating during the *Preclassic Period* (*ca.* 600 B.C.–A.D. 250), a formative era when villages mushroomed to become significant towns, Tikal went on to thrive as the first great Maya state of the *Classic Period* (*ca.* A.D. 250–909), the most spectacular era of cultural growth.

The initial phase of this epoch, the *Early Classic Period* (*ca.* A.D. 250–448), saw Tikal's rise to preeminence largely through outside intervention and the subjugation of surrounding districts. After a decline due to outside military pressure during the *Middle Classic Period* (A.D. 448–682), Tikal's resurgence by the *Late Classic Period* (A.D. 682–909) left it the Maya city *par excellence*, boasting one of ancient America's tallest structures, one of the area's most powerful dynasties, and a political region that covered much of the southern Maya lowlands.

Sometime during the *Terminal Classic Period* (after A.D. 830) everything came to a stunning end. Pyramids stopped being built, monuments stopped being carved, and books stopped being painted. The Maya abandoned the city and wandered away. Eventually the jungle reclaimed the massive towers, concealing them until the city's rediscovery by Europeans and its subsequent archaeological apotheosis.

From excavations conducted by the University of Pennsylvania and the Guatemalan government from the late 1950s to the present day, archaeologists have pieced together the history of Tikal's rise and fall. Additional sources help supplement these findings, including accounts written by European witnesses of the Spanish conquest (*ca.* 1540) and myriad objects of art recovered from ancient tombs. Ancient sculptural programs carved on stelae (upright stone shafts) also help shed light on Tikal's past, in addition to sculptured altars and the famed massive wooden lintels, whose visual imagery offers vital clues to the life of the city. Long thought to be indecipherable, hieroglyphic inscriptions and calendar notations on these pieces record details of battles, rituals, political alliances, and a host of additional historical events.

More than any other source, the Maya script identifies who built Tikal, its culture and people, and what qualities of life experience its residents found important. In their own words, the Maya told how Tikal rose on the political landscape of Mesoamerica—the area of Mexico and Central America that gave birth to the high civilizations of the Olmec (*ca.* 1200–600 B.C.), Teotihuacan (*ca.* A.D. 1–700), the Toltecs (A.D. 800–1100), and the Aztecs (A.D. 1350–1521). Tikal's inscriptions outline significant political relationships, both among the Maya themselves and "internationally" between the Maya and other contemporaneous civilizations. In short, few other sites focus so intensely upon themselves and their contemporary world.

This is Tikal's story. From its Preclassic origins to its Terminal Classic demise, from its abandonment to its archaeological rebirth, these chapters recount how Tikal and its inhabitants prospered, declined, and finally faded away. In this sense biography rather than history, the book evokes life in ancient America more than one thousand years ago and recreates a material culture that was forever lost.

Few endeavors of this sort unfold without weaknesses, including a "Western" approach conceived in cultural paradigms very different from those that the Maya envisioned. That hieroglyphic writing significantly overcomes these limitations no one can deny. Yet history remains a personal view, however hard the historian strives towards objectivity. In the end, this portrait remains my own perspective, informed by the latest scholarship, but shaped by the convictions and goals that have emerged from my individual strengths and weaknesses, and from my profound admiration for the people who built Tikal. If I succeed in evoking Tikal's period and time, then my goals have been met.

PART 1

THE PRECLASSIC PERIOD
(600 B.C.–A.D. 250)

CHAPTER 1

BENEATH THE TREES, BENEATH THE VINES

The Yucatan Peninsula thrusts from the isthmus of Central America like an enormous thumb, a nearly featureless limestone shelf ranging in elevation from sea level to several hundred feet. Blanketed under dense tropical forests that give way in the north to dry thorn and scrub brush, much of the region lacks significant geological features, resembling a vast carpet of green from above. Dry three months of the year, the country is deluged under torrential downpours during the remaining rainy season. This is a harsh, formidable region from which it is difficult to eke a living.

No rivers cross the northern districts, and thus potable water is obtainable only from rainwater collection, caverns, or natural sinkholes called *cenotes.* In contrast, two great river systems wind their way through the southern forests, the Pasión and Usumacinta Rivers, mighty bodies of water that drain into the Gulf of Mexico.

The Yucatan Peninsula has always divided important Precolumbian cultural regions, in particular the volcano-studded mountains of southern Guatemala inhabited by highland peoples and the swamp-infested lowlands of Tabasco (and points west) that gave rise during early Preclassic times to the Olmec. Olmec and other early cultures renowned for their jadework no doubt looked to the Motágua River Valley along the peninsula's southeastern margin for raw materials, whereas the people of Central America turned to Olmec culture for inspiration for their programs of art. Later, a steady stream of trade goods would cross the Yucatan—seashells, obsidian for tools, jade, a variety of minerals, jaguar pelts, and the ornamental feathers of exotic birds.

7

To cross this formidable barrier, those who transported goods could choose from a variety of routes. Unable to circumnavigate the Yucatan by sea for lack of ocean-going vessels, and shunning the north for its lack of rivers, traders very early in the history of the region must have crossed the southern lowland river systems to reach the Gulf of Mexico, the primary route westward from the Caribbean Sea. While the Pasión and Usumacinta Rivers greatly facilitated travel, the very early Maya also traveled a key overland passage: from the Bay of Chetumal along the Hondo and Azul Rivers and southwest into the seasonal swamps of the Bajo de Santa Fe. From this point, traders could cross a simple one or two day portage to the Río San Pedro, draining westward into the Usumacinta and thence the Mexican Gulf.

Uplifted in broken limestone ridges between the Caribbean and Gulf of Mexico, the southern overland trade route traversed an area that offered a convenient and defensive vantage point, a rugged escarpment that dominated the local landscape. Abundant, naturally-occurring flint deposits made the region especially attractive, and by 600 B.C. persons of modest means had erected huts of stick walls and thatched roofs along the marshy western perimeter of the *bajo*, with materials for the houses retrieved from the surrounding forests.

They were no doubt simple farmers, the people who settled here. Probably of Maya stock, they traded for obsidian and quartzite, and supplemented their diet with protein from freshwater *pomacea* snails. Concentrated in three major locations—one near the edge of the *bajo* proper, and at two key points along the ridge to the southeast—their numbers could hardly have exceeded more than several dozen.

These early peoples' origin and identity remains lost to history, as do the names that they bestowed on themselves and their villages. Also unclear is whether they considered themselves a series of villages or a single community. Participants in what may have been ritual sacrifice, they intentionally beheaded one of their victims and dumped him in a simple grave, hinting at the grizzly practices that would later characterize the Classic period. Otherwise unremarkable, this simple aggregate of dwellings would give rise to an extraordinarily powerful city that would endure for the next fifteen hundred years—Tikal.

View from Temple IV.

Thatched House.

THE RAIN FOREST ENVIRONMENT

From the crowns of the highest trees, down through the dark and primal understories, the rain forest setting of Tikal presents an astonishing array of plant and animal life. Comprised of four or five discrete tiers or "stories," the jungle ranges from the shadow-engulfed forest floor to giant trees whose crowns, reaching as high as 150 feet, form an "umbrella" or "canopy." The canopy itself functions as an enormous sunscreen, shielding all the floral and faunal niches of the lower stories. Huge mahogany, Mexican cedar, ramón, guanacaste, gumbo limbo, and other valuable canopy trees serve together to break the wind of violent storms and to deflect torrential downpours. The canopy modulates temperatures and atmospheric conditions within the interior, trapping humidity and energy not unlike a greenhouse. The massive tree trunks and broad, interlocking branches act as giant trellises for the support of pendant lianas and vines, and as aerial highways for monkeys, spotted cats, myriad insects, snakes, and lizards. The crooks of trees and other traps serve as elevated water tanks and airborne gardens, collecting rainfall and nourishing lush bromeliads, epiphytes, dozens of different kinds of delicate orchids, and spawning pupae and larvae of mosquitoes, exotic flies, butterflies, and tree frogs. At once the jungle's foundation and rooftop, the canopy shelters and conceals as a beneficial protector, converting energy into living matter and weaving its abundance into a single, breathing organism. For good reason did forest dwellers conceive of the trees as the axis and foundation of the world.

Local tropical forests do not thrive uniformly across the land. Largely confined to "upland" zones between the seasonal *bajo* swamps, the forests give way to open savanna grasslands farther south. Along the base of a series of hills cutting across the region, numerous freshwater lakes trend from east to west like jungle-shrouded gems, including Sacnab, Yaxhá, and Petén Itzá—the latter located just below the settlements at early Tikal. Certain areas incorporate vast tracts of palm forests comprised of the royal cohune, with much of the area seamed with rugged limestone hills.

The several hamlets in the Tikal area thrived remarkably well in this tropical setting. From the surrounding forests villagers could scavenge palm fronds and branches to build simple huts that had thatched roofs and stick walls, while vines served to lash the poles together. Significantly dependent upon local game for food, the people of these early villages hunted miniature brocket deer and the larger white-tailed mule deer, as well as the collared peccary (wild pig) and tapescuintle (paca). Other animals provided pelts and hide, including big and medium-sized cats. Among the latter were the world's largest spotted cat, the jaguar, the much smaller ocelot and the margay, and the tawny-pelted cougar and dark-brown jaguarundi. Still other local animals that thrived in abundance were coatimundis or pisotes, the perico ligero (tyra), spider monkeys, howler monkeys, and prehensile kinkajoos with large, bulging eyes.

In the nearby *bajos*, which were probably perennial in early times, and in more distant streams, there were fish such as the mojarra and needlefish, while giant tarpon thrived in the deeper waters of the Pasión and Usumacinta. Then, as now, there were deadly snakes—yellowbeards, bushmasters, and rattlesnakes—as well as boa constrictors, iguanas, basilisks, tarantulas, and scorpions. Strange and exotic birds like the banana-billed toucan, the iridescent blue-green mot-mot with its "tennis-racket" tail feathers, and the green parrot, lent flashes of color to an otherwise oppressively dark-green world. Along the rivers and streams thrived the scarlet macaw and caiman, the latter a member of the crocodile family.

Interior of the Rain Forest.

EARLY OCCUPATION

Foraging for animals and other forest products, people were drawn to the jungles of Yucatan by at least 7000 B.C. Although concentrated in coastal zones, especially in Belize, where they thrived off fish and other marine products, the earliest inhabitants known to archaeology soon moved inland along the rivers and streams. They continued to penetrate the deeper forests until, by around 800 B.C., incipient hamlets had been established in isolated areas along the Pasión at Seibal and Altar de Sacrificios. These settlements considerably predate the villages at Tikal.

Who these earliest people were remains uncertain, but they were probably groups of Maya speakers, a language not yet broken up into as many branches as it is today. The Maya, like most Native Americans, belonged to groups that, in the very distant past, had crossed from Siberia to Alaska along the Bering Land Bridge, an isthmus of ice above where the Aleutian Islands now stand. Beginning no later than about 10,000 B.C., and possibly much earlier than that, waves of people crossed into North America and then migrated southward to populate all of the Americas, as far south as Tierra del Fuego. Others perhaps crossed the Pacific Ocean from Asia in small vessels, and not inconceivably over the Arctic from Europe. Stylistic affinities with tools found in North America and Western Europe as far south as Spain suggest the peopling of the Americas may have been a much more complicated process than originally believed.

Whatever the origins of the Maya, the primeval jungles of Central America attracted nomadic hunter-gatherers who, over the course of millennia, settled down into village life or were replaced by other stock. From these hamlets the great civilization of the Maya would be forged.

Much of what archaeologists know about early settlements of the Maya depends on shards from pottery vessels, the containers for food and drink manufactured by these people. At this early time, the pottery in use consisted of plain or simply-decorated basic bowls and storage jars, unsophisticated vessels of the Real Xe complex.[1] Found chiefly in trash dumps ("middens") layered stratigraphically in the ground, these fragments of lost culture provide a method of "relative dating." That is, from them archaeologists can determine an approximate age for associated features like the foundations of houses, hearths, or other evidences of occupation.

Although not precise, ceramic dating techniques allow investigators to organize features chronologically from earliest to latest.

In order to assign a specific date in our Gregorian calendar, however, other means have to be employed. As their chief tool, archaeologists rely on radiocarbon dating, which is based on the rate of radioactive decay in organic material. Bone and charcoal admirably serve this purpose, and from them dates can be established with a margin of error of approximately 100 years.

Another way to tell "archaeological time" is to study the changes that occur in the styles of pottery from one epoch to another, and to determine the *rate* of change. For example, automobiles from the earliest days of the Model T to gas-guzzlers like the Lincoln Continental disclose a range of changes that pinpoint automobile styles down to the year and, in some cases, the month of manufacture. In this same way, investigators can track cultural markers like ceramic vessels and house features, allowing a broad reconstruction of major periods and changes in Maya history, especially in terms of material success.

Within their world of dense forests and swamp, the people who made these ceramics thrived remarkably well. Exploiting the specialized geographical niche of rampant jungle with all its teeming life, they chopped from the forests the clearings to build their necessary houses, settling down to a sedentary life after untold centuries of migrations. Their wanderings would cease, at least temporarily, for the next thousand years.

THE FOUNDATIONS OF VILLAGE LIFE

But the founders of the original hamlets at Tikal exploited their environment for much more than just game, fish, and forage. Mesoamerican peoples for several thousands of years had already known a precious secret, one that had begun to transform life throughout the American continents. By as early as 7000 B.C., they were learning to adapt plant products for cultivation in small plots of earth. The chile and the avocado were among the earliest foods domesticated in the Precolumbian world, followed by maize—the staple of Native American life—beans, squash, tomatoes, and a succession of herbs. Perhaps most importantly, special trees with thick waxy pods that encased small beans were eventually cultivated, with the beans used to make a rich frothy drink that was brown in color and often fermented. Dried and pre-served, the beans became the basis of the Mesoamerican economy, the equivalent of currency. Today we call the product chocolate.

To grow food plants, early farmers in the Tikal area chopped down the jungle to make agricultural plots. Laid out carefully according to the four cardinal directions—east, west, south, and north—*milpas* (plots of land) were cleared with axes that had pressure-flaked stone blades manufac-tured from deposits of local flint. Farmers would allow the downed forest to dry during the three-month dry season, and burn it off to clear the land. Ash enriched the soil with potassium, and from the *milpas* the maize grew to twice the height of a man.

Early agriculturists carefully watched the changing seasonal patterns of rain and sun, meticulously timing their sowing and harvests. The scorching sun of the dry season baked the land under intense heat and sunlight, increasingly extending northward in its apparent passage across the sky until, at the solstice, it would slowly begin to make its way back south. In the east the sun came up, and in the west it set. These movements were not lost on the farmers who eked their living from the shallow jungle soil, and in the layout of their agricultural plots they recreated the path of the sun, perma-nently symbolizing their dependence on its cycles. This was the shape of the world, the universe, and all it contained—a four-part division that ruled the entire cosmos.

They must also have known that in maize, as well as in other products of the soil, lay the foundation of life itself. Corn could be dried and ground on saddle querns to make dough, from which *tamales* and *tortillas* were shaped. Dough could also be dissolved in water for a drink called *pozole* or boiled to make *atole* (corn gruel). Over a fire kindled between three hearth stones, the women of the families would cook their maize for every meal.

One other key feature of *milpa* or slash-and-burn agriculture figured significantly in the daily life of Tikal. After an initial harvest, crop yields would decline, so that within two or three seasons new plots of land had to be cleared. In the Tikal forest setting, a few families rotating crops in this manner could thrive and prosper, increasing modestly in number and pos-sibly attracting new families from outside the region. Yet in this pattern of shifting *milpa* lay another precious secret, far more sinister than life-sustaining agriculture. Although it seems unlikely that early settlers at

Tikal realized anything was wrong, the system of *milpas* on which early Tikal depended contained the seeds of the settlement's own demise.

But this was many centuries in the future, and in the meantime the three hamlets at Tikal grew and burgeoned amid their patchwork quilt of farms and fields.

NOTE

1. Ceramics of this complex and the closely related Swasey ceramics of Cuello, Belize were the earliest pottery vessels manufactured in the Maya lowlands.

CHAPTER 2

THE DAWN OF HISTORY

F̲ar to the west, along the Gulf of Mexico in an area encompassed today by the modern Mexican states of Tabasco and Veracruz, events were unfolding that would profoundly effect the future of Tikal. For the past 600 years, a people evidently unrelated to the Maya had built towns and ceremonial centers, developing a distinctive cultural pattern that would influence Mesoamerica long afterwards. Chief among these paradigms were pyramids, great mounded works meant to recreate the World Mountain. Like those of other agricultural peoples, including the Egyptians, their pyramids represented the point of contact between heaven and earth, a veritable stairway meant to elevate human beings to the height of clouds and gods.

Poorly known and discovered only towards the beginning of the twentieth century, the people of the Gulf Coast have been nicknamed by archaeologists the "Rubber People," a name drawn from ethnohistoric accounts more than two thousand years later.

This was the civilization of the Olmec.

ORIGINS OF PRECOLUMBIAN CIVILIZATION

No one understands how the Olmec rose on the Precolumbian landscape as the first people to employ the hallmark features of Mesoamerican civilization.

Beginning around 1200 B.C., they founded a succession of important towns at San Lorenzo, La Venta, and Tres Zapotes—great thriving centers of population circumscribed by extensive swamplands. Considered Mesoamerica's "mother culture," the first great Mesoamerican state, the Olmec extended their influence as far as southern Guatemala and western El Salvador, and into central Mexico and beyond. Settlements of the Olmec drew their support from farmers in the surrounding countryside, and imported high-quality jade and other foreign goods.

Olmec civilization set the stage for what was to follow in Mesoamerica for the next two thousand years. Originators of such characteristic concepts as paved plazas, pyramids, stone sculptures, and specific symbolic images, they disseminated these features through trade and other forms of influence.

Central to the symbols propagated by the Olmec were images of serpents, exemplified by La Venta Monument 19. Enclosing an Olmec-style figure within its looping body, the serpent displays rattles at the end of its tail, identifying its species. What appears to be a feather crest arches over the reptile's forehead, lending the creature a distinctive bird-like effect. Monument 19 may introduce the god who would figure so prominently in later epochs—Quetzalcóatl, or the Feathered Serpent.

Olmec sculptors drew on materials imported from dozens of miles away. Lacking suitable stone for buildings or works of art, they arranged to quarry hard, nearly black volcanic basalt from the Túxtla Mountains, dragging huge boulders down the slopes to rafts waiting on tributaries of the mighty Coatzacoalcos River. Although they fashioned a variety of art, including the first stone shafts or stelae,[1] the Olmec are best known for their carved colossal heads, enormous basalt boulders sculpted as portraits of rulers, gods, or ball players. Characterized by fat, fleshy lips; broad, flaring nostrils; and penetrating eyes, these colossal heads were buried underneath the civic plazas of key sites, never meant to be seen by human eyes.

Like almost every other civilization in Mesoamerica, the Olmec built homes of thatch and stick that were arranged around private courtyards, where most of the activities of daily life occurred. Oriented to the cardinal directions—east, west, north, and south—Olmec settlements prospered under powerful rulers in a kind of patron-client relationship, presumably organized around important family ties and the structures of lineages and

Olmec Colossal Head.

clans. Here, as elsewhere, maize dominated agriculture, furnishing the "bread of life" for the commoner and the elite alike.

Of particular note was an Olmec penchant for greenstones and an especially bluish-green jade used to fashion figurines of composite animal-men. Thought to portray shamans undergoing spiritual transformations, images in jade evoked characteristic features that include high, domed foreheads, slanted eyes, squared and down-turned mouths, and composite infant-feline features, a sort of "were-jaguar" creature. These and other Olmec jades made their way across Mesoamerica to turn up in elite burials centuries later, the prized possessions of individuals who had laid claim to the Olmec's heritage. Probably never of direct influence at Tikal, Olmec civilization nevertheless contributed to the city's renown in other ways, a legacy that Tikal would adapt and transform into a distinctly Maya one.

THE SPREAD OF MESOAMERICAN CULTURE

Still other centers of population contributed indirectly to Tikal. Arising out of the arid Valley of Oaxaca, not far from Central Mexico, the Zapotecs founded an early state at Monte Alban that overlooked the surrounding country from the leveled plateau of a defensible mountaintop. There can be little doubt that belligerence, violence, and warfare contributed to the city's rise around 600 B.C. Carved panels known as the Danzantes portray leaders of subjugated towns with their genitals mutilated, their entrails exposed, and their bodies limp and lifeless. These pictorial rows from the very dawn of the Mesoamerican world establish the primacy of warfare, the mortar of society's foundation.

These and other monuments at Monte Alban display distinctive symbols in isolation from the portraits of individuals. Possibly captions that identify the depicted prisoner, these symbols represent the earliest use of writing in the Americas, a small inventory of signs that record an aspect of Zapotec language. Just as importantly, the first hieroglyphic bars and dots appear at Monte Alban, incipient elements of the Mesoamerican mathematical system in which bars equal five, and dots one. Furthermore, the first records of the Precolumbian calendar appear here, including components of the famed 52-Year Cycle or Calendar Round.

THE OLMEC LEGACY

By the last centuries B.C., long after Olmec hegemony had passed, Olmec symbols and the pattern of pyramid-plaza compounds had spread considerably. Catching on like wildfire, manifestations of this pattern erupted throughout many areas of Mesoamerica, flowing both towards highland Mexico to the west and Central America to the east.

The Isthmus of Tehuantepec, just south of the Olmec heartland, sustains a heavy tropical environment that extends along the Pacific littoral of Guatemala into El Salvador. Along this natural corridor Olmec styles spread to non-Olmec cultures at Izapa and Abaj Takalik and points farther east. Here the Pacific Coast of Guatemala and Chiapas forms a long, narrow coastal plain and piedmont, the Pacific slope of the highland massif. Although the degree to which this area was penetrated by the Olmec themselves remains debatable, the Olmec legacy diffused in ever-widening circles until many cultures throughout this part of the world had adopted its imagery and, consequently, elements of Olmec society.

Situated along the Pacific piedmont of Chiapas, only a few miles from the Guatemalan border, Izapa sprawls for two-and-a-half square miles. Studded with some 200 monuments, fifty of them carved, the site engendered an intensive stela-and-altar complex consisting of paired upright stone shafts and drum-shaped altars. Sometime after 300 B.C., what were apparently non-Maya peoples had begun erecting stelae with newer, more diverse images nevertheless firmly rooted in Olmec culture. In many ways the precursor to Tikal's symbolic repertoire, motifs appeared at Izapa that, hundreds of years later, Tikal would virtually duplicate. Especially prominent, Izapa Stela 1 portrays a long-snouted god striding through water with a basket in his hands, and with a creel strapped to his back that bears his catch of fish. Clearly a forerunner of the Maya Rain God Chaak, the image would survive the vicissitudes of Mesoamerican history long after Izapa had vanished.

Monuments from this period bear distinctive features that link them together in terms of both composition and theme. Of particular note, principal human figures carry their hands against their chests, with their fingers wrapped around the thumb. Scrolls, serpent heads in profile, skirts overlain with tubular beads in diamond patterns, voluted scrolls, belt trophy-head assemblages, and upper and lower "registers" or panels all characterize these precocious monuments. Perhaps most importantly, stela-altar pairs also made an appearance at Kaminaljuyu, a highland town in the Valley of Guatemala that was situated far closer to Tikal.

Izapa Stela 1.

THE PETÉN CORE

Sculpture seemingly spread from the Olmec heartland over the Isthmus of Tehuantepec then down the Pacific littoral to cross the mountains of highland Guatemala, thence into the jungles of Petén where Tikal thrived. But influence must have penetrated from the north and west as well. El Mirador built massive stone pyramids, sprawling palaces, causeways, and reservoirs long before the Classic Maya. The seat of powerful royal dynasts from roughly 300 B.C. to the first centuries A.D., El Mirador administered a host of Late Preclassic towns that formed an incipient state only now coming to light.

El Mirador built what may well stand as Precolumbian America's largest pyramid, many times more massive than those built several centuries later at Tikal. Surrounded by *bajo* swamplands but linked to the surrounding uplands by systems of causeways, El Mirador dominated northern Petén from its island-like stronghold, probably the largest Mesoamerican archaeological district known from this period. Eventually overcome by unknown catastrophe, the precinct was largely deserted to rain forest before Tikal's Early Classic phase.

Tikal hardly remained indifferent to contemporary events in Mesoamerica. By 500 B.C., trade goods were certainly increasing in demand and crossing the peninsula with greater frequency. No longer simple hamlets in isolation, the settlement at Tikal included another village, east of the original one, together with additional hamlets strung out along the margins of the Bajo de Santa Fe. The two ridge-top locations continued to prosper, expanding from their original core of huts to form an east-west trending strip of sites, an orientation maintained throughout the remainder of Tikal's history.

The first permanent buildings at Tikal reflected paradigms similar to those among the Olmec. Increasingly sophisticated platforms of stone supported perishable huts used for the worship of religious figures, family and "Mesoamerican" gods with roots deep in the Olmec past. By the period 200–100 B.C., the first structures of cut-stone masonry were in place, with the building material excavated from the surrounding limestone bedrock. Walls of masonry and roofs of perishable thatch were being installed, with permanent surfaces plastered and painted inside and out.

These earliest buildings were erected in an area that would play an increasingly important role over the next centuries. Clearly the focus of religious rites and the veneration of prominent, deceased members of the community, this zone would receive permanent features built over burial crypts and, eventually, over stone-lined tombs. Both men and women were buried here, capped with shrines evidently dedicated to them and meant to perpetuate their memory. At first modest in scale, shrines increasingly received sculpted and painted friezes, the makings of an incipient symbol system. Here were tombs and shrines equivalent to Tikal's "Valley of the Kings," a necropolis of picket-like towers known as the North Acropolis.

THE GROWTH OF TIKAL

Increasingly Tikal was becoming socially stratified. Individuals interred in the more elaborate crypts represented heads of families and lineages, marked for special honor due to their status among their peers. No doubt certain individual families were increasing in importance, monopolizing the trade items that flowed in ever-greater volumes from the Caribbean to the Gulf of Mexico. Power and prestige had begun to concentrate in the hands of a few bold leaders, wealthy enough to rally less economically-viable segments of the population to build shrines and other public works of architecture.

Water remained critical on the hilltop locations in the more westerly precincts, and leaders of this time were no doubt organizing gangs of laborers to help carve from bedrock the massive reservoirs that would one day dominate so much of the central precincts. Perhaps attention was also turning towards communal efforts at farming the marginal swamplands, bringing more and more areas of agricultural land under control. The first raised fields in the *bajos* were probably constructed at this time, intensifying agriculture to sustain an increasing population.

Still farther west along the rugged hilltops at Tikal, another area was coming under the sway of communal projects. Known as the Lost World Complex, it contained the beginnings of a radial Olmec-style pyramid, oriented towards a series of three buildings along the precinct's eastern margin. Among the earliest of the Maya's astronomical compounds, the pyramid-shrine orientation allowed for the calculation of the equinox and solstice, the initiation of observations that would form the basis of a solar calendar.

Nor was Tikal developing in isolation from other settlements in Petén, certainly not within its own immediate area. Only about fifteen miles north, the town of Uaxactun had begun erecting monumental architecture like the buildings at Tikal. Renowned for a planned astronomical group similar to the Lost World Complex, Uaxactun would develop and prosper for the next several centuries. Both centers of population would be intimately linked as near "twin cities," all but for Tikal's more spectacular ascent in the future.

THE PROTO-CLASSIC PERIOD

Everything abruptly changed during the first centuries A.D. By about A.D. 1, architects in Tikal had completed the Lost World Pyramid. Soaring to a height of one-hundred feet, it represented one of the most massive structures anywhere in Precolumbian America. On the North Acropolis, tombs of powerful religious and political leaders symbolized an emergent social hierarchy, men and women who were distinguishable from the agriculturists and craft workers by their much higher degree of material wealth. Population soared dramatically, the swelling numbers beginning to congest around the hilltops zones in nucleated groups notable for their lack of streets or avenues, and to sprawl across the countryside surrounding the downtown precincts.

One final major event may have helped spur Tikal's growth: the sudden eruption of distant Volcán Ilopango. Located within fifty miles from El Salvador's Chalchuapa—a mile-long, densely-inhabited zone of Preclassic pyramids, temples, and plazas—the volcano quickly devastated everything for miles. In haste people smashed sophisticated stone sculptures and inscriptions to appease the earth's fury, and then abandoned their town under a rain of ash.

Chalchuapa was left blanketed under two feet of ash, with ash 170-feet thick near the volcanic cone. Thousands had perished, land for miles around had been destroyed. As far as the Pacific and Chiapas Coast, populations felt

Lost World Pyramid.

the effects of the devastation. People fled the heavier areas of ash-flow, leaving much of the region to lay deserted for hundreds of years.

Volcanic particles carry tremendous distances through the atmosphere, scattering on stratospheric winds, blocking sunlight, and increasing local cloud-cover and rainfall. Across the northern highlands of Honduras and the lowland forests of Belize, evidence from river floodplains reveals especially thick deposits from layers after the eruption, testimony to heavily increased rainfall and floods.

People traveled tremendous distances to escape the devastated areas. In Petén and Belize, the introduction of new forms of pottery—especially vessels with "mammiform" supports, polychrome designs, and bowls with ring bases—made an appearance, evidently hybrid types introduced from El Salvador.

Refugees must have migrated northward. That they arrived from the hardest-hit areas seems reasonable. Yet few of the diagnostic ceramic types actually reached Tikal or penetrated the Petén districts, remaining confined instead to riverine areas more easily accessible and perhaps less heavily populated. The true impact of the Ilopango eruption remains debatable, obscured under jungle debris and developments that seeped towards Petén from other regions—those of the Olmec, of Izapa, and of Kaminaljuyu.

THE DAWN OF HISTORY

Preclassic Tikal adapted from its precursors a wide-ranging repertoire of visual symbols and cultural forms. Tikal codified these images to promote powerful individuals in their quest for social and political preeminence. Interred in ever-increasingly elaborate tombs on the North Acropolis, ancestors were linked to emblems of supernatural portent. Eventually the status of these individuals would come to be regarded as divine. In this way, potent symbols initiated by the Olmec would reemerge among the Maya out of the demands for dynastic legitimacy and for the promotion of social cohesion.

Not least of the methods borrowed by Tikal was the idea of keying symbols to speech. Originally pictographic and evidently derived from calendrical signs, hieroglyphic writing formed the documentary basis of the Maya royal charter. Perhaps the single greatest achievement of Precolumbian America, Maya hieroglyphs reflected local dialects like Ch'olan and Yucatec, encoding grammatical elements such as syllables, verbs, nouns, and sentence structure. It thus surpassed all other Native American scripts in versatility.

With tools of monumental art and hieroglyphic writing, Tikal and other centers of Petén went on to forge a series of unprecedented chronological documents towards the end of the second century A.D.—records that would run for more than six hundred years. The first of the public records at Tikal with an unchallenged date commemorates the year A.D. 292. With erection of this freestanding stela, Tikal emerged for the first time into the light of recorded history.

Not for one thousand years would a Precolumbian people leave so clear a record of their times, and never again would Mesoamerican literacy achieve the brilliance of the Classic Maya.

NOTE

1. From the Greek word *stele*, "stone shaft."

PART 2

THE EARLY CLASSIC PERIOD

(A.D. 250–448)

CHAPTER 3

CHILDREN OF YAX EB' XOOK

Marcos López could see an outline of sculptured limestone on the ground. He had been crossing an especially dense area of forest just west of the Great Plaza on this day in 1958, heading leisurely back to the University Museum camp near the Tikal airstrip. For three seasons the University Museum of the University of Pennsylvania had been excavating among the great Maya ruins—one of the most intensive archaeological projects ever conceived and one that would grow larger still in years to come. As he now hustled to claim the prestige of having discovered a new monument, Marcos López ran to tell the project's architect and spread word among the staff.

The whole camp had soon gathered around the sculpture. They excitedly discussed its age, its style of carving, and its condition. The stone was the twenty-ninth carved stela or limestone shaft found at Tikal, but affectionately it was dubbed "Marcos's Stela."

Ed Shook, the project's director, ordered his Guatemalan laborers to strip back the surrounding underbrush and chop down the trees within the immediate area, allowing sunshine through the forest so that the stone would dry. Gradually, his men cleared the area of leaves and branches to carefully expose Stela 29's complete outline on the ground, digging underneath to search for additional carving. Others dug trenches through the surrounding soil to see if additional pieces of the stone shaft could be located. The digging left Stela 29 stranded on a pedestal of earth, with the intention that someone would soon turn and examine it.

As excitement died down and digging in the Great Plaza resumed, however, Stela 29 was left on its elevated perch. Day after day passed until it was virtually forgotten.

On the morning of Saturday, April 4th, members of the archaeological staff returned to carefully clean the stela Marcos had found. After the front surface had been scrubbed with water and small brushes, Shook ordered workers to lift it and set it on one side, intending to photograph the ornate imagery. As they raised the great stone between them, soil fell from the backside, and to the astonishment of everyone present, hieroglyphs appeared that formed a single narrow column down the reverse side. Shook saw bars and dots take shape—numbers from the Maya mathematical system—together with the first hieroglyphs of a Long Count date. Hesitating, he stopped to explain the calendar to his men.

So far, the fallen soil had revealed eight b'aktuns, the period of four hundred years in their positional notation system (not unlike our own calendar statement 2001). What this meant was that, on Stela 29, the Maya had written one of the earliest dates ever recorded by their civilization.

This new discovery caused celebration, as it significantly pushed back Tikal's chronological record. But as Shook turned to reveal the third glyph, still clogged with earth, he explained that it was this one—the k'atun period—that would determine the true extent of Stela 29's age. As everyone drew closer to finish the job, he gave them sharpened sticks; together they pried away the remaining soil very slowly and gently.

Farther off, where excavations were underway in the Great Plaza, members of the archaeological staff could hear someone shouting wildly. Unsure what was wrong, they crashed through the forest to help Shook and his men. In no time, word had spread through the whole University camp, bringing archaeologists, botanists, and laborers.

Shook was standing over the rear surface of Stela 29, examining the k'atun glyph so important to dating this monument. Beside the little head designating "twenty years," two bars and two dots stood out plainly. The University project had just revealed the oldest Long Count date ever discovered among the Maya.

THE MAYA CALENDARS

That the Maya had invented one of the most sophisticated mathematical and calendrical systems in history no one can deny. Comprising three separate calendars, plus additional secondary cycles, the complete calendar notation indicates the equivalent of the day, month, and year. In other words, it provides a date not unlike January 1, 2001 in the Gregorian Calendar.

The Gregorian Calendar is a *decimal* system that proceeds from right to left (though read from left to right) in units of ones, tens, hundreds, and thousands. It keeps track of the years elapsed since the birth of Christ.

The Maya Long Count notation, on the other hand, has five standard positions, including cycles of 400 years of 360 days each (b'aktuns), twenty years (k'atuns), years (tuns), months (winals), and days (k'ins).[1] This system is *vegisimal*, or based on multiples of twenty. Running from bottom to top (though read from top to bottom), the Maya calendar tracks years from the mythical origin of the current epoch in human existence—a date that scholars have determined coincides with August 14, 3114 B.C.[2]

But the Maya went beyond records of years. They wove into their calculation additional cycles of days, weeks, months, and lunar phases, documenting individual moments in time with several different techniques. After the Long Count comes the Tzolk'in, or cycle of 260 days, a constantly revolving round of thirteen numbers and twenty day names (13 x 20 = 260). Possibly related to the length of human gestation, the Sacred Round, as scholars often call it, was so important to the social fabric of the Maya world that it is still in use among the Maya today.

Any number of cycles can follow the Tzolk'in, including a nine-day week called the Lords of the Night, an 819-day count, the age of the moon, and the position in a six-month Lunar Calendar. Most commonly, however, the Tzolk'in co-occurs with the Jaab' cycle, an endlessly permutating series of twenty numbers (0 through 19) and eighteen months, plus an additional five-day unlucky period (20 x 18 + 5 = 365). Meant to approximate the true Solar Year, the Jaab' interlocks with the Tzolk'in to form an additional cycle of fifty-two years. Only after fifty-two years will co-occurring Tzolk'in and Jaab' dates repeat, inspiring the name 52-Year Cycle, or Calendar Round.

Stela 29 from Tikal, unfortunately, suffered major damage in ancient times, with the result that only the Long Count and part of the Jaab' survive.

With the Long Count firmly fixed, however, the full date on Stela 29 can be reconstructed as 8 b'aktuns, 12 k'atuns, 14 tuns, 8 winals, and 15 k'ins 13 Men 3 Sip (conveniently written as 8.12.14.8.15 13 Men 3 Sip)—equivalent to July 8, A.D. 292.

STELA 29

The earliest of Tikal's securely dated monuments, Stela 29 portrays an image of a man on its front, overwhelmed in detail that includes complex costume elements, an overhead "floating" ancestor, and traces of what scholars call a "ceremonial bar," a long, diagonally-held symbol of authority whose ends terminate in serpent heads. From the serpent's yawning maws emerge characteristic god heads, and additional serpent profiles, an image of a bird, and smoke scrolls complicate the seething design.

Scholars originally believed images such as this portrayed gods or priests, pious theocrats that ruled over devout Maya. Those who decipher Maya hieroglyphic writing, or epigraphers, have instead proven that the portraits represent rulers, individuals who were kings and who commanded the cities over which their images kept watch. Stela 29 thus depicts the earliest contemporary ruler known from Tikal, someone who controlled the political affairs of the city at this early date. As supreme lord of the land, he commanded prestige and power well beyond ordinary men, benefiting from the products of increasing trade and agriculture.

Name Glyph of
Foliated Jaguar.

No hieroglyphs that name this man survive on Stela 29, nor do any indications of his history or accomplishments. But later monuments refer to him by name, and epigraphers call him Foliated Jaguar, based on the graphic appearance of his principal hieroglyph. Called the "Kalomte," a royal title of unknown meaning handed down generation after generation as a sign of Tikal kingship, he was an individual who left almost no trace of himself beyond this broken monument. Significantly, supernal images or the "floating" disembodied heads above the principal figure portray the father of the subject, who in almost every instance had ruled as the previous king. On

Stela 29, front.

Stela 29, the "father" floats above Foliated Jaguar with an image of a god in his headdress whose nose terminates in a jaguar's paw, used here in reference to Foliated Jaguar's progenitor. Foliated Jaguar was therefore not the first of the Tikal Classic kings.

Only calendrical glyphs survive on Stela 29, but the front side records an element that was later renowned throughout the Maya lowlands as one of the most significant symbols of dynastic power. Representing the back of an individual's head covered under locks of hair, bound-up with a knotted headband, the sign reads *mutul*, meaning a particular but unknown bird. First appearing on Stela 29, this is the Tikal Emblem Glyph, the ancient name of the city.

In establishing its primacy, Tikal was the first of the lowland Classic Maya districts to document its territory by the use of an Emblem Glyph, a symbol that embodied in visual form the nature and extent of its incipient political power. Over the next several centuries, many other Maya districts would come to embrace emblems for similar reasons, but none would surpass the distinction and longevity of Tikal's.

ORIGINS OF THE TIKAL DYNASTY

In the latter centuries of the Late Preclassic (300 B.C.–A.D. 250), a change took place that would transform Tikal into something far more ambitious and powerful than any of its local competitors. Undoubtedly these changes reflect the emergent ruling class, prestigious men and women who belonged to the privileged levels of society. The focus of Tikal's elite continued to center around the North Acropolis, the site of one of the earliest settlements in the Tikal area. Built up during the Late Preclassic Period, it formed a broad, flat terrace crowned by Early Classic times with numerous sacred shrines.

Early Maya sites include triadic architectural arrangements, three shrines configuring a kind of "U." Thought by some to commemorate the "original three lineages" of Maya society, the arrangement may also relate to the terrestrial counterpart of the three cosmic hearthstones. It was the setting and configuration of these hearthstones that constituted one of the central acts of creation.

The Tikal Emblem Glyph.

These facts notwithstanding, very early in Tikal history the Maya began interring their dead where the North Acropolis would later stand, graduating to more ambitious schemes and eventually to tombs. From that moment onward until Late Classic times, all the great kings of Tikal were interred on the North Acropolis, successively buried under increasingly grandiose architectural schemes. Ascended by monumental staircases along its southern facade, the burial place of the Tikal royalty came to include huge polychrome jaguar masks, guardians of the dead rulers' sanctity. The North Acropolis was to be rebuilt over many centuries—ten, fifteen, twenty times—becoming a two-and-a-half-acre sacred precinct more holy than any other location at Tikal.

IN THE NAME OF THE FOUNDER

Whether Foliated Jaguar and his father, Jaguar Paw, were among those interred on the North Acropolis remains uncertain. The last Preclassic tomb at this location, Burial 125 was established on the central axis *ca.* A.D. 150. Roofed with logs instead of the more common corbelled arch, it was buried under hundreds of pounds of chipped flint debitage, a characteristic of royal tombs of the later Classic Period. The tomb was found empty except for the skeleton of a five-foot, seven-inch tall adult male, who was evidently buried naked and without offerings of any kind. Instead, what seem to be his grave gifts were interred farther east, evidently establishing the central axis of an entirely new and revamped acropolis. Whoever he was, the individual was certainly a powerful one, worthy of especially high esteem to be so honored.

Tikal inscriptions mention an individual from whom all later kings claimed descent. Deciphered well over two decades ago, the "Successor Glyph" keeps track of a ruler's order of succession—eleventh, twenty-second, twenty-ninth, and so forth. Sites that record the "successor glyph" include the name of an individual specific to that particular city, generally identified as the "dynastic founder" of the royal line. Tikal's founder takes a variety of names, but characteristics of the most common include the head of a long-nosed god with a stingray-spine tooth and a segment of a wooden scaffold or stairway—or Yax Eb' Xook, in effect "First Step Shark."

North Acropolis.

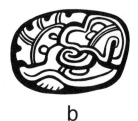

a   b

Name Glyph of Yax Eb' Xook.

Yax Eb' Xook's interment in Burial 125, just before the close of the Pre-classic Period, accords with his position as "first ruler" of the Tikal dynasty, to judge from later "successor" statements and the number of generations implied by these.[3] Unfortunately, no contemporary inscriptions from monuments carved during the ruler's lifetime have survived. All references to Yax Eb' Xook post-date his reign, with many written centuries after he lived and died. But in their reverence and emphasis for this man, the Maya were remarkably clear in years to come.

Tikal's founder may have established the first dynasty at Mutul, while wresting control of Petén from the poorly understood center at El Mirador. However, it appears that Tikal prospered at the expense of El Mirador, probably gaining its full independence under Yax Eb' Xook. This ruler may also have seized from El Mirador the trans-Petén route for traders crossing the Yucatan to points westward.

Following Yax Eb' Xook's Burial 125, no tombs were installed on the North Acropolis for two centuries, long after the Early Classic had dawned and dated monuments had been established. What would emerge from this "burial hiatus" were rulers more powerful than any before, an unprecedented dynastic sequence unrivaled in ancient America. But other competitors loomed large, emerging on the horizon in step with Tikal's Early Classic success. The next century after Foliated Jaguar would prove crucial, a trial by fire, as the political landscape of Mesoamerica shifted and realigned.

ORIGINS OF TIKAL SCULPTURE

The vast, only partially explored southern lowlands of the Maya include those areas west of the Caribbean, north of the Guatemalan highlands, east of the Chiapas Mountains, and south of where the Yucatan merges into Central America. Archaeologists well know that the area remains too extensive to rule out the possibility of monuments that predate Stela 29. They almost certainly do exist.

By the same token, too much lies sealed under Classic architecture to rule out the discovery of additional monuments at Tikal. Tremendous Early Classic and Preclassic levels extend down to bedrock, vast quantities of construction that include rubble of every kind of material. Zealous in their architectural projects and always ready to remodel existing shrines, the Maya constantly demolished obsolete buildings, beautiful sculptures, and polychrome stucco friezes, burying them as construction fill for ever-increasing projects. To the Maya, nothing lasted for ever.

Archaeologists constantly turn up new finds—overlooked remains lying buried under jungle debris, shattered sculpture interred as architectural fill. Ground-breaking discoveries regularly overturn accepted beliefs or claims of the "first" or "earliest."

Indeed, sculpture earlier than Stela 29 has come to light, discovered sometimes in archaeological contexts, sometimes in private collections of Precolumbian art in Europe and elsewhere. As a rule, most remain problematic for one reason or another: an inscription may be eroded or incomplete, or a date may be written in non-Classic style and therefore remain unreadable.

One such monument may be Altar 1 of Polol, a small, insignificant site in the savannas below Lake Petén Itzá. Though its Long Count no longer survives, the imagery of the altar—two figures seated below scroll-work and facing an intervening glyph panel—recalls earlier monuments at Izapa, Abaj Takalik, and Kaminaljuyu, Preclassic towns well outside the Maya lowlands. Detail that overwhelms the design, hands held against the chest where the fingers curl around the thumb; down-gazing "protector," "father," or "ancestor" motifs; distinctive multiple-scroll patterns; and the profile stance where one foot advances before the other,[4] all tie early Petén sculpture—at El Mirador, Polol, Tikal, and other locations—to Pacific piedmont styles of the Late Preclassic.

Yet the differences remain clear and striking. Izapa depicted mythic tales, humans and gods amid natural environments that incorporate trees, water, or other elements. Several include parallels to the Quiche Maya's *Popol Vuh*, or *Book of Council*, just as monuments would in later times at Tikal. Nevertheless, Tikal took these conventions and presented humans as historical portraits, as semi-divine leaders, and charged them with cosmic symbols, reflecting a more thoroughly institutionalized office of kingship.

These associations tied Tikal and central Petén not only to new sources of imagery, but almost certainly to newer and more distant sources of wealth. They symbolized the concentration at Tikal of political and economic control. Social structures were developing rapidly, a new era had dawned, and for a time Tikal *was* Classic civilization. It had developed as the focal point of Maya prosperity, a concentrated energy that would propel this jungle-shrouded land toward many greater deeds.

NOTES

1. Note that, rather than approximating the true length of the 365-day year, the tun includes only 360 days.
2. All dates given in this book correspond to the Gregorian Calendar, rather than the Julian Calendar traditional among scholars.
3. Another contender for the tomb of Yax Eb' Xook is the somewhat earlier Burial 85 (Martin and Grube 2000: 70). In light of the new axis established for the North Acropolis with the probable redistribution of the contents of Burial 125, it seems more likely that this was the final resting place of the founder.
4. Stela 29 would surely have had this stance had the lower fragment survived.

CHAPTER 4

THE RISE OF
TIKAL'S JAGUAR DYNASTY

Although no tombs survive on the North Acropolis that are unequivocally attributable to the immediate successors of Yax Eb' Xook, monuments and unprovenanced ceramic vessels from later in Tikal history mention individuals who lived during these times.

El Encanto, located about six miles northeast of the site-center, erected its own stela during the k'atun (twenty-year period) that followed Stela 29. Mentioning the first woman in local inscriptions, "Lady Skull," the monument commemorates her son Siyaj Kaan K'awil I or "Sky Born K'awil," called the son of "Animal Headdress."

Some sense can be made out of Tikal's early affairs from key ceramic texts, the most important of them being the "Successor Vase," which indicates that Siyaj Kaan K'awil reigned as the eleventh successor of Yax Eb' Xook. It then follows that Animal Headdress ruled as the tenth in line, with Foliated Jaguar eighth or ninth. If Burial 125 on the North Acropolis received the worldly remains of Yax Eb' Xook, then thirteen successors during a period of two hundred years—the length of the "burial hiatus"—provides an average reign of slightly more than fifteen years. Given the probability that, out of these thirteen, some reigned longer than others, two hundred years seems a reasonable span to accommodate all of the numbered rulers.

Another obscure individual who turns up during this period of "missing kings" goes by the name of Une B'alam, or "Jaguar Tail," one of the first ladies

*Name Glyph of
Lady Une B'alam.*

in inscriptions from the Tikal area and a woman who played a major if still uncertain role in local affairs. Evidently Tikal's nominal queen, she overseered an event at 8.14.0.0.0 (September 1, A.D. 317), and likely figures as the twelfth but uncounted ruler. Lady Une B'alam probably failed to enjoy the support of Tikal's patrilineages, and her accession no doubt precipitated a crisis, accounting for her lack of a succession number. This crisis was evidently resolved when the thirteenth ruler acceded, an individual known as Muwan Jol, or "Bird Skull."

Name Glyph of Muwan Jol.

Another of Tikal's burgeoning satellite centers offers the primary information about this man. Corozal, only about four miles east of the downtown zone, near the edge of the Bajo de Santa Fe, records Muwan Jol's death date as 8.16.2.6.0 (May 24, A.D. 359). Whoever he may have been, he merited remembrance outside the main urban zone. But no monuments directly attributable to him survive in Tikal's downtown area.

Inscriptions from the earliest phase of the Classic Period remain some of the most difficult to understand. Fortunately, with the advent of the fourteenth successor, the situation clarifies itself, even while posing much greater challenges.

GREAT FIERY CLAW

With the death of Muwan Jol, a ruler took the throne who would represent something of a climax in Tikal affairs, a peak moment in terms of the city's political sovereignty. Named as Muwan Jol's son on Stela 39, a miraculously preserved if somewhat fragmentary sculpture from the Lost World Plaza, the fourteenth successor at Tikal takes the skull with jaguar paw nose from El Encanto, but was clearly someone other than the subject of that monument. Prefixed with CHAK, the sign meaning "red" and "great,"

Stela 39, front.

a   b

Name Glyph of Chak Tok Ich'aak I.

the individual's name similarly reads Chak Tok Ich'aak. Because of his role at Tikal and to distinguish him from others of the same name, epigraphers refer to him as Chak Tok Ich'aak I, or Great Fiery Claw I.[1]

As with many Early Classic kings, information about Chak Tok Ich'aak turns up on numerous looted pottery vessels, including polychrome cylinders, blackware cache vessels, and lip-to-lip cache lids. Key texts about this king also survive outside the downtown zone at an Early Classic satellite center—in this case Uolantun, located about three miles southeast of the site-center. As if defining Tikal's boundaries, these very small and relatively distant suburbs attest to Tikal's expansion, a centrifugal movement in the face of increasing population pressures.

THE JAGUAR PAW LINEAGE HOUSE

For the first time, surviving records tie the ruler of Tikal to a specific architectural compound without funerary associations. To the south of the royal necropolis, another collection of buildings had begun to take shape, an area of scattered residences in Late Preclassic times that came to define the southern boundary of the Great Plaza. Emerging by the time of Chak Tok Ich'aak I as substantial masonry structures of the "range" or "palace" type, the Central Acropolis prospered as the seat of royal power and the administrative center of an increasingly complex political hierarchy. Here the ruler held court and housed his sundry officials, his sons and daughters,

Portrait of Chak Tok Ich'aak I, from an unprovenanced cache vessel lid.

The Palace of Chak Tok Ich'aak I (Structure 5D–46).

and his royal wives. As the royal palace, the Central Acropolis would emerge in Late Classic times as a labyrinth of private courtyards, concealed passageways, and complicated rooms.

Excavations have identified a particular palace structure on the Central Acropolis as the king's residence. Called by archaeologists Structure 5D–46, the building consisted of components universally associated with Maya architecture—a supporting platform, vertical walls, and a pitched roof—abstracting qualities of the common house type of poles and thatch but executed in stone. Stairways surmounted the platform from the east and west, and provided access to the two-story building on top, the latter installed with corbelled vaults and stone benches.

Primary access to the palace in Chak Tok Ich'aak I's time was probably from the east. Aligned with the stairway's axis, a stone bench positioned against the rear wall of the inner chamber probably served as the ruler's throne, with the throne room organized to accommodate court officials and scribes. As shown on polychrome "palace" scenes much later during the Classic Period, rulers received guests in similar rooms, dignitaries who approached via the staircase and across the upper landing. Cushions covered in jaguar pelt, plaited palm mats, textiles, and bevies of servants made the ruler comfortable.

That the building served as Chak Tok Ich'aak I's primary residence has been confirmed by the discovery of the building's dedicatory caches, buried beneath both staircases. By far the most important, the west cache included precious objects sealed within the confines of a beautifully carved lidded blackware vessel. Modeled in relief, the ceramic's lid identifies the palace as belonging to Chak Tok Ich'aak I, calling him the "nine generations lord" of Yax Eb' Xook, and firmly tying Ich'aak to the dynasty founder.

TIKAL SOCIAL AND ECONOMIC ORGANIZATION

The emergence of the Central Acropolis as the chief seat of government, the Maya's incipient art style, and the expansion of Tikal's population indicate that society was becoming heavily stratified by this point, if not by the time of Yax Eb' Xook. Several tiers of status were in evidence among the nobility. At the pinnacle of society stood the ruler, the chief of the site. Although royal titles that would distinguish him were slow to come into use, the cache vessel from Structure 5D–46 refers to Chak Tok Ich'aak I as a *k'uj'un* or "bookkeeper," one of the titles of certain members of the upper nobility throughout the Classic Period. The cache vessel also calls him *ajaw*, or "lord."

Ajaw distinguishes higher nobility of every sort but, as the Classic Period progressed, the ruler came to be distinguished as "sacred," "holy," or "divine"—in other words, a "divine *ajaw*." Individuals immediately below the ruler continued to refer to themselves as simply "lords."

Later inscriptions from the river valleys of the Usumacinta and Pasión speak of the high-status office of *sajal*, meaning essentially "underlord."[2] *Sahalob'* attended rulers in their palace, while others ruled in their own right over smaller, outlying secondary centers of the same class as Uolantun and Corozal. Though this title never occurs at Tikal, or anywhere else in central Petén, it indicates that the political hierarchy associated with Maya cities was stratified in ways only just beginning to be understood.

Special titles refer to women, while others identify "sages" or "learned men" (*itz'at*), "bookkeepers" (*aj k'uj'un*), "prominent artists" (*aj tz'ib'* and *aj uxul*), and "first warriors" (*b'a lom*). Presentation scenes depict court dwarves, hunchbacks, courtesans, and musicians, as well as hosts of guards and attendants. Especially complex artistic scenes included assemblies of individuals possibly representing royal councilmen, not unlike the Councils of Four and Twelve who would advise the emperor of the Aztec Triple Alliance hundreds of years in the future.

Less prominent positions included architects, surveyors, and engineers. Labor gangs undoubtedly had their foremen and their skilled and unskilled laborers. Artisans sprang up among the surrounding residences, while others manufactured specialized pottery, costume elements, and jewelry. Workers in all the sundry crafts that Maya artistic sources imply—including those who worked with leather, feathers, precious stones, jewelry, mats, textiles, and stone tools—must have fulfilled the basic needs of the population and the pageantry of increasingly elaborate religious spectacles.

Tikal households probably were organized by lineage or "family" ties, as were Aztec towns when Europeans first reached the shores of Precolumbian America. Commoners owed allegiance to higher-status individuals, the lords who resided in better-constructed dwellings and who collected percentages of the household crops, personal services, or other commodities in tribute. These items were remanded to still higher lords and, in turn, reached the ruler in the downtown zone. Heads of lineages dispensed back to their subjects usufruct rights to farm land, with choice plots differentially distributed as rewards for especially meritorious service.

Likely organized along the lines of what might be called the "patron-client" state, Maya social organization resembled feudal Europe in that it relied on complicated personal obligations and kinship ties. While obligations were more or less burdensome, social mobility could be achieved by honorable service, especially on the field of battle. Later "count of captive" titles, tallying the number of prisoners an individual warrior had personally taken, suggest that rank and prestige depended upon success in warfare—a potent theme already established on monuments such as Tikal Stela 39.

Still other nobility must have transcended social constraints by organizing long-distance trade. Both Maya and Aztec accounts at the time of the Spanish conquest indicate international trade belonged to the realm of specialized merchants, called in sixteenth-century Yucatan the Ek' Chuwajob'. Responsible for the large-scale collection of utilitarian and luxury items in "foreign" countries such as highland Guatemala, they dealt in exotic obsidian, seashells, cacao (or chocolate beans), salt, pottery, and textiles. Tikal no doubt grew rich from its share of goods crossing the Yucatan, channeling trade across the southern lowlands and monopolizing local transportation routes.

BURIAL 22

For more than two hundred years, since the burial of Yax Eb' Xook in *ca.* A.D. 150, no tombs on the North Acropolis had been sacred enough to escape renovation. Probably ripped out to make room for later construction, any burials during this period had succumbed to Tikal's relentless urge to rebuild and revamp.

Burials in the Lost World Plaza, most of them sumptuous in grave contents and clearly of high-status individuals, may account for some of the "missing" rulers between Burial 125 and the next major North Acropolis tomb. Pottery from these tombs display innovative, even playful motifs that incorporate detailed animal imagery in polychrome colors, mostly "ring-stand" or "basal-flange" bowls with dome-shaped lids.[3] Purely Maya motifs prevail, the form of the vessel itself the standard local shape. Among the most beautiful vessels, an example from Structure 5D–88's Tomb 1 depicts the head, legs, and tail of a turtle, with the domed body and lid representing the animal's carapace. Designs around the sides indicate that the turtle swims in water. Over the lid rears the head of a water bird with composite serpent-bird wings, the head and beak modeled to form the lid's handle.

Most epigraphers agree that Chak Tok Ich'aak I did not break tradition by having himself interred outside the ancestral graveyard of the North Acropolis. The first burial rich enough on the North Acropolis for a ruler since the founder, Burial 22 was installed on the main axis overlooking the staircase from the Great Plaza. Built about 8.17.0.0.0 (A.D. 375), according to seriation and radiocarbon dates, Burial 22 accords with dates given on the monuments of Tikal for Ich'aak I's demise. Stripped of its jade hundreds of years later, at a time when trade networks were breaking down and the material had grown scarce, the tomb had been ransacked long before archaeologists arrived. What survived, however, offers vital clues to the identity of its occupant.

Burial 22 had been cut through an earlier structure on the now very high platform of the North Acropolis, down through construction fill, and then covered under a more modern temple-shrine with a vaulted corbelled ceiling. Inside the crypt an adult male was put to death, no doubt to accompany the ruler on his journey into the Underworld. Besides the missing jade, the tomb contained sixteen pottery vessels, thorny oyster shell, obsidian flakes, and part of a quartzite saddle quern for grinding corn, probably imported from the relatively distant region of Belize.

Two painted polychrome basal-flange bowls, like those from the Lost World Plaza, were modeled with animal imagery that depicted jaguars. Both had lids with jaguar heads for handles, one with the body of the great cat spread-eagled over the lid in relief and with its claws bared. Before sealing the tomb, funeral attendants dusted everything—walls, bodies, grave gifts—with bright powdered cinnabar, coating everything in red. Chak Tok Ich'aak I was very old when he died, perhaps seventy or eighty, an age consistent with his associated hieroglyphic record.

THE DATE OF
CHAK TOK ICH'AAK I'S DEATH

Tikal Stela 31 bears the clear statement, almost perfectly preserved, that Chak Tok Ich'aak I "entered the water," a well-known metaphor for "death." The Maya of Tikal evidently held the belief that an individual's life resembled a cosmic canoe journey, with the span of an individual's lifetime determined by the length that the canoe traveled. When the canoe descended beneath the waters of the cosmic ocean, the person's life came to an end.

But despite the fact that Chak Tok Ich'aak had lived an honorably long time, inscriptions suggest that his reign did not end peacefully. That trouble had festered since the time of Lady Une B'alam (the early fourth century A.D.) seems certain, hinting at an unstable rulership. No longer the chief power, Tikal was gradually being eclipsed by its nearest neighbor, Uaxactun. Whatever the trouble between the two dynasties, by the time of Ich'aak's death, Tikal had thrown up formidable defensive earthworks. Massive, and penetrated only at key points, the ditched earthworks closed off the site to the north and provided a bulwark, presumably a first line of defense against any Uaxactun aggression.

Yet signs indicate that threats other than Uaxactun were beginning to plague Tikal by this time. Not only were the northern margins sealed off, but similar defensive earthworks appeared on Tikal's southern flank as well, with both earthworks running between impenetrable swamps on the west and east. More than that, subtle changes were taking place in local architecture, the introduction of forms from well outside the Tikal area. South of the Lost World Plaza, laborers had been busy constructing an elite residential compound with private ceremonial shrines and other vestiges of ritual. Amid these, unobtrusive and nearly overlooked, workers installed a little platform with distinctive terrace profiles. Called the *talud-tablero*, the feature includes upper outset rectangles (the *tablero*) positioned over battered or sloping lower walls (the *talud*). This radial platform belonged to the stylistic set of a very distant and aggressive foreign power, hundreds of miles in the west.

THE END OF THE JAGUAR DYNASTY

For slightly more than seventeen years, Chak Tok Ich'aak I had ruled in central Petén. During his lifetime, all the salient hallmarks of Maya tradition had emerged, a purely Maya surge of building and artistic energy that had brought Tikal to the brink of greatness. Already tremendous in stature, surely among the most powerful and influential cities of the Mesoamerican world, Tikal could look forward to a bright future. Chak Tok Ich'aak I's fame would spread exponentially, to judge from monuments of succeeding generations, especially beyond the Petén heartland where Classic signs of Maya civilization were still modest and precocious.

Tikal continued to maintain its original primary east-west axis, extending from the *bajo* settlements across the higher hilltops, from the North Acropolis-Great Plaza complex to the Lost World Pyramid. Residential districts surrounded this monumental urban core, mostly house platforms that supported buildings of perishable materials. More extensive structures with stone vaulting emerged as well, the houses of heads of lineages and other important officials. And while considerable jungle survived, especially in more distant areas, the whole vast downtown district was giving way inexorably to continuous pavements, plazas, and temple-shrines.

During the reign of Chak Tok Ich'aak I the stela cult of erecting stone shafts spread north to Uaxactun, and for a while Tikal and Uaxactun were the only independent centers of Petén recording the Long Count calendar. All this would change with Jaguar Paw's successor, as new institutions and new forms of economic prosperity emerged. By the time of Ich'aak's death, Maya civilization was quietly developing according to its own standards, polishing the great traditions of the Preclassic and reinvigorating them in a fresh, Classic configuration.

NOTES

1. Also referred to as Great Jaguar Paw or Jaguar Paw the Great.
2. Literally "one who fears," in reference to the individual's subordinate status to a "divine" or other high lord.
3. "Ringstand bowls" refer to vessels that have a ring around the bottom.

CHAPTER 5

THE ARRIVAL OF STRANGERS

Maya hieroglyphic inscriptions encode information about the people and events of history, but there was a time when no one could read them. For decades epigraphers labored to unlock the secrets of the strange, complex emblems. Late in the nineteenth century, Cyrus Thomas discovered that reading order progressed in double columns from left to right; and by the first decades of the twentieth century, most of the calendars were understood and could be correlated with our own dates. But differences of opinion stymied further work, with the most aggressive scholars succeeding in thoroughly silencing genuine developments. Among the most outspoken was J. Eric S. Thompson, who fought against attempts to read the glyphs phonetically or to interpret them as historical documents.

All theories nevertheless have their die-hards. Beginning in the 1950s, Heinrich Berlin identified Emblem Glyphs, nominal statements that function as lineage names or toponyms. He went on to isolate the names of individuals at Palenque and elsewhere, providing a rationale for an "historical approach." Others went on to notice similar patterns on other monuments, chiefly Tatiana Proskouriakoff, who identified the glyphs for "birth," "accession," "death," "capture," and a host of royal titles. It was Proskouriakoff who first tackled the inscriptions of Tikal, identifying the principal rulers and their primary dates.

Tatiana Proskouriakoff took under her wing a graduate student named Clemency Coggins, who went on to write her dissertation on Tikal art history. Proskouriakoff shared Coggins' ideas about Early Classic succession and its major players, and helped her shape the first Tikal dynastic sequence. Together, they identified the burials of most of Tikal's kings—research that is still valid today—while Coggins wrote the first history of the Maya lowlands.

Newer, more dynamic work eclipsed Proskouriakoff as phonetic decipherments gained momentum, and much of the script could be read in Mayan. Despite the fact that the historical background developed by the two women became the basis of later translations, few scholars bothered to cite their work at Tikal. When they did, it was largely in token deference.

Proskouriakoff died in 1986, while writing the summation of her life's work, *Maya History*. The book lacks the depth that characterizes modern phonetic and historical decipherments, yet it contains innumerable insights into ancient dynastic life. One such observation centers around a controversial moment—the death of Chak Tok Ich'aak I. Purely dependent upon standard Preclassic and Early Classic motifs of definitively Maya character, monuments of this period went on to thoroughly influence Maya aesthetics for generations to come. Yet, with the death of Chak Tok Ich'aak I, new ideas infused the royal dynastic art at Tikal and many additional locations throughout the lowlands. With the introduction of these motifs, one of the more intriguing episodes in Maya history begins.

THE BURIAL OF NUUN YAX AYIN (BURIAL 10)

For more than seven hundred years, the North Acropolis had served as the receptacle for tombs of the Tikal elite, especially the burials of kings. Yax Eb' Xook had certainly entered his Afterlife from there, as had the first thirteen successors. But with the passing of the successor to Chak Tok Ich'aak I, Nuun Yax Ayin, the focus of tomb construction shifted dramatically, taking the first of a series of steps that would scatter the royal funeral shrines of Tikal throughout the downtown districts.

Built along the western end of the North Terrace, the projecting slip that fronts the North Acropolis proper, the temple-shrine for the new ruler's tomb would set the precedent for adding funerary shrines against the front staircase from west to east. Subsequent builders followed this example until the

Late Classic period, building repeatedly over these original temples until great towering spires were raised.

Supported on a wooden funeral bier, the dead king was carried into the tomb resplendent with jades and textile finery. As they set him on the tomb floor, his attendants arranged turtle carapaces beside him "marimba fashion," that is, from smallest to largest like a xylophone. To this offering they added pigmy owls, green jays, and an ant tanager—the first birds included in a tomb at Tikal[1]—in addition to stingray spines used in blood-letting rites, thorny oyster shell, and the headless skeleton of a crocodile. Executioners dispatched nine sacrificial victims to accompany the ruler into the Underworld.

Name Glyph of
Nuun Yax Ayin I.

Those sealing the tomb left behind the small head of a crocodile—quite possibly an "Olmec dragon"—carved from jade, its snout curled tightly back on itself, representing the namesake in hiero-glyphic inscriptions of the fifteenth ruler of Tikal. For lack of another name or translation in Mayan, epigraphers initially called this man Curl Snout.[2] Recent decipherments indicate that his name reads Nuun Yax Ayin, or "First Great Crocodile."

Imports from the Valley of Guatemala figured among the thirty-two ceramics found in Burial 10. The most outstanding, a three-dimensional effigy representing the so-called Old Fire God seated on a stool, comes apart under the arms so that incense can be burned inside, and allows smoke to escape through its fore-head tube. The Old Fire God proffers a human skull on the palms of its extended hands and wears an especially impressive beard.

Old Fire God Figurine, Burial 10.

KAMINALJUYU, "PLACE OF THE ANCIENT ONES"

The massive mountains of Guatemala and Chiapas extend from west to east along the continental divide. Down their southern margin march the cones of numerous volcanoes both active and dormant, testimony to a violent region plagued since the beginning of time by eruptions and earthquakes. Populations settled in Preclassic times along the Pacific Piedmont between the mountain massifs and Pacific Ocean, but the richer valleys of the highlands attracted even denser populations that built far more impressive architectural centers.

Modern Guatemala City in the Valley of Guatemala engulfs one such ruin, Kaminaljuyu, approximately five square miles of buried architecture alongside the Pan-American Highway. In the late 1930s and early 1940s, the Carnegie Institution of Washington conducted excavations in two of the Early Classic pyramids there, both of which overlay earlier Preclassic ones. Originally earthen mounds when work got underway, the pyramids were found to have distinctive *talud-tablero* architecture, and to form part of a network of regular streets.

Some dozen elite tombs were found within the mounds, mostly of high-ranking males interred sitting on the remains of boxes or wooden litters. Quantities of jade and other jewelry adorned the deceased, while stacks of pottery were crammed into the vaults—tripod cylinders of foreign design covered in stucco and painted, including vessels imported from the Zapotec capital at Monte Alban, and others from El Salvador.

Not only were the final tombs of Mound A, the ones associated with *talud-tablero* architecture, roughly contemporaneous with that of Nuun Yax Ayin, but both interments contained similar pottery and nearly identical artifacts: turtle carapaces, crocodiles, and the same kind of birds.

Kaminaljuyu, or "Place of the Ancient Ones," exhibited extraordinarily close cultural and economic ties to Tikal. Kaminaljuyu controlled trade in obsidian procured from the surrounding hills, mass-producing "blanks" (or unfinished slabs) at the quarries, and distributing these to distant areas throughout Mesoamerica, where local craft shops worked them into finished products. Originally an indigenous government, Kaminaljuyu administered dozens of scattered villages and farming hamlets throughout the valley and pine-covered slopes.

Sometime during the third or fourth century A.D., Kaminaljuyu came under the sway of outside political forces, the source of foreign architecture and other elements both there and at Tikal. Either through conquest, through trade associations, or through subtle alliance and intermarriage— or all three—Kaminaljuyu bound its wealth to this more powerful rival. Foreign domination would overshadow the city for the rest of its Classic days.

BURIAL 10'S COSMOPOLITAN FLAVOR

Although Kaminaljuyu contributed heavily to Nuun Yax Ayin's grave assemblage, gifts probably brought by the Kaminaljuyu branch of the ruler's family to pay their last respects, there were other vessels from the Guatemalan coast. The most notable, a black-brown cylinder with a lid, includes as the lid's handle a "diving god" who balances on his arms as he somersaults. The little acrobat wears cross-hatched tabs along his loincloth that sprout leaves, seemingly depicting cacao pods, the source of chocolate.

Classic monuments of the Guatemalan Pacific Coast in particular depicted cacao, and like Kaminaljuyu came under the sway of foreign influence throughout much of their history. Vast hordes of foreign pottery turn up at this time throughout much of this region, including mold-appliqué incense braziers, with distinctively non-local features and symbolic imagery traceable to areas far in the West.

As Mesoamerica's basic currency, cacao beans played an enormous role in local and international economies. Transshipped from the cacao-producing centers of the Maya area and Central America, where ideal environmental conditions prevailed, cacao rose dramatically in price once the precious cargo reached arid central Mexico. Soaring populations throughout the Classic world furthered demand for the product and fueled long-distance trade. Control over production of family and state-run plantations, and over cacao merchants, probably remained one of Mesoamerica's primary sources of wealth. To ensure monopolization of money that literally "grew on trees," elaborate political and family ties were fostered. It was these ties that no doubt formed a major source of financing for Tikal's nobility.[3]

But ultimately Burial 10's strongest contributor was the source of foreign influence itself, the real power behind the throne. If political events in the Precolumbian world resembled big fish swallowing smaller ones, then Tikal was about to be swallowed by the biggest fish of them all: Teotihuacan.

CENTRAL MEXICO

In the initial centuries A.D., the Valley of Mexico far to the west of the Maya world began to attract enormous populations, concentrated in a spur of the valley off its northeastern flank. This first truly urban population in America came to embrace eight square miles of structures and as many as one to two hundred thousand inhabitants. Their city was Teotihuacan, the "Home of the Gods."

The impact of this huge concentration of pyramids, streets, apartment buildings, and concourse plazas on the rest of the Mesoamerican world must have been incalculable. Dominated by its Pyramid of the Sun, some thirty million cubic feet of rubble and cut stone 230-feet high, its structures stood among the tallest Precolumbian monuments ever built. Slightly higher than any pyramid at Tikal, the Sun Pyramid ranged as large around its base (about 700 feet along each side) as the great pyramid of Cheops in Egypt.

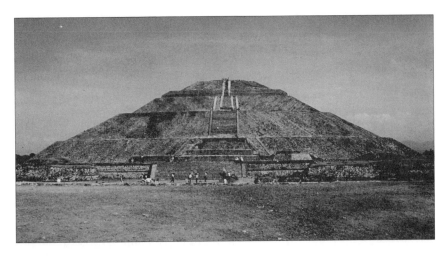

Pyramid of the Sun, Teotihuacan.

Unlike the founders of Tikal, whoever built the city of Teotihuacan did so according to a carefully maintained plan. Organized along avenues and streets, Teotihuacan preserved its layout in strict orientation to the cardinal directions, deliberately skewed seventeen degrees east of north. At its heart lay the intersection of two broad avenues that divided the city into four quarters and established the basic orientation of every avenue and building, even those that were miles from the downtown zone.

The Street of the Dead served as the city's main axis, originating at the Pyramid of the Moon in the north and running south for two miles, well beyond the major buildings. All along the most important segment of this avenue, fronting the minor pyramids and the Sun and Moon Pyramids, *talud-tablero* architecture distinctively shaped this most important of locations, the most massive display of such architecture ever conceived.

Not nearly as massive as the Pyramid of the Sun, but in many respects more important for its decoration, the Temple of the Feathered Serpent embraced ideas that Teotihuacan emissaries and traders carried to the far corners of Mesoamerica. Emblazoned with full-frontal serpent heads with feathered necks, and eighteen scaled or mosaic serpent "warrior helmets," the Feathered Serpent Temple occupied the heart of the Ciudadela Complex, where the Mesoamerican "New Fire" ceremony took place. As depicted in hieroglyphic books from later Aztec times, the fire kindled every fifty-two years required stick bundles, or fasces, that would themselves become emblems of Mesoamerican lineage founders. This fire, originally engendered by primordial gods, would keep the generations alive, rekindled in the renewal of life and the rebirth of the sun.

Crowded into the central districts and beyond, Teotihuacan's inhabitants occupied compact one-story apartment buildings secluded from other compounds by high windowless walls. Over two thousand apartments have been identified by archaeological mapping projects. Populations lived in neighborhoods organized by the crafts they manufactured. Foreign enclaves occupied private districts representing Oaxaca, the Gulf Coast, the Yucatan, and Guatemala. More than five hundred workshops mass-produced pottery, finished obsidian tools made from imported blanks, and practiced other crafts that were in demand throughout the Mesoamerican world.

Teotihuacan traders traveled the far-flung provinces of Mesoamerica to fill Mexican workshops. Commerce brought merchants to the Maya area to trade for jaguar hides, colorful feathers, cacao, jade, cotton, rare shells, and exotic marine materials, but especially obsidian for the large-scale tool industry. Developing deep inroads into Maya culture, Teotihuacan eventually dominated such thoroughly Maya cities as Kaminaljuyu, which consciously transformed itself into a less spectacular replica of Teotihuacan. All along the Pacific Coast, Mexicans left massive quantities of pottery, often careful copies but otherwise excellent trade imports from the workshops of Teotihuacan itself. With royal estates of cacao trees along the Pacific Coast within its dominions, Teotihuacan dominated all the major sources of Mesoamerican wealth.

To manage transshipment across Petén, Teotihuacan must have set its sights on Tikal, understanding that to control the lowland Maya was to control trade itself. Teotihuacan unquestionably functioned as an economic empire, the center of a "world economy" that commanded allegiance and tribute from subjects through far-ranging distribution networks and kinship ties. In size, population, and the density of its buildings, the highland Mexican metropolis evolved into the greatest urban zone, the most complexly stratified society in Mesoamerica, and quite possibly in all of the New World.

TEOTIHUACAN'S CONTRIBUTION TO BURIAL 10

Some of the most beautiful Teotihuacan vessels, found either in Mexico or anywhere else, come from Nuun Yax Ayin's Burial 10. Some were direct imports, others locally-manufactured imitations of exceptional quality. As usual in royal tombs at Tikal, there were ring-based or basal-flange bowls, each with a domed cover; but these were painted with ring-eyed Tlalocs, the principal Mexican Rain God, and Xipe Totec, the Mexican "flayed" god, rather than with Maya jaguars and other animals.

In numerous respects, these vessels resemble the renowned Teotihuacan stucco murals, as if a bit of the city's signature mural work in portable form had become the currency of gift exchange.

Another vessel combines bird and conch shapes, undoubtedly a direct import from Mexico[4]. Feathers and shells were among the most highly

*Ring-Stand Bowl, with dome lid painted with
the Mexican Rain God (Tlaloc), Burial 10.*

prized luxury items from the Maya world, no doubt used in quantity by
Teotihuacan and other workshops in the densely settled regions of Mexico.
Featured prominently in murals on the walls of the Tetitla compound at
Teotihuacan, shells and birds repeat with wallpaper-like regularity as possible emblematic devices. In the same compound, an old man sits surrounded by shells, recalling the Old Fire God from Burial 10. These and
other associations suggest direct ties between Teotihuacan and Tikal at
some close and very personal level.

THE ARRIVAL OF SIYAJ K'AK'

But at Tikal, the most powerful evidence comes not from unseen artifacts
hidden in tombs, but architectural and sculptural monuments marked con-
spicuously as "Mexican." Nuun Yax Ayin himself stares back from Stela 4
arrayed in extraordinary foreign style, wearing feathers and shells. No previous ruler had displayed these features, conspicuous in the necklace and

Stela 4, front.

the fantastic spray of headdress plumes. Contrary to previous stelae, he faces directly at the viewer, enthroned with only his lower body in profile. He cradles in his arm something not before seen at Tikal—the weapon of choice from central Mexico, an *atlatl* or spearthrower.

Name Glyph of Siyaj K'ak'.

Stela 4 preserves Yax Ayin's accession date as 8.17.2.3.16 (September 13, A.D. 379), only slightly less than two years after the death of Chak Tok Ich'aak I. Key information follows with the identification of who presided over the affairs of Tikal during this interregnum. That information comes in the form of a personal name, the head of an "up-turned frog" preceded by flame—Siyaj K'ak', or "Fire-Born."

Siyaj K'ak' figures as the most enigmatic character in Tikal's early days. As related much later in the dynastic sequence, his presence follows a possible local war and the "conjuring" or "appearance" of an individual who takes a "spearthrower" for his name. Also conjured was the War Serpent Waxaklajun U B'a, a creature made manifest during bloodletting rites and associated with Teotihuacan's scaled war helmet (reproduced eighteen times along the facade of the Feathered Serpent Temple).

To make sense of the forces behind these changes, sculptured monuments from districts surrounding Tikal and somewhat farther afield offer vital clues. Seventy-five miles to the west, El Peru guarded one of the principal overland approaches to Petén, restricting access to Tikal's western perimeter and its incipient political centers. Within a generation of Chak Tok Ich'aak I, El Peru had erected the first of its surviving monuments: Stela 15, which notes Siyaj K'ak''s involvement in an event only eight days before the death of Chak Tok Ich'aak I.

Another clue from Uaxactun, one of the original Petén core districts approximately fourteen miles north of Tikal, involves Siyaj K'ak''s "arrival" there, where Stela 5 depicts a warrior in the uniform of Teotihuacan who brandishes an *atlatl* (spearthrower). Over his "balloon" headdress perches a quetzal bird, its long spray of tail feathers cascading down his back. 11 Eb' (8.17.1.4.12, or January 16th, A.D. 378) marks the warrior's arrival.

The "arrival" of Siyaj K'ak' figures in key inscriptions at Tikal itself, in particular the so-called "Ball Court Marker," or "Marcador." Among the

Tikal Ball Court Marker, now in the National Museum, Guatemala City.

most unusual Maya sculptures, the Marcador represents the stone version of a distinctive war banner, carved as a cylindrical shaft and spherical upper area with a feather-bordered disk. Emblems within the feathers depict the name of the Mexican Rain God—a bracket and three circles that pervade murals throughout Teotihuacan, and an owl behind a hand that holds the Mexican spearthrower.

Few monuments in Precolumbian America resemble the Marcador. Although Teotihuacan painted ball game scenes with similar objects, actual counterparts in stone survive, carved with cylindrical bases and spherical-disk arrangements like the one at Tikal. Tikal's Marcador originates from one of the major Tikal residential districts south of the Lost World Complex, where buildings early in the Classic Period were heavily remodeled in Teoti-huacan *talud-tablero* fashion.

The Tikal Marcador bears two hieroglyphic texts carved in panels that include very strange, possibly foreign glyphs. Their featured statements provide Siyaj K'ak''s parentage—his mother was a local woman of Maya stock, his father the man who takes the Mexican "spearthrower." The opening date falls on 11 Eb' 15 Mak,[5] the "arrival" at Tikal of Siyaj K'ak' the West Kalomte', the same day of his arrival at Uaxactun.

Chillingly, this date—June 16th A.D. 378—also marks the death of Jaguar Paw, the ruler Chak Tok Ich'aak I.

STELA 31

References to Siyaj K'ak''s Petén "arrival," together with later notations from Palenque, suggest that he arrived from outside the territory under Maya control. Having left his place of origin probably in A.D. 377, and after the "conjuring" of whomever or whatever takes the "spearthrower" glyph, he reached El Peru nearly seven months later. After an additional eight days, he arrived at Tikal and Uaxactun.

Siyaj K'ak''s arrival at Tikal may be portrayed on a cylinder tripod man-ufactured in Teotihuacan style, depicting an on-going journey of Teoti-huacan warriors. Marching in file around the body of the vessel, they brandish *atlatls* and spears, but bear gifts from an obviously Mexican

talud-tablero temple towards a purely Maya one. Frieze-like and impersonal, the warriors arrive with friendly intentions, but arrayed in military
paraphernalia and posed ready to engage in combat. Inscriptions indicate
Siyaj K'ak''s arrival in Petén involved travel from west to east through the
western Maya lowlands, the western rivers district, and then into Tikal. His
western arrival may account for his title "West Kalomte'," tying Fire-Born
to an origin in Mexico.

One other monument from Tikal sheds crucial light on these events,
among the most remarkable stelae ever carved. Commissioned by Nuun Yax
Ayin's successor in the years following Burial 10, Stela 31 carries on its
reverse an exceptionally long inscription of more than two hundred individual glyphs. Concerned largely with events surrounding the reign of the
son of Nuun Yax Ayin, its early passages relate in detail the circumstance
of Chak Tok Ich'aak I's demise and the arrival of the stranger Siyaj K'ak'. Not
only does it feature prominently the 11 Eb' "arrival," it relates Siyaj K'ak''s
relationships and hints at the identity of the man who takes the "spearthrower" sign.

Side panels on Stela 31 portray Nuun Yax Ayin dressed in the warrior
uniform of Teotihuacan. Diminutive and slight, as though a young man, he
bears the Mexican spearthrower in each portrait, both marked with the
ring-eyes of the Mexican Rain God Tlaloc. He wears on the left the scaled
feathered-serpent helmet indicative of Teotihuacan, like one found inside
his tomb, and carries on the right side a shield emblazoned with Tlaloc.
Both representations of Nuun Yax Ayin and Tlaloc wear the pectin shells
introduced on Stela 4. The two representations include rear bustles of multiple coyote tails, ubiquitous in Teotihuacan murals and Mexican stuccoed
and painted pottery.

Inscriptions carved above each side portrait on Stela 31 identify Nuun
Yax Ayin by name. He was simply a "k'atun ajaw," someone who ruled (or
lived) for less than twenty years, an epithet reminiscent of the Spanish
Colonial books called the Chilam Balams and their references to foreigners
as "two-day" and "three-day" lords. In other words, by Maya standards
Nuun Yax Ayin's longevity was short-lived, without precedence, and not
fully acceptable. The overhead texts describe his father—the man who
takes the Mexican spearthrower as his name.

Stela 31, right side.

THE ACCESSION OF JATZ'AM KU

It thus follows that Nuun Yax Ayin and Siyaj K'ak' were brothers, offspring of the man named "spearthrower." On Stela 31 this hand-held weapon surmounts a shield-like device, and elsewhere surmounts an owl. Phonetic spellings suggest the name reads Jatz'am Ku.[6]

The motif of owl and spear, or owl and spearthrower—with the latter sometimes grasped by a human hand—pervades painted and sculptured images at Teotihuacan, especially the polychrome murals added as decoration to the more elaborate residential compounds. Called the *lechuzas y armas* motif, or "owl and weapon" sign, it conveys in especially strong terms the direct ties between Teotihuacan and Tikal.

Jatz'am Ku, father of Siyaj K'ak' and Nuun Yax Ayin, acceded in A.D. 374, and "oversaw" his son's arrival on the day Chak Tok Ich'aak I died. Whatever the motivation, Fire-Born's journey to Tikal took place under his father's auspices. Jatz'am Ku's other son, Nuun Yax Ayin, then acceded when he was very young, possibly too young to rule Tikal alone—the direct result of Siyaj K'ak''s arrival and the death of Chak Tok Ich'aak I. Jatz'am Ku still lived and ruled at the time of the succeeding king, and his death took place during this later period, in A.D. 439. Since his accession happened when Chak Tok Ich'aak I still ruled Tikal, Jatz'am Ku could hardly have been Tikal's ruler.

The question remains, over which site did Jatz'am Ku accede?

a

b

c

Name Glyph of Jatz'am Ku.

Lechuzas y Armas *Motif, from an unprovenanced mural from Teotihuacan.*

PLACE OF THE CATTAIL REEDS

There seems little doubt, given Teotihuacan's pervasive emblems, that the "strangers" Siyaj K'ak' and Nuun Yax Ayin originated in central Mexico. That Jatz'am Ku acceded and died on specific dates—an extraordinarily long reign of sixty-five years—suggests that he ruled over an actual location. All doubt vanishes with the "foreign" hieroglyphs in the inscriptions at Tikal, especially the pervasive Mayan name for Teotihuacan—the logogram that translates *pu*, or "Cattail Reed." This fact, and the widespread presence at Teotihuacan of the *lechuzas y armas* motif, points to this city as the place over which Jatz'am Ku reigned.

"Place of the Cattail Reeds" served not only as the sign for Teotihuacan in manuscripts during later Aztec times, but it designated one of the most prestigious and enigmatic locations in Mesoamerican lore and legend. This was Tollan (the Aztec name), more commonly Tula, which was founded by the Toltecs, Teotihuacan's Terminal Classic successor in central Mexico.

The Toltecs were an ephemeral people, the product of northern "Chichimeca" barbarians and easterly Nonoalcans, the latter the people of a land that included much of the western Maya world. It was the Toltecs from whom later Aztec emperors claimed descent, recognizing them as the people who introduced high art and craftwork to the world, as well as knowledge and ritual. In short, the Toltecs founded civilization itself, bequeathing to the rest of Mesoamerica the fruits of an ordered society. Toltec descent lent legitimacy to aspiring kings and dynasties, bestowing honor and prestige; and it was the Toltec cultural hero who received the highest honors—the renowned Quetzalcóatl or Feathered Serpent.

The key to Toltec history concerns their migration, their dispersal from Chicomoztoc or Place of the Seven Caves, which was intimately related to the Aztec mythical homeland, Aztlán. From this area migrated the Toltecs and all the other Mesoamerican people who came to settle in the diverse locations where most of the great civilizations arose.

Scholars have long debated the location of Tollan, with no indication that their arguments will abate any time soon. Originally Jorgé Acosta, the renowned Mexican scholar, identified Tula in the Mexican state of Hidalgo as Toltec Tollan, basing his argument on the correspondence between hieroglyphic place signs, ethnohistoric references, and the surviving names of the surrounding towns. Nevertheless, Tula lacks the scale and monumentality implied by legendary Tollan. Relatively poorly constructed and mostly unimpressive, Tula appears an unlikely candidate for a great military empire—one that would dominate the hearts and minds of Mesoamericans for the next three hundred years.

Teotihuacan, on the other hand, fits Tollan admirably. Clearly a huge economic and probably military empire, Teotihuacan left its mark on the arts and crafts, the political organizations, and the religious beliefs of every culture with which it came into contact. Thus it was influential not just for several hundred years, but for the remainder of Mesoamerican history. In recent years, consensus has mounted for the identification of several Tollans, for in general "*tollan*" meant "great city." Teotihuacan was the greatest and most formidable Tollan of them all.

Stela 31 with its exceptionally long text evokes the flavor of the Toltec migration history, a hint that the Mexican arrival at Tikal exceeded straightforward historical events. Bound up with the myth of Tollan, it conveys an epic quality redolent of the heart and soul of Mesoamerica.

EXPANSION OF THE PETÉN CORE

With the arrival of Siyaj K'ak', the original Maya core district irrevocably fell under the sway of Teotihuacan, falling into the lap of the great central Mexican metropolis by the time of the inauguration of Nuun Yax Ayin in A.D. 379. As Teotihuacan's king, Jatz'am Ku perhaps sent his son to rule Tikal, after Siyaj K'ak''s successful reduction of the local lineages. Texts from later in Tikal history hint that the rationale for Mexico's intervention involved an on-going dispute over the reign of Chak Tok Ich'aak I. While Teotihuacan certainly moved to capture Tikal's political power, exactly how it succeeded remains unclear. The mother of Nuun Yax Ayin belonged to the local Jaguar Paw lineage, and since no evidence survives that Jatz'am Ku himself lived at Tikal, the mother no doubt resided and gave birth at Teotihuacan. As a legitimate member of the royal lineage on his mother's side, Nuun Yax Ayin could manipulate the intricacies of Tikal politics more so than any completely foreign king. To be sure, Siyaj K'ak' arrived with Teotihuacan warriors to back up Teotihuacan's ostensibly peaceful trade activities with formidable military might.

As Teotihuacan expanded into the Maya lowlands, seeking to control trade goods, its expeditionary members appropriated shells and feathers—among the most important ritual Mesoamerican trade items—as lineage symbols, and as familial insignias of rank.[7] To emphasize these signs, they recreated on the walls of their residential compound at Teotihuacan the environment and setting of their source of wealth. Nuun Yax Ayin wore shells and feathers for their emblematic value, as seen so frequently on his Maya portraits. In this way, Nuun Yax Ayin identified himself with the families who resided in the Tetitla compound so distinctive for Teotihuacan.[8]

Solidifying control over the Maya by acceding at Tikal, Nuun Yax Ayin emblazoned the downtown with Mexican symbolism, probably far more than currently survives. In addition to his own accession monument, he installed a formidable portrait of his father, the Teotihuacan ruler Jatz'am Ku. Stela 32 survives only in fragmentary condition, but portrays Spear-thrower Owl with the ring eyes of the Mexican Rain God, bearing on his chest the head of an owl and wearing a typically Teotihuacan headdress.

Stela 32.

The presence of Jatz'am Ku, Nuun Yax Ayin, and Siyaj K'ak' in the Tikal inscriptions, as well as the pervasive nature of Mexican ceramics, artistic motifs, and costume elements, all point to the tremendous impact Teotihuacan had on the Maya world. With Teotihuacan's expansion, the Maya stela cult expanded as well. The first great wave, initiated after Chak Tok Ich'aak I, distributed monuments largely within the immediate surrounding districts, bearing Tikal's official state art style to smaller, secondary centers. At least one image carried the jaguar paw emblem as far as southern Belize and the minor center of Uxbenká.

Not content with Tikal alone, Siyaj K'ak' went on to lead Teotihuacan merchant-warriors into other areas of Petén. Monuments during the second wave of expansion turn up at Bejucal and El Zapote, engraven with this warrior's name. Río Azul especially came under heavy Mexican influence. Warriors under Siyaj K'ak' descended upon this minor site and sacked it, capturing at least six of its local lords. Sculpture at Río Azul depicts these individuals bound and tied, subdued under an expanding wave of Teotihuacan military might. As far as distant Honduras in the southeast, Siyaj K'ak''s name would spread and be recorded by subsequent generations who would link him to the founding of Copán. Nearly all the monuments of this period extol Fire-Born, the Teotihuacan warrior who installed his brother, Nuun Yax Ayin, at Tikal.

THE DEATH OF NUUN YAX AYIN I

Shortly before completion of the half-k'atun, or half-period of twenty years (8.18.10.0.0), Nuun Yax Ayin passed away after a reign of slightly more than twenty-five years. During his lifetime, or soon afterwards, the practice of erecting sculptured stone shafts to commemorate the passage of time, especially the passage of the twenty-year k'atun period, would continue to spread from its origins at Tikal and Uaxactun. The practice reached Balakbal and possibly Xultun in the north, El Zapote to the east, Uolantun to the south, and Yaxhá to the southeast.

B'aktun 8 monuments, erected during the eighth period of four-hundred years, cluster around the headwaters of the Holmul River, which rises from feeder streams of the Bajo de Santa Fe not far from Tikal. A tiny area responsible for about fifteen monuments between them after Stela 29—

from approximately 8.12.0.0.0 to 8.14.0.0.0—the central Petén district produced a homogeneous sculptural style, almost always employing the same stance in which the figure strides with one foot before the other, and the same hand position in which the fingers press against the chest to curl around the thumb. Despite their ties to Tikal, each varied in peculiar ways, maintaining their individualism and innovative features.

Nuun Yax Ayin and his reign introduced Mexican imagery to Petén, where it was erected alongside purely Maya styles. Over the next generation, Tikal would forge an artistic legacy from these elements that had lasting results on the Classic Maya. Although descended from local stock on his mother's side, Nuun Yax Ayin remained something less than a legitimate blood member of the ruling lineage. In order to stabilize his authority, he married a daughter of Chak Tok Ich'aak I soon after his arrival, thereby binding Tikal and all that it controlled to the sovereignty of the Mexican state. Very young when he acceded in A.D. 379, he was still young for a major ruler when he died in *ca.* A.D. 404; but his influence, and that of the men who installed him in power, would endure for generations.

Nuun Yax Ayin introduced a "golden age" that outstripped his own fame, one that saw not only the Maya world transformed but every region in Mesoamerica touched by Teotihuacan. Quickly reaching its maximum territorial extent in terms of what it directly influenced, Teotihuacan would continue to thrive and prosper as the most powerful of all Precolumbian urban zones.

Many years would pass before Mesoamerica saw such unity again.

NOTES

1. Problematical Deposit 87, from the Late Preclassic Period, included two dozen quetzal wings. The tail feathers from this bird were later used at Tikal as costume ornaments.
2. And alternatively "Curl Nose." I am reading the order of glyphic elements as NUUN YAX AYIN, rather than the more accepted YAX NUUN AYIN, largely for editorial purposes. Certainly the latter more likely conforms to the actual reading order.
3. Coggins 1975.
4. Coggins 1975.
5. Written evidently in error 11 Eb' 10 Mak.
6. As argued by the Dutch epigrapher Eric Boot.
7. Coggins 1975.
8. Although originally proposed by Coggins (1975), my review of the data suggests that her idea remains a viable one.

Stela 31, front and sides.

Nuun Yax Ayin I in the "Sky" or "Protector" Position

Name of Siyaj Kaan K'awil II In Headdress

Name of the Founder Yax Eb' Xook Over the Earflare

Accession Helmet

Trophy Heads on Belt

CHAPTER 6

SKY-BORN "ANCESTOR"

J ust after completion of the Eighth B'aktun—the turn of a Maya "millennium"—Tikal introduced an innovative Teotihuacan arrangement on Stela 31, representing in many ways Tikal's crowning Early Classic achievement. Progressing vegisimally, or by multiples of twenty, the higher order of time changed only twice during the Classic Period—from the Eighth to the Ninth B'aktun in A.D. 435, and from the Ninth to the Tenth B'aktun in 830. Rare by any standard, the B'aktun change represented a great milestone, a cause for celebration and the dedication of special monuments.

Stela 31 bears the dedicatory date 9.0.10.0.0, ten years after this major calendrical node. Presented in narrative form in an extraordinarily long text on the rear surface, the extensive hieroglyphs on Stela 31 suffered damage in later times, resulting in the loss of one-quarter of the inscription from the lower portion of the monument. Nevertheless, the passages that survive provide much of the early history of Tikal.

The long text on Stela 31 extends as far back as the reign of Lady Une B'alam (8.14.0.0.0; A.D. 317), and then steps forward to the arrival of Siyaj K'ak' and Nuun Yax Ayin ca. 378. Its extraordinary sides identify the two flanking portraits of Nuun Yax Ayin dressed in the warrior uniform of Teotihuacan.

But the true innovation of Stela 31 lies in the way Nuun Yax Ayin's side portraits flank the central image, bracketing the detail-encrusted likeness of his son and successor. Rigid and impersonal, the warrior-father guards and protects his son, Siyaj Kaan K'awil II, with the full might of the Teotihuacan state.

Overwhelmed in detail, the new ruler faces left on the front surface while holding aloft his grandfather's accession helmet, heralding his inauguration under the auspices of Jatz'am Ku. Tied together to form a chain, jade earspools hang from the helmet's chin guard, ornaments probably taken from enemy war captives as souvenirs. The helmet displays Jatz'am Ku's heraldic device—the owl carrying a spear and shield—mounted over its crown.

Siyaj Kaan K'awil wears heavily encumbered belt devices balanced left and right with the heads of the God of Number Seven and the Jaguar God of the Underworld, the latter supporting the name of the ruler's mother, Lady Une B'alam. The second woman to use the "scroll-baby" with umbilical cord, she bears an earlier queen's namesake, tying the new king to indigenous factions at Tikal. Both heads include dangler plaques of jade, while the belt carries a series of segments denoting the royal mat—emblematic devices that signify the ruler's throne and consequently his source of power.

The ruler bends his curled hand against his chest in the traditional style of the Early Classic period, maintaining canons of Maya portraiture and embracing in the crook of his arm the purely Maya God of Number Seven. Heraldic like his grandfather's name, Tikal's Mutul emblem rides the head, surmounted by the *ajaw* title that means "lord," and backed by a jaguar's tail—again, all devices emblematic of early Tikal. Yax Eb' Xook, Tikal's founder, emerges with his saurian head and lashed scaffold segment, to angle over the ruler's enormous earflare and to reinforce his ties to the indigenous royal lineage. In the "sky position" reserved for ancestors, Nuun Yax Ayin peers down to "protect" and "oversee" his son, his headdress the curl-nosed Olmec dragon that was his namesake.

The new king was a potent ruler, one charged with all the sacred emblems of the city as well as foreign ones not yet fully absorbed by the people of Tikal. By commissioning Stela 31, imbued with both Maya and Mexican symbols, he declared the dual nature of his allegiance, upholding traditional Maya sources of power while championing those of his father and grandfather.

THE SIXTEENTH SUCCESSOR

Nothing so perfectly reflects the goals and aspirations of this ruler than the hieroglyph for his name, the long-nosed patron of royal lineages known as K'awil. Vaulting from the cleft image of the sky with his little arms bent at right angles, K'awil bears a mirror infixed over his forehead, and from this an ax extends with smoke or fire scrolls streaming out of the tip in opposite directions. Installed over the ruler's head on Stela 31, the name depicts K'awil being born literally from the sky, hence he is Siyaj Kaan K'awil—"Sky-Born K'awil."

As patron of royal bloodlines, K'awil would become the chief heraldic device of rulers in succeeding generations, held commonly as the king's scepter. Used in these contexts the god's leg terminates in the body and head of a snake to form a handle, hence his essentially one-footed nature. Full-figure representations depict him in a fashion similar to Lady Une B'alam's "scroll-baby" device, with K'awil reclining on his back below an umbilical cord that identifies the god as an infant. Since the Mayan name for "lineage," or *ch'ok*, also means "youth" or "sprout," it may be that the "infant qualities" of K'awil relate to his patronage of royal lineages, and that lineage was conceived of as the "root" or "sprout" of a particular blood line. His name may be interpreted therefore as "Sky-Born Lineage."

Siyaj Kaan K'awil probably erected Stela 31 on the North Terrace footing the North Acropolis, near the area of his later funerary shrine. Towards the west, near the end of the terrace, Nuun Yax Ayin's Stela 4 would have stood before an early shrine covering his Burial 10, with the two monuments positioned nearly side by side for the next several generations. Other monuments

a

b

Name Glyphs of Siyaj Kaan K'awil II.

attributable to Siyaj Kaan—Stelae 1, 2, and 28—pose the ruler in the same manner as Stela 31, with sculptural programs embracing all four sides of the stones. These monuments clearly present Siyaj Kaan's rationale for himself and the power he wielded, an attempt to establish his legitimacy after his father's disruption of the Jaguar line. The "sprout" of a Maya mother but Mexican father, he represented a compromise, a melding of foreign and Maya traditions, a dynamic new personality who claimed the best of both worlds. In some ways the restorer of the Jaguar line, his power base and economic wealth nevertheless embraced Teotihuacan's far-flung trade network, a commercial empire that backed his claim to the throne with force. Considering that he succeeded his father only after a lapse of seven years, he may have called on that force more than once.

As with Chak Tok Ich'aak I, Yax Ayin, and many other rulers of early Tikal, pottery vessels looted in modern times from the peripheries of the site or from Tikal's dependent satellite centers supplement the local inscriptions. The most important identify Siyaj Kaan K'awil as the sixteenth successor of Yax Eb' Xook. In addition to his Mexican heritage, he was careful to maintain associations back to the founder of the line, painstakingly establishing his claims, if in reality only quasi-legitimate ones, to rule Tikal. While superficially the situation appeared very different from previous generations, his succession, he was quick to note, had proceeded out of an "unbroken" past.

THE FOUNDING OF COPÁN

Teotihuacan's presence increased under Siyaj Kaan, and for a time Mexico established its own suburb at Tikal, just as the Maya had established barrios representing Guatemala and the Yucatan at Teotihuacan. Laid out with extensive *talud-tablero* architecture, the Teotihuacan suburb had its own monuments, including the exotic Mexican Marcador. The Teotihuacan residential district south of the Lost World Plaza thrived remarkably well, increasing in complexity and population and commanding resources from master craftsmen of every sort. Nearby, Teotihuacan established its own cemetery, an area infused with unusual burials including gifts of non-local iron pyrite mirrors, rare Mexican green obsidian, and other signs of continuing contact.

Farther afield, much farther than Petén-style motifs had ever before traveled, Classic civilization was reaching one of the more distant outposts of the Maya world. In the fertile Copán Valley of western Honduras, an area of rugged pine-clad mountains interspersed with jungle-shrouded valleys, a burgeoning population recorded the founding of its royal dynasty by another obscure figure, a man named Yax K'uk' Mo', or First Macaw-Quetzal. Yax K'uk' Mo' makes an appearance in inscriptions of some of the earliest Classic Period remains at the site, in particular the contemporaneous Xukpi Stair buried under the Main Acropolis. Found in association with *talud-tablero* architecture, concentrations of Mexican green obsidian, and the tomb of the founder himself, the Xukpi stone relates the origins of Copán's own line of rulers.

Installed at the very core of the Copán kingdom, on the central axis of the acropolis proper, these early Mexican remains attest to heavy Teotihuacan influence in the affairs of the local dynasty, at the crucial moment when the stela cult was being introduced. Principal figures on Copán monuments, strongly iconic and impersonal, press their hands against their chests with fingers curled—a motif identical to early Petén monuments and their Preclassic antecedents. Figures at Copán employ left and right hands in this manner to grasp the royal ceremonial bar, now a flaccid double-headed serpent reminiscent of Teotihuacan's monumental Coatlicue statue. Rulers stare straight ahead in full frontal view, not unlike Nuun Yax Ayin on Stela 4 or Jatz'am Ku on Stela 32, vertically stiff as if more emblem than flesh and blood.

Long after Yax K'uk' Mo' had passed away, rulers at Copán continued to trace themselves to the founder. Monuments regularly portrayed the founder wearing goggle-eyes like Tlaloc, Mexico's preeminent rain god, as though to establish the primacy of Teotihuacan long after the city itself had lost its splendor.

Copán flourished along the swift-flowing river of the same name, a tributary of the Motágua River of Guatemala. Linked to sites downstream, it sought to control key access to jade mines along the lower Motágua. It occupied the strategic northern flank of a major Mesoamerican source of obsidian, mined from the Ixtepeque Volcano off the Motágua Valley's eastern rim and one of the primary sources of material for fine cutting tools. The Copán Valley itself specialized in cultivating tobacco, as it does today, an important trade item destined for the Mexican Gulf Coast and beyond. Chocolate from cacao plantations also probably played a key role in the seizing of Copán.

With Yax K'uk' Mo' in power at Copán, Siyaj Kaan K'awil installed at Tikal, and Mexican merchant-warriors at Kaminaljuyu, Teotihuacan guaranteed for itself regular access to all the vast array of Mesoamerican trade items. With its sources of wealth ensured, the highland Mexican city waxed fat, its growth seemingly limitless and unstoppable. As Teotihuacan grew, so did Tikal—the prosperous, dynamic populations of Petén soaring as never before.

THE DEATH OF JATZ'AM KU

Near the crucial break in hieroglyphs along the bottom of Stela 31, scribes recorded that on 9.0.3.9.18 (June 11, A.D. 439), the Teotihuacan ruler Jatz'am Ku "entered his road." The Maya employed more than one metaphor for death. At Tikal, one was the concept of life as a canoe voyage, the passage over the surface of the earthly world until the vessel of the soul slipped beneath the primordial waters. Another, similar metaphor saw death as a journey along the great white road of the Milky Way, the primordial *sakbe*. To die was to enter this road and journey back among the ancestors, back to the beginning of time and creation.

On Stela 31, Jatz'am Ku "entered his road" after an unprecedented reign of some sixty-five years. He must have had an impressive funeral, conducted at the heart of downtown Teotihuacan within sight of the Pyramids of the Sun and Moon, not far from the Ciudadela with its Temple of the Feathered Serpent and fire hearth. To judge from royal Aztec funerals recorded much later, dignitaries from all over the Mesoamerican world would have attended, arriving from the steamy cacao-producing lowlands of Guatemala's Pacific Coast, the Copán highlands, and the city of Tikal. No burial certainly attributable to Jatz'am Ku survives, no royal crypt of any kind at Teotihuacan. Indeed, signs of "rulers" remain remarkably scarce, enough to lead scholars to conclude Teotihuacan must have supported a theocracy.

But the remains of inscriptions at Tikal, the wealth of textual information among the Maya, makes it clear that Teotihuacan was ruled by an exceptionally powerful lord, one with unequaled kinship ties and personal resources.

Jatz'am Ku left Teotihuacan unsurpassed in grandeur, bringing that city quite possibly to its Early Classic apogee. Remarkable in longevity, unsurpassed in diplomatic skill, and supreme at manipulating elite alliances, he left an indelible mark on the world he governed and forever altered the course of Mesoamerican history. Although who he was, where he came from, or how he achieved his initial power may remain forever lost, the few personal traces that survive attest to an individual strength not unlike the gods.

His empire would outlast him, stabilizing under unknown, unnamed successors. But with his passing the heart of the Mesoamerica world would briefly skip a beat, the barest murmur in an ever-expanding rhythm of grandeur. With his passing would appear the first symptoms of a terminally fatal disease.

THE DEATH OF SIYAJ KAAN K'AWIL

Siyaj Kaan K'awil, grandson of the Teotihuacan ruler, continued his Mexican ties even as he entered his own road. Like every important ruler since Late Preclassic times, including his father Nuun Yax Ayin, Siyaj Kaan was interred on the North Acropolis. But like his father, he would break tradition by bringing his burial down onto the North Terrace, the narrow platform fronting the North Acropolis staircase with monumental polychrome masks of jaguar gods. Here, before the tomb of his maternal grandfather Chak Tok Ich'aak I, under the lip of the North Acropolis proper, workers dug through the staircase to hollow the tomb from bedrock. Once finished, they covered the walls with stucco and painted them, adding with broad black brushstrokes hieroglyphic talismen and the Long Count 9.1.1.10.10 (March 20, A.D. 457), commemorating the ruler's interment. As a final, grisly addition, attendants sacrificed two teenage youths, and positioned their bodies along the floor to flank the dead ruler.

Siyaj Kaan K'awil entered his tomb missing his head and hands, his body wrapped in textile as though inside a sack, in the manner of mummy bundles painted on polychrome ceramics and in Mixtec and Aztec painted books. Among his offerings was a saddle quern that would allow the deceased, or the sacrificed attendants, to grind corn in the Hereafter. Pottery vessels contained quantities of drink—maize beer, chocolate, *atole*, and such—and residue from birds evidently prepared ritually as food. Sea shells and stingray spines were contributed, in addition to rare green obsidian from the mines of Teotihuacan, massive earflares, and hundreds of jade beads, disks, and tubes.

Thirty pottery vessels stocked the tomb—cylinders on tripod supports stucco-covered and painted in Teotihuacan style; incised and polychrome bowls; and an alabaster bowl with stucco around the rim, incised with hieroglyphs and wrapped in gauze. Mexican designs dominated. One stucco-covered cylinder included butterflies, a wide-spread Teotihuacan emblematic device, and bore skulls that vomit blood.

Ties to Kaminaljuyu also continued. The tombs from that site included astonishingly parallel grave gifts, among them stuccoed and painted cylinder tripods, artifacts with butterfly motifs, alabaster cups, green obsidian from Mexico, *oliva* and thorny oyster shell, and quail imported from Petén. Siyaj Kaan wears on his Stela 31 an image of a quail, heralding kinship ties no doubt inherited through his father.

The funeral of Siyaj Kaan K'awil must have rivaled the burial of his grandfather. Members of the family probably arrived from locations as distant as Teotihuacan, and from Kaminaljuyu, Copán, and other sites with close ties. Although no concrete evidence survives, the preparation of grave gifts and offerings and final arrangements inside the tomb probably lasted for days before the king was finally laid to rest.[1] On the day of his interment, a procession no doubt bore him on a sumptuous litter in ceremonial finery, advancing along the several causeways that criss-crossed Tikal by this time. Participants in feathered headdresses, flowing robes, and animal uniforms, would have marched in file, including members of the family, prominent warriors of the king's generation, and bands of musicians. Priests probably fumigated the crowds with billowing clouds of incense, the pungent smoke roiling skywards from modeled incense braziers. Singers would have chanted dirges, funeral notes to speed the ruler on his way. Among the plazas and concourse pavements great crowds would have watched, as the procession mounted the North Terrace and carried their king to his final resting place.

Cylinder Tripod, Burial 48.

THE LEGACY OF SIYAJ KAAN K'AWIL

During the weeks that followed Siyaj Kaan's interment, new stairs were added across the North Acropolis to conceal the tomb shaft, the final stair-case built at this location. The great jaguar masks were obliterated, the old facade buried under new construction. Over the area, workers erected Stela 31, and at the top of the stairs additional stone monuments—twin Siyaj Kaans who faced each other before the ancestral shrine of his grandfather Chak Tok Ich'aak I. Stelae 1 and 2 imitate Stela 31's wrap-around design, extending the front panel along the sides and bearing long inscriptions on the rear. On both monuments, wearing sandals and other elaborate foot gear, Siyaj Kaan advances one leg before the other in typical Early Classic style, cradling in his arms dual-headed serpent bars—the ruler's scepter-like authority symbol. The heads disgorge bearded and fanged supernaturals from yawning jaws, and earspool chains drop past the belt. Siyaj Kaan wears feather back-shields and bustles, sprays of the precious quetzal bird imported from the Central American highlands.

Identical Stela 28 also seems posthumously dedicated to Siyaj Kaan, but only his stance and the jaws disgorging the God of Number Seven survived damage inflicted on it in Late Classic times.

Inaugurated at Tikal when relatively young, while under the auspices of the Teotihuacan ruler Jatz'am Ku, Siyaj Kaan K'awil had probably reached his mid-sixties by the time he died. Mexican ideas had dominated Maya culture for a generation, touching every aspect of Tikal life and the most hallowed of its traditions. As the inheritor of the Teotihuacan legacy, he remodeled local social institutions after those of Teotihuacan so that, on balance, the Maya would never again be the same. By the closing k'atuns of B'aktun 8, Mexican power had become absolute, its enclaves had been established, and a Mexican suburb and graveyard had been founded west and south of the Great Plaza. Vessels, sculpture, and architectural facades depicted Mexican emissaries in Teotihuacan bustles and panaches, in the Waxaklajun U B'a mosaic war helmet, and sporting spear-clusters and *atlatls*. From an impressive assortment of Mexican and Maya monuments, the goggle eyes of the Rain God Tlaloc stared out.

Siyaj Kaan K'awil was the most successful ruler Tikal had ever known, precisely because he controlled an ability to manipulate both sides of

Stela 1, front.

his heritage. The great esteem in which his subjects had held him led to the great drive to erect his posthumous monuments, a nostalgic remembrance as Tikal entered a very different phase. Around his stelae, themes would emerge that would endure for centuries as the basic repertoire of Maya symbolism.

Siyaj Kaan represented a high point for Tikal, a great resurgence of the indigenous line of rulers after a crisis under Chak Tok Ich'aak I and the arrival of "strangers." His was a legacy few rulers, anywhere in Mesoamerica, were entitled to share.

But with the passing of Siyaj Kaan went something of the greatness of Early Classic Tikal. Siyaj Kaan and his times were a continuation of his father's "golden age," Tikal's finest moment, a genealogical link to the legendary ancestors and power of the past. Rulers that would inherit the turbulent times ahead would forever associate themselves with his symbolism and the luster of his Early Classic Sky Dynasty. But centuries would pass before anyone emerged who would recapture the fame and glory, the political fortune of this brilliant age.

NOTE

1. I have based this speculative account of the burial of Siyaj Kaan K'awil largely on the sequence of events proposed by Shook and Kidder, 1961.

PART 3

THE MIDDLE CLASSIC PERIOD

(A.D. 448–682)

CHAPTER 7

THE CHILDREN OF K'AN CHITAM

No histories of the Classic Maya survive other than those from monuments and ceramic vessels, the occasional artifacts tagged with hieroglyphic texts. Nothing like the Roman histories have been found, nothing equivalent to medieval libraries of manuscripts. The closest approximations are the codices, pictorial manuscripts made from sheets of bark paper that were folded accordion-fashion in long, continuous strips, and then sandwiched between covers of wood and jaguar pelt. Pounded smooth and coated in stucco, Maya paper was painted in multi- or polychrome colors, along with columns of hieroglyphs.

Four genuine, legible Maya books have been found, plus an assortment from ancient tombs that are too damaged to read. Numerous at the time of the European conquest, books were destroyed by the dozens by over-zealous Spanish missionaries, confiscated from their native owners as "lies of the devil." Most famous of all was the *auto de fe* of the Franciscan priest Diego de Landa, later Bishop of Yucatan, who burned as many books as he could find—an act that led to accusations and his eventual trial. The four books that survive deal almost exclusively with calendrical and ritual divination, containing virtually nothing about secular matters or history.

Histories were first written down in the sixteenth century, using the Latin alphabet but recorded in Mayan, in particular the manuscripts called the Chalam Balams. They offer important clues to Classic civilization, but their episodes deal largely with events that post-date the Classic Period and add little about the great period of Maya history. Enterprising Spaniards also set

93

down personal impressions at the moment of European contact, notably Diego de Landa, but with little direct relevance to the Classic Period.

Whoever seeks to understand Maya civilization must therefore rely on "dirt archaeology," the digging of trenches and test pits and other survey techniques. They have to establish sequences in architecture, pottery, and trash, the latter the most readily available material related to everyday life and therefore vital to the reconstruction of Maya social organization. They have to search for traces of how the Maya made their living, how they acquired food, what they did in their spare time, and how these activities changed over time. They have to study sculpture, paintings, craft goods, hieroglyphic inscriptions, accounts of the way the Maya live today, and descriptions of how they lived in the past.

Correlated with the Maya calendars, all this accumulated information divides neatly into several main periods of development. The Maya rose on the Precolumbian landscape during the Preclassic, an era of gestation. The Classic Period followed, or the great epoch of Maya achievement. Then came the Post Classic, when the Maya reorganized themselves along new economic lines.

The Classic Period itself reflects sharp divisions, in particular the way sculptured monuments changed. Sometime during the generations following Siyaj Kaan K'awil, the stance and profile view of rulers became predominantly a frontal pose. In this later style, the upper torso turns towards the viewer but the feet turn sideways and opposite each other. Conversely, the entire figure could stand in profile with feet side by side and with one leg hidden behind the other.

But Tikal's tombs and hieroglyphic inscriptions make it clear that there was a middle period after Siyaj Kaan, an era intermediate between early and late Classic events. After Siyaj Kaan died, construction declined, rich tombs stopped being made,[1] luxury goods stopped arriving, and the power of Siyaj Kaan's Sky Dynasty waned.

All over Mesoamerica during the Middle Classic Period there was an introduction of heavy Teotihuacan traits—Mexican architecture, religious motifs like Tlalocs, bird and butterfly imagery, military regalia, methods of pottery manufacture and design—lasting from about A.D. 400 to 550. An imitative phase followed from about A.D. 550 to 700, when Mesoamerica adapted, transformed, and absorbed Teotihuacan motifs, even as Teotihuacan declined and collapsed.

Significantly, Teotihuacan intrusions began and ended earlier at Tikal than at other locations, lasting from the reign of Nuun Yax Ayin (*ca.* 379) until the death of Siyaj Kaan in A.D. 456. Influenced by a Maya renaissance, pottery in tombs now maintained purely local traditions, preferring strictly Maya ones until much later in the Classic Period. With this absence of Mexican traits, the true Middle Classic Period begins.

THE FALL OF TEOTIHUACAN

The collapse and abandonment of Teotihuacan sometime between A.D. 600 and 700 must have begun slowly and required time to gather strength, but the end was sudden and dramatic. Barbarian hosts from the north, probably Chichimeca and other groups, plagued Teotihuacan's final days, succeeding in sacking and destroying the city around A.D. 700. People were slaughtered, palaces burned, and temples reduced to rubble.[2] Not content with the Ciudadela, the heart of Teotihuacan, the invaders dismantled and burned the Street of the Dead, reducing everything to rubble along both sides of the avenue for more than a mile. Sweeping onward, they carried their rage into the lesser districts and suburbs, tearing down even local temple compounds in outlying districts and turning at last against residential apartments. Whoever began the destruction made certain Teotihuacan would never rise from it ashes. As René Millon described it, "ritual destruction and desacralization unprecedented in scope and scale in Mesoamerica was carried out until the heart of the city was in flaming ruins."[3]

Though destroyed by a final spectacular conflagration, the city had been in decline for some time, perhaps as early as A.D. 500. With its mercantile network breaking down, its once formidable array of patron-clients in revolt, and uncivilized Chichimecs pressuring the city from the north, Teotihuacan's population must have begun to leave quite early for less troubled regions. As the city's influence waned, its craftsmen and laborers dwindled away. What followed was a great diaspora, its inhabitants cast to the four quarters of Mesoamerica.

Teotihuacan's withdrawal from Petén presaged what would happen on a grander scale during the seventh and eighth centuries, an early symptom of the fatal disease that was weakening the city's lifeblood. Whether decline resulted from Jatz'am Ku's passing, or pressures too ephemeral to detect, Mexico now retreated from Tikal and concentrated its resources at Kaminaljuyu and its coastal enclaves. Teotihuacan continued to dominate there, maintaining its grip over highland obsidian mines and Pacific cacao plantations, hanging on until Teotihuacan was no more.

Freed from constraints imposed by Teotihuacan, Tikal found itself able to make its own decisions. Thus empowered, Tikal rejected everything Mexican. A surge of local motifs emerged, a revival of purely Maya norms. Local culture became ascendant, and a great new period ensued.

Above all, Mexican cylinders—those portable "fragments" of Teotihuacan murals distributed all over Mesoamerica—disappeared from the repertoire. Polychrome vessels resurfaced in their place, especially graceful, typically Maya plates painted with colorful native motifs.

THE ERA OF K'AN CHITAM

There were other influences less easily shed. New forms of wealth had emerged, new elements of the political structure that focused chiefly on commercial affairs. With the rise of Teotihuacan, parvenu families had risen to power, more complexly stratifying the original patron-client society. Tikal's population was soaring, congesting the downtown precincts and extending into the hinterlands. Where a lesser, weaker institution of government had once stood, a great new state now took its place. Like amoebic probes, its relationships were extending beyond the Petén heartland to encompass Belize in the east, Copán in the south, and quite possibly budding populations in the west.

But how to balance the distribution of power achieved by Siyaj Kaan K'awil must have soon led to problems. Indigenous and non-indigenous factions were competing against each other. For the next century and a half, power vacillated between those factions that championed the old and venerable patriline established by Nuun Yax Ayin and those that centered around an even older veneration of Jaguar Paw, the blood of whom still continued in the matriline.

Mexico had given Tikal greatness, bestowing an unprecedented degree of political authority over Maya affairs. But with Teotihuacan's eclipse, the

Mexican factions stood alone, without their powerful ally to "protect" and ensure stability.

Only four years after Siyaj Kaan's inaugu-ration, an heir was born who would take as his name the head of a collared peccary infixed with "yellow"—phonetically K'an Chitam, "Yellow Peccary." But two and a half years fol-lowed the death of his father before K'an Chitam himself took control, hinting that he was not initially powerful enough to succeed. Even when he did, K'an Chitam was less pow-

Name Glyph of K'an Chitam.

erful than sedate, unremarkable in terms of his sculptural or architectural programs. Acceding on 9.1.2.17.17 (August 9, A.D. 458), he erected his first monument eleven years later, perhaps the first and last inspired expression of his reign.

Stela 40, discovered on the North Terrace during the 1990s, retains Siyaj Kaan's wrap-around design from Stela 31. Side figures portray K'an Chitam's mother and father flanking his own portrait on the front, occu-pying the left and right surfaces, respectively. K'awil, the little infant god of royal lineages, rears over the sign for "sky" in the left portrait's head-dress, identifying him as Siyaj Kaan K'awil II. His mother takes the head of a long-nosed crocodile, identifying her as Lady Ayin.

K'an Chitam, wearing his own name infixed over his headdress, con-tinues Siyaj Kaan's Stela 31 pose by bending his arm against his chest and curling his fingers in Early Classic style. Instead of a god-head, he clasps the traditional serpent bar with dual heads that disgorge patron deities from their jaws, braided its length with symbols of the royal mat. All of the usual, nearly overwhelming welter of detail encumbers the design, nearly sub-merging K'an Chitam under unrestrained symbolic images.

Despite close ties to Stela 31, the imagery of Stela 40 appears more rigid, less fluid in its flow across the stone. Details seem more angular, squared-off, and segmented. Its sculptor seems to have lacked the vision of the earlier artist, missing his chance to balance the dense detail of his sub-jects against the plain areas of background, and failing to achieve the kind of coherence seen on the earlier stone.

Whoever he was, and despite his knowledge of Stela 31, the sculptor of Stela 40 probably carved other monuments in K'an Chitam's suite of sculptures, vastly reducing its imagery to the more basic details of royal portraiture. Both Stelae 9 and 13 belong to a group of carved monuments called the "Staff Series," eight or nine monuments commissioned by K'an Chitam and at least one of his children, in particular the successor Chak Tok Ich'aak II. Differing only slightly from each other, each consists of simplified portraits who stride one foot before the other with the aid of a staff, barely suggestive of movement. The sculptures lack basal registers, unlike traditions of the past, so that K'an Chitam and Chak Tok Ich'aak II stand on bare ground. No down-gazing ancestors, typical since Late Preclassic times, protect the portraits from overhead.

These traits certainly flowed from traditions begun on Stela 40, where all of the essential features of the Staff Series make their first appearance: the form of the headdress, the staff-like flaps pendent behind the back, and the figures' rigid, angular pose. These details suggest that its sculptor emerged under the patronage of K'an Chitam and continued under the succeeding king.[4]

MASUL AND THE LAST DAYS OF K'AN CHITAM

As the son of Siyaj Kaan K'awil, K'an Chitam must have enjoyed enormous prestige during his lifetime. His own record of monuments, if increasingly uninspired, rivaled those of his father. The legacy of his reign survived at the heart of Tikal, the ancestral Great Plaza and its surrounding area, when monuments of other, much earlier rulers were dumped or reerected outside the downtown zone.

Not long after K'an Chitam's inauguration, his younger brother died, one of the sons of Siyaj Kaan installed as governor at Río Azul. There, amid first-rate civic districts that consisted of pyramids on par with Tikal's, at the frontier outpost of Tikal's northeastern approach, local administrators commissioned a lavish tomb. Covered in cream-colored stucco, the tomb walls were painted with red talismens very much in the tradition of Burial 48, but now much more spectacular in nature. To the back wall scribes added the Long Count date 8.19.1.9.13 (September 29, A.D. 417), recording the deceased's birth date, which was nearly two years after K'an Chitam's

Stela 9.

birth in A.D. 415. In successive years, other members of the Río Azul administration would pass away, their bodies similarly dispatched into the Underworld in painted tombs.

During the second k'atun of K'an Chitam's reign an event transpired that, although at first insignificant, suggests that not everything was under control. In A.D. 486 one of K'an Chitam's military leaders raided Masul, probably the large but poorly understood site of Naachtun northwest of El Mirador, just under the present border with Mexico. In itself not unusual—captives had appeared on Maya sculpture since very early times—the written record of this raid comprises the earliest direct reference to warfare, and the beginning of repeated and increasingly more frequent references over the duration of the Classic Period. From this moment forward, the record preserves a series of almost continuous and escalating battles that would end, seemingly, only with the cultural exhaustion of the lowland Maya.

Tikal's raid almost certainly resulted from much deeper problems, unrecorded antagonism that had festered since Nuun Yax Ayin and the Teotihuacan invasions. Masul, the object of the Tikal raid, bore strong ties to another, superior power farther north in the modern state of Campeche, one that was only just then establishing itself as a rival claimant to the trans-Petén trade routes. Calakmul, in the centuries ahead, would emerge as one of the most potent Mesoamerican cities ever known, one of the true mega-cities with civic districts larger perhaps than Tikal's. Over the course of the Classic Period, Calakmul erected more carved stelae than any other Maya city—nearly one hundred and twenty[5]—extolling its own line of rulers and royal consorts.

Calakmul and its dominions largely resisted domination by Tikal's Teotihuacan-backed rulers, channeling goods from the Caribbean Coast farther north than Tikal. The object, just as in later Post Classic times, was to transship goods as far as the Laguna del Terminos, for centuries one of the major transshipment points where goods changed hands for the final journey to Mexico. What was at stake was the most efficient means of achieving these goals. By passing through Calakmul and its dominions, the more laborious southern route could be avoided—the tedious ascent of the New River system from Chetumal and then the descent of the Río San Pedro. More importantly, passage through Calakmul maintained trade in purely Maya hands.[6]

Trouble between Calakmul and Tikal must have been brewing for some time. Perhaps a bastion of traditional Maya culture, Calakmul no doubt felt threatened from the moment Siyaj K'ak' arrived in A.D. 378. Tikal's Mexican usurpers established their eastern frontier outpost at Río Azul, a fortified administrative center without supporting populations. Between Tikal and Calakmul a kind of no-man's-land developed, a sparsely populated farming region that extended eighty miles from east to west, and twenty miles from north to south.[7] Calakmul's own frontier settlement at this time, Masul, lay on the edge of this buffer zone.

Problems perhaps fell out along racial lines. Although the linguistic picture in the lowlands remains clouded, the latitude of Tikal was possibly the rough dividing line between Ch'olan speakers in the south and Yucatec speakers in the north. Yucatecans were perhaps bulging southwards as low-land populations expanded and crowded against each other, driving wedges and pockets of linguistically diverse peoples into the two major northern and southern zones, with Tikal sandwiched between them. Tikal itself may have become more linguistically diverse and cosmopolitan as the years progressed, with Mexican Nauhuatl speakers mingling with speakers of both Yucatec and Ch'olan. From this milieu would emerge the special-ized "scribal" language of the hieroglyphs, the *lingua franca* that all regional dynasties of lowland Maya could understand.[8]

The situation with no-man's-land soon changed, and Calakmul encroached deeper into areas under Tikal control and closer to Tikal itself.

There was one final feature of the Masul raid that had implications down the line for the future of the Tikal dynasty. The raid was led by Tikal's military leader, so that K'an Chitam himself may not have participated. After the demise of K'an Chitam's successor, this military leader would reemerge under the name Kalomte' B'alam. Whether by coincidence or incompetence, his appearance would mark a precipitous change in Tikal's fortune, as the city was struck down by the rising stars of other, less stable political forces.

CHAK TOK ICH'AAK II

No death date survives for K'an Chitam, but on 9.2.11.10.6 (October 10, A.D. 486) his son celebrated his "first bloodletting," an event interpreted generally as "heir designation." Perhaps ailing, the old king hoped to ensure that his kingdom would pass to his son. At seventy-one years old, he would guarantee his son's smooth transition, an event that ultimately took place without trouble by 9.2.13.0.0. On this date, Chak Tok Ich'aak II celebrated the completion of thirteen tuns by erecting Stela 3. Executed like the prevailing Staff Series, Chak Tok Ich'aak II strides with the help of his ceremonial bar, but treads upon a narrow basal panel of vertical and horizontal bands.

Other monuments followed, attesting to Chak Tok Ich'aak II's out-pouring of sculpture, an *oeuvre* probably much more extensive than what survives. For the k'atun-ending 9.3.0.0.0 the new ruler commissioned no less than three stelae, each repeating his father's "staff monuments," with only one that depicts the king facing right.

In A.D. 504 and 508, respectively, the wives of Chak Tok Ich'aak II gave birth to a daughter and a son: Na Kalomte' ("Lady Leader") and Wak Kaan K'awil ("Stood-Up Sky God"). Within months Chak Tok Ich'aak II would be dead, however, evidently the victim of bad judgment on the field of battle. For the first time in Maya history, the western rivers region, the area of the Usumacinta, and points farther west would come into play. Toniná erected later histories noting the death of Chak Tok Ich'aak II at 9.3.13.12.6, only nine months after the birth of his son. Generally, foreign references to the deaths of kings mean the ruler's capture and eventual sacrifice, suggesting Chak Tok went to war and lost. That Chak Tok Ich'aak II died violently can be confirmed by the capture of his *yajawte*, or vassal lord, thirteen days later, as mentioned retrospectively at Yaxchilán.

The western rivers region would figure strategically in later events, one of the most venerable and important avenues of trade. Directly flowing into the Laguna del Terminos and the Gulf of Mexico, its shores had long ago given way to thriving settlements poised to join the swelling tide of Classic dynastic records. Yaxchilán itself, only years away from initiating its own sculptural traditions, commanded a strategic bend in the Usumacinta, and farther inland, astride the transitional mountains of Chiapas, Toniná guarded the Classic world's southeastern margins. Significantly, whatever happened to Chak Tok Ich'aak II, his vassal succumbed to the spreading influence of Tikal's more northern neighbor. Yaxchilán Lintel 37 records the ultimate source of Jaguar Paw's demise: the city of Calakmul.

THE LEGACY OF K'AN CHITAM

No rich tombs survive at central Tikal during the first hundred years of the Middle Classic (A.D. 448–558). During this century, two new shrines were built over the location of Burial 48, the tomb of Siyaj Kaan K'awil II. One probably housed the remains of K'an Chitam, the other Chak Tok Ich'aak II. These tombs have never been found, and were more than likely ripped out when two chambers were installed prior to construction of the final shrine at the end of the Middle Classic. Maya laborers evidently missed Burial 48 in the process, or considered it too sacred to disturb.

If succession following Siyaj Kaan K'awil had precipitated a crisis, it deteriorated hopelessly with the death of Chak Tok Ich'aak II. For the first time no suitable male heir came forward, and no leader of mature age appeared to take control. Wak Kaan K'awil, Chak Tok Ich'aak II's infant son, lacked support. His sister, not yet four years old, represented the least acceptable choice. Traditionally, succession had passed through the male line, as it had since the days of Nuun Yax Ayin.

For three years no successor emerged. Members of the ancient patri-line may have migrated eastward during this turbulent time, carrying the king's young son with them as far as Xultun, a relatively minor site near Tikal's northeastern frontier with strong ties going back to the days of the first Chak Tok Ich'aak. Here, in this northeast bastion of Tikal's family ties, Wak Kaan K'awil may have waited for his chance to accede, maturing in the political conflagration that had swept his father from power.

But Tikal's expanding residential districts prospered despite behind-the-scenes political manipulation that threatened to deepen. Migrations continued, with more settlements filling every available district. For years scholars have believed that rulers of southeastern cities like Quirigua, located near jade mines of the Motágua River Valley, and Copán, closer to highland obsidian mines, were founded by migrants from Petén. Recent reassessments of Teotihuacan's role in the development of the Maya confirm that Copán's dynastic founders traced their descent to Mexican "strangers" probably led by Tikal's Siyaj K'ak'. Quirigua also recorded its dynastic founding by Copán's founder Yax K'uk' Mo', with its earliest monuments dramatically reflecting their origins at Tikal.

In the crises opening the Middle Classic Period, events in the Motágua and Copán Valleys may have kept alive Teotihuacan's vital links to highland resources. But at the same time, these movements from Tikal may have preserved something much more vital—the young heir to the Tikal throne, Wak Kaan K'awil.

NOTES

1. Or they may have been ripped out later to make room for new construction activity.
2. My account of the destruction of Teotihuacan is based on Millon 1993: 32–33.
3. Millon 1993: 33.
4. A more careful analysis suggests for Stela 40 the possibility of several sculptors. The left portrait, depicting Siyaj Kaan K'awil, was perhaps executed by the same artist who carved most if not all of the Staff Series, whereas each of the front and right sides were perhaps carved by different sculptors. In other words, three sculptors may have carved Stela 40, not counting its rear inscription.
5. Most of them badly eroded and illegible.
6. The nature and degree of Teotihuacan influence at Calakmul remains uncertain, and the present situation could have resulted from the differential preservation of materials at sites such as Tikal.
7. Adams 1999.
8. Stuart et. al. 1999.

CHAPTER 8

HUBUY MUTUL:
THE "DOWNING OF TIKAL"

As never before in its 350-year dynastic history, Tikal faced an almost insurmountable problem. How to resolve the lack of male issue from the legitimate royal patriline continued to plague its ruling families after the death of Chak Tok Ich'aak II. As with Lady Une B'alam, before the succession of Chak Tok Ich'aak I, the break in the patriline left only a female to uphold the dynasty.

The crisis in succession temporarily resolved itself when Tikal's old military leader came forward, championing Chak Tok Ich'aak II's young daughter. Kalomte' B'alam, the man who had attacked Masul during the reign of K'an Chitam, pressed to take the throne alongside Lady Kalomte'. On 9.3.16.8.4 (April 21, A.D. 511), Chak Tok Ich'aak II's daughter became Tikal's queen at the age of six. Tikal had narrowly averted disaster, at least for the time being.

Lady Kalomte' and Kalomte' B'alam celebrated the subsequent k'atun ending, dedicating two separate carved stelae to the date 9.4.0.0.0 (A.D. 514). Three other monuments survive from their reign, suggesting they were in office as late as 9.4.13.0.0, a period of at least sixteen years. Stela 23 depicts Lady Kalomte' on its front surface wearing a *huipil*, the traditional garment of Maya women, woven of cotton and decorated with brocade or embroidery. On her honored right stands her father, Chak Tok Ich'aak II, brandishing a scepter or baton as his symbol of authority. On her left stands her mother, an unknown woman in jaguar skirt and wrap-around element, her shoulders hidden under a mantle.

Stela 23, front.

Stelae 10 and 12 functioned as "twin stelae," mirror images of each other probably erected someplace on the North Terrace where they stood side by side, similar to Siyaj Kaan's Stelae 1 and 2. Although the one may portray the queen, Lady Kalomte', Stela 10 no doubt depicts her consort or protector Kalomte' B'alam, Tikal's former military leader, who stands imperious over the prostrate form of his bound prisoner. Texts on the sides and back relate the conquest of Masul and other information from his early days, while Stela 12 identifies him as nineteenth in the line of succession at Tikal.

But these were increasingly troubled times. To the west, where El Peru guarded access to Petén near the Río San Pedro, another prominent woman celebrated an unknown act, her name given in the text as Na Ek', "Lady Star." Unremarkable in character, her event set the tenor for the future, for Lady Ek' was the wife of the Calakmul king, ruler of the territorial districts to the north. Thus, by 9.4.5.6.16 (A.D. 520), Tikal's former western ally, El Peru, had fallen into the orbit of Calakmul, Tikal's most bitter enemy.

More drastic events unfolded. In Lady Kalomte''s uncertain, final days, an act of violence erupted that was unprecedented in Tikal's early history. Along the Río Azul, Tikal's frontier garrison in the northeast was attacked by unknown assailants who spared nothing in their fury. Long held by relatives of Siyaj Kaan K'awil II, and bearing strong ties to Mexico, the administration at Río Azul faced an overwhelming raid.[1] Its palaces were burned and its tombs looted. Its Early Classic monuments with their records of Siyaj Kaan and Teotihuacan were mutilated and burned. In its wake, the sacking of Río Azul left the remaining center abandoned. Buildings fell into disrepair, vaults and walls came crashing down. The jungle surged back. For 130 years no one would occupy its downtown zone.

Located along the eastern edge of "no-man's-land," Río Azul fell victim to the intensification of hostilities that had been festering between the northern and southern linguistic boundaries since Siyaj Kaan's time. Within a generation, these hostilities would degenerate into open warfare.

Stela 10, front.

Stela 12, back and right side.

Lady
Kalomte'

Kalomte'
B'alam

19th
Successor

BURIAL 160

One of the great mysteries of Tikal concerns the identity of an individual buried in an outlying community of modest proportions, located about a mile off the Great Plaza's southeastern margin. Excavations in Group 7F-1 during the 1960s by the University Museum of the University of Pennsylvania revealed a sumptuous elite tomb rich enough to be that of a king. Stelae 23 originally stood before the principal shrine that covered Burial 160; Stela 25, on the other hand, was dumped near the tomb long after the interment, when the sculpture had become "obsolete."

The deceased, a man approximately fifty years of age, journeyed into the Underworld in the company of young boys slain as companions. His funeral gifts included jade, thorny oyster shell, stingray spines, red cinnabar, imported obsidian, but less than a dozen plain pottery vessels. As with Siyaj Kaan K'awil, the tomb contained a single vessel of rare alabaster.

On its rear wall, over a covering of stucco, scribes painted gigantic hieroglyphs in black, drawing an Initial Series Introducing Glyph that marks dates of the Long Count, and the single notation of nine b'aktuns, not improbably meant to record the Period Ending 9.4.0.0.0 (October 18, A.D. 514). In all, the Classic world saw less than a dozen tombs painted in this manner, most notably Siyaj Kaan K'awil's Burial 48 and several tombs for the lords of Río Azul.[2] Here, undoubtedly another of Siyaj Kaan's relatives was laid to rest, one of his many sons or nephews or some other closely-related noble.

Between the legs of the man lay a quetzal bird, bearer of the most sought-after feathers in Precolumbian America. Native to cloud forests of the highlands of Guatemala, and ranging as far as Costa Rica, the elusive quetzal bird was heavily protected in later times, when poaching was punishable by death. Male tail feathers grow up to three feet long, blue-green iridescent and shimmering with reflective surfaces. Marked by a red and white breast and an iridescent crest, the quetzal was the most prized bird from the Maya lands, its feathers commonly used as headdress and backshield sprays, from Teotihuacan through Aztec times.

Apart from portraiture, and a Preclassic cache of thirteen quetzal wings, Burial 160 represents the first and only evidence for quetzal feathers at Tikal until much later in the dynastic sequence. Even on monuments these plumes remained rare, limited to images that portray

Nuun Yax Ayin on Stela 31 and Stela 4. Stelae 23 and 25 represent some of the first prominent examples since that time, incorporating long plumes that radiate behind the headdresses in fan-like arrays, falling from the waist in backshields and presaging the dominant costume elements of the Late Classic.

Over the deceased's face, a greenstone death-mask idealized the individual's features, fashioned from broad mosaic tesserae carefully modeled to form contours around the cheekbones and mouth and cemented together with bitumen. Details were made of shell, including specimens of white and black for the eyes and orange-red thorny oyster for the lips. Jade earplugs were further added, along with a quetzal-beaked headdress. In light of the quetzal specimen and death-mask, scholars have nicknamed the deceased "Quetzal."[3]

Greenstone Mask, Burial 160.

His identity and the presence of two major monuments in this location has stymied investigators for years. Suggestions range from Lady Kalomte''s husband, either the aged Kalomte' B'alam or a possible second husband, to one of the "missing" Middle Classic kings who theoretically ruled some years later. As a male from outside the royal line, Kalomte' B'alam was perhaps seen as illegitimate, an usurper who reigned long after propriety allowed. As Lady Kalomte''s regent, or guardian, he was perhaps expected to step down when she came of age, or when Chak Tok Ich'aak II's legitimate heir acceded, after a long exile at Xultun. That Kalomte' B'alam failed to step down seems clear, a position highlighted by his inauguration of Stela 12 when his ward was fully twenty-three years of age. The identity of the person in Burial 160, however, remains unresolved.

BURIAL 162

Possibly within a year or two of Burial 160, an underground chamber immediately to the southwest received another interment, this for a woman in her late twenties and her infant. The chamber, a type known as a *chultun*, already existed at the location, though its purpose remains unknown. Always carved from bedrock in one or more bell-shaped cavities with often restricted, multi-level orifices, *chultunes* were used for a variety of purposes. Filled with trash, burials, and possibly foodstuffs for storage, the ubiquitous chamber defies categorization, especially since regional uses existed, divided into intriguing geographical contrasts.[4]

At Tikal, the Group 7F-1 *chultun* doubled as the woman and infant's tomb. Along with the two bodies, a spider monkey was added, together with carved thorny oyster shell usually exclusive to males, and a single deep, red-painted dish with faint traces of a long-nosed skull painted in black.

The two burials and pair of monuments bear ties to an area prominent much later in Maya history, but that by this time must already have acquired significant buildings and dynastic art. The long-nosed skull from the polychrome dish in Burial 162 resembles stucco friezework fashioned along the walls of the Palace structures at Palenque. Although the death-mask later worn by Janaab' Pakal at Palenque would attain much greater fame among scholars, "Quetzal" wore a better-crafted and more power-fully evocative example far earlier at Tikal. Iconographic and sculptural similarities were perhaps coincidence at both sites, including the well-known Petén tube-and-bead skirt. But in light of the seemingly centrifugal dispersal of Classic regalia, it remains likely that here, as elsewhere, Tikal directly intervened in the foundation of the Palenque realm.

The individuals buried in 7F–1 were perhaps members of an elite family related to the Tikal royal line, one of Chak Tok Ich'aak II's or K'an Chitam's brothers, or some other closely-related family member. In any case, they bore ties to the western rivers region, linking them with crucial events soon to commence in those districts. Not eligible to rule, these family members possibly migrated west,[5] founding dynasties and producing sculptures and other forms of art with Tikal antecedents. As the Middle Classic progressed, these areas would succumb to the temptation of Classic opulence, drawn to the flame that was enveloping the Lowland Maya.

EXPANSION OF CLASSIC CIVILIZATION

During the reign of Lady Kalomte', the highly individualistic city of Yaxchilán joined the stela cult, erecting its initial carved stone shaft for the k'atun-ending 9.4.0.0.0. Early monuments make it clear, nevertheless, that the city's history goes back much earlier with records of dates well before Chak Tok Ich'aak II. By 9.3.13.12.19 (August 9, 508), at least nine kings had ruled, doc-umented with "successor" glyphs similar to Tikal's count from Yax Eb' Xook. The founder of Yaxchilán takes the name Yoat B'alam—"Penis Jaguar."

The Usumacinta River, Mesoamerica's largest by volume, flows north-east into the Gulf of Mexico, arising out of the combined flow of the Pasión, Chixoy, and Lakantun Rivers. Lined with sandbars and climax rain forest and home to a colorful array of waterfowl and aquatic life, the Usumacinta makes its way slowly and without hurry, one of the timeless aspects of the western region.

But after only a few miles the Usumacinta narrows, anticipating con-strictions farther downstream in the more porous canyon country. Hills rise along both shores, gradually higher and steeper. The river sweeps round to form an enormous omega, geologically enroute to creating an oxbow lake some centuries beyond our modern times. On the western, currently Mexican side of this omega, across natural river terraces and multiple levels of the several hillsides, the Maya built one of the most magnificent of all Precolumbian cities—Yaxchilán.

During the Early Classic, Yaxchilán rose as an offshoot and artistic dependent of Tikal, which had already governed as the regional capital of central Petén for some 250 years. But Tikal's control of this growing center remained short-lived. Yaxchilán gained its independence relatively early, acquiring its own Emblem Glyph—Siyaj Kaan K'awil's "split-sky" sign—and its own artistic medium.

Much of Yaxchilán's architecture still stands, in tribute to exceptionally fine architects and their tradition of employing stone lintels. Maya buildings at sites throughout the lowland districts incorporate mostly wooden lintels, as did Tikal. But these decayed over time, falling prey to wood-devouring insects, high humidity, and torrential rainfall. Stone lintels can break under the crushing weight of the roof material, but by and large buildings produced with lintels of stone survive much longer than those with wooden ones.

So it was that, with convenient, ready-made surfaces for sculptural displays, Yaxchilán began carving its stone lintels with figural scenes, among the most beautiful and dynamic narrative compositions ever conceived by the Maya. Yaxchilán's fifty-six lintels provide an extraordinary historical record, arrayed uncharacteristically with princesses and queens, scenes of warfare, and a multitude of alliances with lesser nobles.

Yaxchilán's independence faded quickly, however, with the rise of still another great Usumacinta city. During the early years of Lady Kalomte''s reign, Piedras Negras inaugurated its own innovative series of monuments, largely exterior wall-plaques inset into the terrace risers of temple-pyramids, and the ubiquitous stelae. Built on the eastern shore of the river near an enormous sinkhole, the city known hieroglyphically as Yokib' quickly drew Yaxchilán into its political sphere, capturing its ninth king, Knot-Eyed Jaguar, and consolidating its control. Significantly, behind Piedras Negras stood Calakmul, extending its political ties to control the riverine trade networks.

Trade served as the chief motivation for expansion along the Usumacinta, and great cargo canoes plied the length of the Usumacinta and Pasión Rivers. From the highland sources of the Pasión and other tributaries comprising the Usumacinta, dugouts made their way from city to city until they reached the Gulf of Mexico. From Caribbean ports in Belize and Quintana Roo, goods ascended much smaller, often intermittent rivers—in particular the Belize, Sarstoon, and Hondo—eventually reaching the western rivers district likewise enroute to Gulf ports.

Not only were the river systems heavily involved in long-distance trade, but they gave rise to extensive agricultural terraces that functioned perhaps as "bread baskets" for the larger regional capitals. Seibal, the Petexbatun, the Pasión, and areas of Belize, perhaps all sustained Tikal's exceptionally large populations, contributing quantities of produce to make up for the capital's limited supply. Similarly, the Río Bec area may have contributed to the upkeep of Calakmul, a heavily occupied zone with populations at least equal to that of Tikal.

By the final years of Lady Kalomte' and Kalomte' Balam, Classic Maya monuments were approaching their maximum geographical distribution. The Maya's state art style had crystallized, given strength by Tikal, and numerous regional capitals had begun to emerge, centered around the stela cult and the glorification of rulers. Cities in Belize had taken up the call, with stelae noting dates at Nimlipunit and, more importantly, at Caracol. As far north as Oxkintok in Yucatan, there were Classic dynasties who carved histories. Closer to home, more towns in central Petén were erecting monuments than ever before—Naachtun, Naranjo, Calakmul, and Tres Islas to name the most prominent. Although Mexican motifs initially survived, these had all but disappeared as the era closed.

Clearly, Tikal's rulers and its political policies had played a major role in carrying Classic ideals to the far-flung corners of the Maya world.

THE RETURN OF WAK KAAN K'AWIL

No monuments survive to elucidate what happened to Lady Kalomte' or the elderly Kalomte' B'alam. If Group 7F–1 did contain the pair's remains, along with those of an infant daughter, then conceivably Lady Kalomte''s power base evaporated upon the death of her consort. This possibility, combined with her premature death, suggests that she my have been exe-cuted.[6] Subsequently, members of her family may have been barred from power or forced into exile.

Just as time has obscured these circumstances, allowing only a tentative reconstruction of events, so too has it obscured the succeeding king. In fact, there are no extant records of the twentieth ruler of Tikal. Only with the twenty-first ruler, Wak Kaan K'awil, does the historical record begin to clear somewhat.

Name Glyphs of Wak Kaan K'awil.

After an exile of at least twenty years at Xultun,[7] Lady Kalomte''s younger brother ascended to the throne by 9.5.3.9.15 (December 31, A.D. 537). Approximately thirty years of age and with legitimate claims to Tikal, Wak Kaan K'awil restored the local patriline and returned control to the factions that had ruled since the days of Nuun Yax Ayin. A fairly long reign followed, and he may have ruled into his eighties.

Too young to accede upon the death of his father, Chak Tok Ich'aak II, Wak Kaan had been forced to await his chance to seize the position lost to Lady Kalomte''s consort. Wak Kaan represented the ancient dynasty of Tikal begun by Nuun Yax Ayin and Jatz'am Ku. As the great grandson of the now long-deceased Teotihuacan ruler, his ascension restored legitimacy to the royal line, unifying the struggling factions of the power structure and restoring order. But although he enjoyed considerable success in office, there were signs that it was already too late.

Stela 17, Wak Kaan K'awil's only known monument, portrays him facing left but with his body in frontal view, holding his staff or scepter and wearing a headdress that radiates feather sprays. His great beaded necklace barely survives, as do traces of inscriptions on the back and both sides. Two Long Count notations and the ruler's name remain legible, noting that Wak Kaan K'awil was twenty-first in line from Yax Eb' Xook.

During the reign of Wak Kaan K'awil, an insignificant site only several miles to the east recorded the installation of a ruler named Aj Wosa. Although accessions had taken place by now at numberless towns across Petén, what made Aj Wosa important was his installation under the authority of a city only just then coming into its own, a regional capital located in the southwestern districts of Belize. Aj Wosa of Naranjo acceded "under the authority of" the ruler of Caracol, evincing direct ties to this dynastic center. Independence would have allowed Naranjo to install its own ruler. That it did not suggests that Caracol placed Aj Wosa on the throne to politically manipulate Naranjo.

Wak Kaan K'awil himself installed a new ruler at Caracol some years later, elevating Yajawte' K'inich to that position and implying a chain of fealty that ran from Tikal at the top down through the lesser sites of Caracol and Naranjo.

But something intense was developing between the three sites. While Yajawte' K'inich celebrated the k'atun ending 9.6.0.0.0 by commissioning Caracol Stela 6, the traditionalism inherent in his act embodied the calm before the storm.

Things changed rapidly when, for reasons unrecorded, Wak Kaan K'awil of Tikal attacked the ruler of Caracol on 9.6.2.1.11 (April 11, A.D. 556). Whether in response to Caracol's recalcitrance, its rebellion, or its defection to the political sphere of Calakmul, the armies of Tikal descended upon the impressive city and presumably inflicted heavy damage. From this blow to its civic pride, Caracol must have reeled. Long the preeminent capital of the district, it controlled extensive agricultural terraces used to increase production and maintain the regularity of harvests. Conceivably, Tikal depended in part upon this and other "breadbasket" districts to feed its rapidly increasing populations, relying on patron-client relationships and family ties for its basic foodstuffs in exchange for "civilization" and the symbols of status. An area heavy with "middle-class" inhabitants—Maya who occupied a "middle" social rung in terms of material wealth—Caracol may have prospered precisely because of its ability to export maize, beans, cacao, and other items crucial to Petén's economy.

Captives from Caracol were dragged off, bound and humiliated, for display back at the capital. Conceivably slaves were taken, herded back to Tikal to help in construction projects or to labor in service positions.

Caracol undoubtedly faced few options in terms of recourse. But the city's moment would come. Six years after its crushing defeat, Caracol erected another monument—one of its renowned circular limestone altars—that reveals through extensive hieroglyphs many key details of what transpired.

On 9.6.8.4.2 (May 1, A.D. 562), the combined armies of Naranjo and Caracol, under the authority of Calakmul, advanced against the Tikal kingdom. Unlike the punitive raid carried out by Wak Kaan K'awil, however, the goal of this conflict was far larger. Caracol Altar 21 records the now famous "Star-Over-Earth" war event, possibly read *hubuy* "the downing of," followed by the name of the place attacked. As armies surged into Tikal's zone, bringing destruction and chaos, probably burning and sacking and carrying away prisoners, the end must have seemed foregone. Monuments were battered, mutilated, and destroyed; civic temples were torn down. As the aggressors packed Tikal's central precincts[8] arrayed in fantastic animal uniforms, flames no doubt engulfed the city, rearing over the white expanse of stucco and the painted emblems.

Calakmul had organized its strategy well, steadily encircling and encroaching upon Tikal over the course of decades with political allies in the west and then in the east. Only the target was no frontier outpost, no vulnerable secondary center isolated miles from any help. The enemy city was far grander and prestigious.

Caracol Altar 21 records in amazingly terse prose *hubuy Mutul*—the "downing of Tikal." After one hundred years of antagonism, the conquest of Tikal was complete.

NOTES

1. Adams 1999: 144–145.
2. At least one other similar tomb was discovered at Caracol (Martin and Grube 2000: 91).
3. Coggins 1975.
4. For example, *chultunes* in northern Yucatan were paved inside and used as water catchment facilities.
5. As originally proposed by Coggins (1975).
6. A conclusion reached independently by Stanley Guenter (2000).
7. The putative "exile" remains tentative and was originally offered by Simon Martin as a suggestion, not a statement of fact (1998). See Martin 2001 for a more recent and cautious assessment of the evidence.
8. Inferred from the punitive nature and success of the attack.

CHAPTER 9

THE SECOND MUTUL

W ak Kaan K'awil's sole surviving monument, Stela 17, would be the last stela erected at Tikal for nearly one hundred and fifty years. Impoverished, isolated, and laid to waste by Calakmul, Tikal would lack effective leadership for an equally long time. No portraits survive after Wak Kaan K'awil, and no major architecture or burials would commence for nearly seventy-five years.

The fate of Classic monuments varied widely after the collapse and abandonment of Maya civilization. Few stelae survived intact in their original locations, where wind and rain attacked relentlessly and where encroaching jungle ate away at foundation cysts. Monuments toppled down, broken perhaps by fallen trees or branches or undermined by shifting ground. The more fortunate stelae collapsed face forward, or were protected by fallen debris, their delicate surfaces sheltered under the resurgence of plant life.

Monuments were sometimes objects of deliberate destruction in ancient times. The Maya often mutilated sculpture, sometimes in the natural course of demolishing areas to begin new construction projects, at other times out of hatred for the subject portrayed. Sometimes only the ruler's face was sheered off, indicating desecration and disrespect. Possibly the ruler's portrait was "alive" and required ritual "killing" before it could be destroyed. Sometimes monuments were demolished wholesale, broken up and ritually interred along with offerings of precious objects.

Often broken up and buried as construction fill, sculptured fragments regularly come to light during excavations. Even after years of scouring

Tikal, workers still discover remains of sculpture.[1] Any gap in a sculptural sequence can be filled in at any time, leaving speculation a very risky business. Arguments about the significance of any missing monuments should proceed with caution, or preferably not at all.

Yet Tikal's "missing" stelae from the final years of the Middle Classic Period have long been considered far more than mere chance. So striking and extended is Tikal's absence of stela-production that scholars long ago dubbed this period "The Hiatus," recognizing that monuments were either destroyed and scattered, or never commissioned at all.

The discovery that Calakmul attacked Wak Kaan K'awil considerably strengthens the likelihood that it was the sack of the downtown zone that began Tikal's hiatus. Calakmul and its allies broke up the histories of Tikal, defacing architectural sculpture and dragging monuments away to dump them in garbage depots. Possibly Calakmul imposed its own ruler on Tikal, installing the next king to ensure the delivery of tribute and to maintain the city's compliance.

E TE'

That E Te', Tikal's twenty-second ruler,[2] posed no threat to Calakmul and its great new "alliance block" seems certain, given his reign of approximately sixty-five years. Certainly E Te' made no objection when Lady Batz' Ek', an aristocrat from Calakmul, married into the Caracol dynasty of southwestern Belize. Mother

Name Glyph of E Te'.

of the later Caracol ruler K'an II, she would solidify ties between Calakmul and Belizean sources of quartzite, granite, slate, and food stuffs.

With Tikal suitably docile under E Te', Calakmul turned its attention westward to solidify its status in the flood-plain districts of the Usumacinta. Already firmly in control of the city of Yokib' (Piedras Negras), Calakmul set its sights on Lakam Ja' (Palenque) just west of where the Usumacinta vaults from its canyon onto the Tabasco Plains. Beautifully situated along ledges of the Chiapas mountains, overlooking the Gulf of Mexico, Palenque had yet to make its mark with significant monuments, though its histories document kings far back into the Maya past. Like many cities of the Classic Period, Palenque probably had been founded by factions from Tikal, and heavily influenced by trade and interactions. Very likely, direct familial ties bound Palenque with the family living in Group 7F–1. In the years to come, these ties would deepen.

In A.D. 599 Calakmul struck with vengeance, attacking Tikal's western ally in the first of multiple raids. Probably the longest-range war recorded in Maya texts, Calakmul maneuvered its armies some two-hundred miles to cross the Usumacinta River and deliver its blow. Twelve years later it struck again, likewise with success, reminding Palenque of its vulnerability despite its location in the distant west.

Palenque had been undergoing its own crises in succession, teetering under the quasi-legitimate rule of a woman. To the credit of its dynastic line, these crises would find resolution when an heir was born in 9.8.9.13.0 (March 26, A.D. 603), ensuring stability for the next two generations. Under Pakal the Great and his children, the ancient center of Palenque at Lakam Ja', or "Banner Water," would evolve to become one of the most spectacular cities of the ancient world. Pakal would champion central Petén for the rest of his long life, remaining among Tikal's staunchest allies. Only with Palenque's help would Tikal overcome the catastrophe that threatened to engulf and consume it.

THE SECOND MUTUL

Nor was E Te' disposed to protest when Piedras Negras advanced against Palenque some eight years after the accession of Pakal, again raiding with cooperation from Calakmul. One by one Calakmul picked off Tikal's allies, hedging it round to ensure that this sleeping giant would remain cooperative and submissive.

That E Te' harbored aspirations of his own and could act when opportunity arose appears borne out by his founding of a new kingdom at this time, when he sent elements of the royal line south into the Petexbatun region. Already the focus of Classic monuments for the past several years, the Petexbatun region extended westward from the lake of the same name to encompass an especially rugged area of escarpments, "haystack" lime-stone hills, and labyrinthine caves especially revered in ancient times. Lake Petexbatun flows north to join the Pasión River as part of the "western rivers region," one of several major trade routes connecting highland Guatemala with lowland civilization that were crucial to the Mesoamerican economy.

Like many regions of the Maya lowlands the Petexbatun and Pasión River districts developed extensive Late Preclassic and Early Classic settle-ments, communities of farmers who thrived along the alluvial terraces of the river systems. Badly depopulated during Tikal's Middle Classic Period, the Pasión River and other pockets remained sparsely populated during the troubles at Tikal after Siyaj Kaan.

Migrations from Tikal that established themselves along rivers and at other key locations were perhaps sent there specifically to establish control of trade along these routes. Alliances were shored up through marriage ties, and through the bestowal of high-status symbols and the trappings of dynastic art. Artists and sculptors must have played key roles in estab-lishing new dynasties. Evidence from later in the Classic Period suggests that they contributed their services to dependent centers, either by trav-eling there or by devoting workshop production to the dependent site. To record off-shoot lineages and cadet lines, royal sculptors from the capital produced magnificent works of art for lords of the dependent centers, signs of the lesser lords' ties to the more powerful regional capital.

By the seventh century, the closing century of the Middle Classic, branches of aristocratic families may have migrated into the river districts specifically with the aim of establishing agricultural "breadbaskets." Faced with mounting populations, basic resources may already have been growing scarce in the heavier-settled peripheries of Tikal. Slash-and-burn, the preferred method of farming when settlement remained low, had prob-ably long ago given way to more intensive techniques. In the Bajo de Santa Fe, the great seasonal swamp modified by Early Classic times, sophisticated drainage ditches formed raised fields for cultivation. Caracol, northern Belíze, and probably areas around Seibal on the Pasión River became zones of extensive agricultural terraces and raised-field complexes, tracts meant to retain soil fertility and produce multiple crops. Seed beds were probably being maintained in specialized environments, fertilized with human waste and food by-products.

Around Pulltrouser Swamp in northern Belize, massive stone-tool production developed around intensive farming techniques. Vast beds of naturally occurring flint deposits were being exploited around Colhá, associated with nearby raised-field "plantations." Sophisticated features like check dams and reservoirs were also making appearances by now, labor-intensive infrastructures crucial to the support of the region's heavy settlement.

Areas formerly abandoned after the opening centuries of the Classic Period were being selectively resettled now, targeted for new dynasties or reestablished by members of older ones. It was therefore unremarkable that E Te' should send his son, Balaj Kaan K'awil, to revive settlements at Dos Pilas and key secondary centers. Formerly under the sway of the venerable city of Tamarindito and its twin capital at Arroyo de Piedra, Dos Pilas quickly established its own dynastic records, which proclaimed close connections to the greater district of central Petén. With his accession, Balaj Kaan K'awil took the same Tikal Emblem Glyph as his father, the sign *mutul* that signified the regional capital.

For subsequent rulers at Tikal, the founding of the second Mutul would prove an enormous blunder. One hundred years later, on the eve of the Maya collapse, it would prove to be the most crucial move of all.

MAYA WARFARE

Scholars once believed the Maya were a peaceful people, the "Greeks of the New World." Industrious, devout, and concerned with time and science, they were thought to be the perfect preindustrial people.

Things changed rapidly after the 1940s with the discovery of the Bonampak murals, well-preserved battle scenes and depictions of the disposition of prisoners. Executed very late during Classic times, they nevertheless made it difficult to ignore the role of warfare. Scholars have learned that full-scale battles raged, horrendous affairs that involved the burning and sacking of towns, prolonged attacks over periods of days, and the torture and execution of prisoners.

Not only did the Maya wage war with all the ferocity of other people, they played for keeps, sometimes with very deadly results. Their cadres of warriors—armed with javelins, spearthrowers, axes, slings for hurling stones, knives, and obsidian-edged swords called *makannahs*—probably included thousands of individual combatants, great hosts of armies willing to attack on open ground or assault the downtown districts of recalcitrant foes.[3] Fortifications protected districts that were especially vulnerable to attack, and included dry motes and earth embankments surmounted by palisades. Island-like high ground in the middle of seasonal swamps helped to insulate downtown districts, with access restricted to causeways or narrow necks of land. In their feather-arrayed helmets, colorful cotton-quilted armor to stop stone projectiles, and bearing wickerwork and wooden shields to deflect blows, attacking armies advanced in brilliant uniforms of jaguars, eagles, and quetzals.

Certainly key resources such as food, stone for tools, cacao, and other elements of trade became objects of war, sought to bolster increasingly dwindling resources. As competition increased, enemies targeted both local resources and trade items, especially portable goods to seize and carry back home. Populations themselves became viable spoils of war, and slaves were taken to sell, to perform manual labor such as construction projects, to act as servants, or to die under the sacrificial blade as offerings to the gods.

Towns and individuals became targets of retribution for their defiance, for acts of rebellion, for failure to deliver trade, or for their own earlier raids. Heavily ritualized, Maya warfare probably proceeded with declarations of war under the proper circumstances, including the giving of quantities of weapons and uniforms as symbols of aggression.

By late Middle Classic times, hieroglyphic inscriptions record a marked intensification in the frequency and ferocity of warfare. Battles shifted from simple raids to full-scale attacks on mega-cities such as Tikal. Often timed with astronomical events to lend battles a mythical overtone, warfare changed in bellicosity with the aim of solidifying political control, both to enlarge effective territory and to increase the personal security of individual kingdoms. Once started, warfare became increasingly difficult to stop. Gradually, the prize increased to encompass the entire Maya lowlands.

Warfare proved incredibly destructive over the long run. Anger and resentment mounted, inflicting lasting wounds that only greater bloodshed was able to staunch. Achieving temporary resource gains, kingdoms over-looked the diminishing returns of the long term.

Increasing rivalry over prestige, trade, and food production drove regions toward systems of greater political integration, forcing the rise of regional states.[4] Warfare accelerated this rate of change until, driven into the political spheres of the larger districts, more and more "alliance blocks" or federations of subjugated towns began to form.

THE FIRST CARACOL-NARANJO WAR

During the desperate years of the Middle Classic, Tikal saw central Petén come under the sway of Calakmul. By 9.9.12.0.0 (A.D. 625), many different sites had installed rulers "under the auspices" of this mega-city—inaugurations "witnessed" or "accompanied" by Calakmul kings and other nobility. Cancuen on the upper Pasión, El Peru in western Petén, Naranjo only miles to the east of Tikal, and Caracol to the southeast all entered the Calakmul domain with little protest. Even Dos Pilas, founded so recently by E Te''s son, defected and declared its allegiance in contradistinction to Tikal's tradi-tional loyalties.

Those sites rebelling against the super-extensive block of the Calakmul alliance suffered heavy punishment. When Naranjo's old king died and rulership changed hands, Calakmul descended upon it with Caracol and crushed the new successor mercilessly. When his replacement also defected four months later, Caracol administered another punitive blow that unseated the Naranjo king.

Naranjo proved much more stubborn than Calakmul ever imagined. The king of Calakmul mobilized Caracol still a third, unprecedented time within the same year. It must have proved the charm. Naranjo lay down among the pacified, seemingly quiet at last.

Old E Te' himself had developed ambitions late in life. Probably in his sixties, he extended Tikal control as far as Altar de Sacrificios, near the con-fluence of the Pasión and Usumacinta Rivers. The move to the Pasión must have figured among his last acts, assuming the inscriptions there record a contemporary event. Alternatively, the monument memorializes the Tikal king in retrospect, long after he was dead.

BURIAL 195

Only one burial after the days of Lady Kalomte' was rich enough to have been that of a ruler. Vaulted with masonry and intruded deep within bedrock under the southeast corner of the North Terrace, Burial 195 held the body of an elderly man who was surrounded by some of the most unusual contents known from any Maya tomb. Distinctive in a period when no other elite burials are known, it reflects Tikal's relative poverty in its lack of imported gifts for the deceased. Although Burial 195's grave furnishings represent high artistic achievements, they never approach the cosmopolitan wealth of the tombs of Nuun Yax Ayin or Siyaj Kaan K'awil. The vast majority of goods were locally manufactured by Tikal craftspeople.

Furnishings consisted largely of wooden objects coated in stucco and painted.[5] Among the finest were images of four seated gods a little over a foot high, carved with axes or cigars in their foreheads that identify them as K'awil, the patron god of royal bloodlines. Covered in eggshell-thin light blue plaster, they were intended to be affixed atop staffs in the manner of Manikin Scepters depicted in Maya portraiture, where one leg transforms to become the serpent-handle. Related objects included stucco-coated ceramic vessels and rodent effigies of alabaster.

Wrapped in textile amid what few items of luxury he possessed, the ruler reclined on four wooden palettes that formed a litter or table-throne, its surfaces and legs carved with cartouches and medallion glyphs all coated in stucco like the K'awil gods. The cartouches and glyphs were painted red, the surrounding smooth surfaces light green. Cartouche designs included seated rulers cradling ceremonial bars, the bicephallic serpent used in conjuring rites held rigid in their arms.

Glyphs on the palettes retain only portions of an Initial Series (9.8.?.?.?), plus the ruler's age of between forty and sixty years old. Texts from two polychrome plates among the grave gifts name the ruler E Te', the twenty-second successor of Tikal, and identify his father as "Black Fire Cross," some obscure lord whose relationship to the Tikal royal line remains unknown. Sometimes called Animal Skull, E Te' figures in the texts of numerous looted plates similar to those in Burial 195, all repeating the same or similar hieroglyphic formulae around the rim.

K'awil Effigy, Burial 195.

EXPANSION OF THE PERIPHERAL KINGDOMS

Tikal's artistic motifs continued their ties to the west—especially with Lacanjá, Bonampak, and Palenque—including E Te''s K'awil scepters and wooden panels, and the style of Wak Kaan K'awil's Stela 17. Lacanjá Stela 1 shares with Wak Kaan's monument the same pose and similar costume elements, in particular the bead necklaces, hinting at the dynastic relationship between these regions. Above all, the ruler of Lacanjá wears the mosaic Teotihuacan headdress with Tlaloc eyes and Mexican year sign, continuing the legacy of Nuun Yax Ayin and Siyaj K'ak'. Mexicanized Maya in much of their artistic repertoire, the western rulers extended some unknown influence over Tikal sculpture, and by extension some influence over E Te' and his successors, as if distantly and subtly steering the direction of the artistic legacy of Tikal.

Ties with Palenque and Copán at opposite ends of the Maya world continued. The K'awils from E Te''s Burial 195 resemble early stucco reliefs of the Palenque palace, in particular the pier sculptures where rulers port Manikin Scepter staffs. Early Palenque reliefs in stucco depict rulers on table thrones like E Te''s wooden palettes, carved with glyphic medallions along their front edges and legs—similarities in individual motifs, not stylistic forms.[6]

Far in the southeast, in the Honduran highlands, Classic Maya Copán became the next major city to include an Emblem Glyph in its inscriptions, configuring a sequence that probably reads "*xukpi*," possibly in reference to the exotic mot-mot bird. Linked closely with Petén through art, religion, and architecture, Xukpi-Copán nevertheless developed distinctive polychrome vessels and retained archaic poses discarded long before in central Petén. By Late Classic times, only Tikal and Palenque rivaled Copán's architectural sophistication, monumental art, and thriving political domain. In the end, the waning power of Xukpi would help push Classic civilization over the edge, with Copán among the first to decline and die out.

While conquest halted much of the vitality of Tikal, migrations from Petén and other intense relationships at the elite level continued. By the death of E Te', Classic manifestations had extended along the Yucatan's east coast to Tulum, Ixpaatun, and Cobá, carried outward during disturbances of the era. Beyond, Altar de Sacrificios, Chinkultik, Toniná, and Comitán in central Chiapas all helped bring Classic ceremony and dynastic trappings to fringe areas of the western highlands.

Beyond the Petén "core," the traditional nucleus of Classic civilization, monuments carried similar Initial Series dates, the usual Petén motifs, and the traditional Classic organization of upper, middle, and lower registers. At Cobá, the subjects were predominantly women, their costume the clothing of great lords. Women played expanded roles outside Petén, cementing alliances with the Tikal and Calakmul dynasties and annexing territory to one or another of the major alliance blocks. As provinces absorbed emigrants from the heavier-settled central Petén, they adopted the ceremonial legacy of the core as an expression of their own dynasties, adapting the government strategies that had allowed Tikal and other mega-cities to prosper. From these districts came trade items and labor, serving to fuel Tikal's political ambitions.

Not all alliance involved such innocuous forms of coercion. Palenque wielded military power to rein in its districts, waging war through such dependent centers as Tortuguero. By 9.10.16.13.6 (July 28, A.D. 649), Tortuguero's Lord B'alam had secured Palenque's western frontier as far as Comalcalco—the farthest western expansion of the Maya world. Abutting areas of major linguistic change, and overlapping cultures very different from the Maya, Comalcalco secured important transfer points for bulked trade goods.

Dominions controlled by the Classic Maya became a near perfect radius. In the k'atuns following E Te', the Yucatan's west coast adopted manifestations of the stela cult, burgeoning at Edzná and influencing northwestern Campeche.

As the last phase of the Middle Classic unfolded, lesser peripheral sites interacted more intensely with the Petén heartland. For the second time since Nuun Yax Ayin, inscriptions point to outside meddling, hinting at the great power shifts to come. For the first time, succession at Tikal becomes impossible to follow, with nothing at all to indicate who ruled—no portraits, no inscriptions, and no burials or tombs.

THE WARS OF THE TWO MUTULS

If Calakmul had imagined its dependent center at Naranjo would submit to administrative control after an unprecedented three punitive raids, it was badly mistaken. With the death of E Te', Naranjo deemed it safe to attempt one final break with its overlords, seizing its chance to defect from the alliance block of the Calakmul "superpower." But this time Calakmul would take no chances. In an action later recorded at both the vanquished and conquering sites, Calakmul moved against its erstwhile upstart and administered the final, devastating blow. 9.9.18.16.3 (December 27, A.D. 631) marks Caracol's occupation of Naranjo on behalf of its Calakmul overlord, and for the next twelve years the lesser site once more came under the jurisdiction of its Belízean neighbor. The victors dragged Naranjo's recalcitrant lord back to Calakmul, where he was tortured and eaten. There would be no chance he would defect again, scattered, as he was, in the soil of central Petén.

The situation did not immediately improve at Tikal, however. No records of the twenty-third or twenty-fourth rulers survive, either in monumental inscriptions or on portable artifacts. Either the rulers of this period were too ineffectual to govern properly, too impoverished to erect their own monuments, or their works were destroyed to intentionally dishonor them. Alternatively, their monuments were used for construction fill, but given the nature of the hiatus, there were probably no monuments erected at this time.

But E Te' had fathered another son, probably one younger than Balaj Kaan of Dos Pilas and who was born to a woman of the older Tikal line. Nuun U Jol Chaak, or "Great His Rain God Skull," never erected stelae at Tikal, to judge from surviving monuments. Known only from later parentage statements, fragmentary ceramic shards, and monuments from outside the Tikal state, Nuun U Jol Chaak was probably the twenty-fifth ruler and the last king to rule during the Middle Classic Period, sometimes called "Shield Skull" for the graphic components of his name. Although birth or accession dates are missing, Nuun U Jol Chaak figures on the ceramic shards of MT25, where his

Name Glyph Nuun U Jol Chaak.

father takes the head of a bird with something in its mouth. Similar to E Te"s name, and identified as Vulture Head, the father of Nuun U Jol Chaak has been interpreted by epigraphers as E Te' himself.

If in truth E Te"s son, then Nuun U Jol Chaak was the brother or half-brother of Balaj Kaan K'awil, leader of Tikal's cadet lineage at Dos Pilas. In light of what would soon transpire, their interaction would create the pivotal moment in Petén history.

As must have happened among many royal lines during the Classic Period, Balaj Kaan K'awil had taken control over Dos Pilas long before he was eligible to rule Tikal. Impatient, he needed his own kingdom while his father lived. But Tikal remained the premier prize, if not Balaj Kaan's actual birthright, and he expected to accede over the regional capital once his father died.

When that moment arrived, however, Nuun U Jol Chaak was already installed at Tikal. Probably of the old line through one of E Te"s high-placed wives, he must have proclaimed himself king above Balaj Kaan, precipitating a rift in succession and triggering a dynastic war. The political position of Dos Pilas has always struck epigraphers as strange—at once Tikal's dependent center yet unexpectedly autonomous. Proclaiming itself "Mutul" with an Emblem Glyph identical to Tikal's, the Dos Pilas aristocracy must have considered itself the political inheritors of the greater capital, or rulers of an extension of that city.

Certainly Nuun U Jol Chaak represented the older ruling families, the ones disrupted by the Calakmul wars and the reign of E Te', the latter a king whose father was a non-ruling member of the lineage. Perhaps thinking he was a restorer of the families of Nuun Yax Ayin and Siyaj Kaan K'awil, Nuun U Jol Chaak offered the perfect opportunity to regain Tikal's independence, and to recapture the glory that Calakmul had stripped away. At the same time, he offered the perfect target.

On 9.11.4.5.14 (January 15, A.D. 657), before the end of the rainy season, the new ruler of Calakmul struck. As at Naranjo, where Calakmul and its allies had successfully captured the king and executed him, the invading armies penetrated the central districts, and once again occupied the downtown zones to install their own sovereign lord. Balaj Kaan K'awil then entered to take the throne, restored to his father's kingdom.

Nuun U Jol Chaak beat a hasty retreat. Inscriptions declare he was "driven out" and forced to flee for his life. Again taking no chances, Calakmul pressed its advantage to pursue the would-be ruler, chasing him westward to administer the same fate as befell the king of Naranjo. If Nuun

U Jol Chaak fell into their hands, torture would follow, then decapitation or the extraction of his heart. His enemies would doubtlessly "consume" him in the cannibalistic rites that characterized Mesoamerican warfare. With Nuun U Jol Chaak one step ahead of the vanguard, he was driven beyond the Usumacinta River and out of Petén.

He was given refuge among family members of the western rivers region, to judge from later texts. Palenque's hieroglyphic stairway records the "capture of the prisoners of Nuun U Jol Chaak," an event that included help from the heir to the throne of Yaxchilán. Only eleven years old at the time, Itz'amnáj B'alam was himself perhaps in exile, championed by Pakal the Great in his seemingly invulnerable kingdom. Other ties may have bound Tikal and Yaxchilán in their struggle against Calakmul. Nuun U Jol Chaak's own son must have been not much younger than Itz'amnáj B'alam, and perhaps the two were playmates in the court of Pakal where no armies could find them. Over the course of the following sixteen years, Nuun U Jol Chaak would bide his time.

Dos Pilas, under the authority of Calakmul, meanwhile expanded into the upper reaches of the Usumacinta, its bellicosity reaching as far as Kob'an in the Guatemalan highlands and no doubt triggering alarm among its larger ally.[7] The calendrical node 9.12.0.0.0 (July 1, A.D. 672) arrived and passed, celebrated all over the lowlands with the erection of more stelae than at any other time in the past. For the king of Calakmul, Yuknoom Ch'en or Yuknoom the Great, this date marked his second k'atun in office—his second period of twenty years.

Eight months after the Period Ending, Nuun U Jol Chaak counter-attacked against his brother, catching Balaj Kaan K'awil at Dos Pilas and driving him out just as he himself had been driven from Tikal nearly a k'atun earlier. Filled with occupation troops,[8] Dos Pilas labored under the burden of forced government. The exile of Balaj Kaan would last five years.

Meanwhile, Itz'amnáj B'alam of Yaxchilán, now grown and struggling to gain and secure his own kingdom, floundered into the midst of local wars along the Usumacinta. Capturing Bonampak, he made headway in battling against an array of enemies, only to be checked against the gathering tide of Calakmul's alliance block.

Amid these tightening hostilities, the final moves for ultimate control played out. Balaj Kaan delivered his own counter-attack on Dos Pilas. For seven days the battle raged, with Calakmul repeatedly attacking and burning and bringing the full measure of its armies to bear. To so stubbornly resist, Nuun U Jol Chaak must have fought back savagely. But again he succumbed, driven off from the pressure of his enemy's persistence.

Nuun U Jol Chaak girded himself for the blow that must inevitably follow. Although inscriptions imply the attack came from Calakmul, directed against Tikal itself, Dos Pilas was once more the site that declared victory, recounting the "missing history" of the last days of the Middle Classic. Nuun U Jol Chaak reeled from the decisive blows of his enemy's combined assault. Battered under the weight of superior forces, he had suffered repeated attacks, twenty years of antagonism and exile, twenty years of seeing all that he had deemed rightfully his slip into oblivion. This time he would refuse to give ground. He would gamble everything, the whole prize of Tikal, risking it all to gain control.

Inscriptions recount that on the day 9.12.6.16.7 (April 23, A.D. 679), great victory celebrations ensued—"the caching of the bones of the Mutul Place." Exactly one k'atun after Nuun U Jol Chaak's exile at Palenque in the court of Pakal, his struggle would end. After this date, Maya inscriptions never again mentioned this ruler. From this moment forward, the would-be ruler of Tikal, Nuun U Jol Chaak, simply disappears.

BURIAL 23

The burial of Nuun U Jol Chaak almost certainly did not take place at Tikal. An usurper and conquered ruler, he was probably humiliated and executed. His bones no doubt were destroyed, and the man himself dispatched in sacrificial rituals of conquest.

In the early years of the Late Classic Period, the resumption of elite tombs and monumental art reflect profound changes in Tikal's ceremonial patterns. After the conquest of A.D. 679, Caracol was perhaps rewarded with stewardship over the Mutul realm. Not only did this possibility have precedence, with Caracol's earlier administration of a defeated Naranjo, but it would be consistent with the appearance of Caracol motifs in Tikal after the reign of E Te'. After intruding Siyaj Kaan's Burial 48 through bedrock at the front of the North Acropolis, along the main axis of the North Terrace, Tikal had super-imposed over the location a series of important temples. The very last, built during the Middle Classic-Late Classic transition (9.11.0.0.0 to 9.13.0.0.0), coincided with the intrusions of Burials 23 and 24, the tombs of extremely tiny adult males.

During construction of Burial 23, the Maya ripped off the fronts of the structures built over Siyaj Kaan's tomb, possibly destroying the tombs of K'an Chitam and Chak Tok Ich'aak II in the process.[9] They excavated through the North Terrace down into bedrock, installing benches at both ends of the resulting pit. Over the opening, after the body had been interred, masons added the celebrated corbelled arch, sealing the tomb by adding a capstone painted on its underside with a red disk. They buried the whole cavity under flint and obsidian chips, razor-sharp flakes heaped over the area in the usual manner of royal tombs.

Only about five-feet tall, the deceased was surprisingly small for an elite male and closer to the stature of a woman. Buried alongside him were carved ornaments of jade, beads of shell, pearls, and thorny oyster shell that probably decorated a cape or shroud. There were objects of wood, plaited palm mats, textiles, and traces of jaguar pelt, as well as exotic marine materials that included seaweed, fish vertebrae, and stingray spines. The entire tomb had been dusted with red cinnabar, including the walls, the corpse, and the buried artifacts.

Burial 23 contrasted dramatically with the few sparse tombs since Siyaj Kaan, particularly in the quality and quantity of its ceramics. Luxury importations were present, contributed from sources previously unrepresented at Tikal. Of twelve examples, three extraordinarily large tripod plates had been painted dark opaque red with superimposed repeating glyphs in lucid white and black outline. The glyphs represent the day sign Ajaw, linking them to the well-known phenomena of "Giant Ajaw" altars commissioned in southwestern Belize.[10] Surely no coincidence, Tikal's first tombs in over a century display ties to the administrative center of the eastern Calakmul alliance block, Caracol.

BURIAL 24

The man in Burial 24 was even smaller, just over four-feet tall, and probably a hunchback with jade-inlaid teeth. The practice of dental modification among the Maya was widespread and could include simply filing the sides to make the teeth pointed or step-shaped. Other modifications included drilling holes in the front surfaces and inlaying these with disks of green jade or silvery iron-pyrite. At Tikal the practice of inlaying teeth with jade was virtually nonexistent, and in the entire history of the site only this little hunchback from Burial 24 boasted jade inlaid teeth.

That the little man played an important role in the Tikal royal court was reflected by an unusual array of grave gifts. Included in his burial were small jade animal pendants, the skeletons of *pisotes*[11] and owls, crystalline hematite, and red pigments that included other hematites and cinnabar. Most singular of all, the corpse rested on a wooden litter under a shroud of mud and textile. At least one vessel demonstrates continued contact with Caracol.

The man in Burial 24 was almost certainly an *itz'at* or "learned man," someone who worked with paints and other aesthetic endeavors—in short, an artist. Accorded special status, he was held in high esteem and cherished as a vital member of the royal line. Not inconceivably, however, Burials 23 and 24 were installed for the twenty-third and twenty-forth successors of Yax Eb' Xook, the two "missing" kings who ruled after E Te'. And not impossibly, although unlikely, one was the tomb of Nuun U Jol Chaak.

Soon after the restoration of local control over Tikal, all importation of elite vessels and other influences from Caracol abruptly stopped. These two tombs, and Burial 200 somewhat later, were the last tombs built on the North Acropolis for the remainder of the history of Tikal.[12]

THE LAST DAYS OF THE MIDDLE CLASSIC

The Middle Classic Period saw the steady decline of the Tikal kings, a period of more than 250 years when the city's influence waned, when more powerful rulers emerged in Petén, and when great "alliance blocks" circumscribed Tikal. Called Tikal's "dark ages," these were the bleakest years in the city's history.

However, one bright spot on the political horizon loomed momentarily. On 9.12.8.14.1 (February 25, A.D. 681), Itz'amnáj B'alam of Yaxchilán, the "Shield Jaguar," ended his years of struggle when he vanquished his most important enemy, someone named Aj Nik—"He of Flowers"—from an area that had contributed a bride to the dynasty of Piedras Negras. Long under the sway of Calakmul, the city of Piedras Negras had fought bitterly against Itz'amnáj B'alam to prevent him from gaining control, probably one of the chief reasons the heir to Yaxchilán had struggled during so many wars. Himself an ally of Palenque and Tikal, Itz'amnáj B'alam may have finally broken free of the Calakmul hegemony with the decisive capture of Aj Nik, gaining in this battle the independence of Yaxchilán. Thus it was that Itz'amnáj B'alam finally attained his goal within the year, acceding at long last over Yaxchilán and the Usumacinta trade routes that were the life-blood of the western rivers.

Amidst this gathering storm, the great Calakmul political block gave no outward sign of any trouble. On the half-k'atun ending 9.12.10.0.0 (May 10, A.D. 682), Yuknoom the Great, the chief architect of the loosely-based Calakmul superstate, took time to dedicate his *k'an tun eb'* ("precious stone staircase"), celebrating and dancing in honor of his personal monument. There were other allies who celebrated along with Yuknoom Ch'en, in particular Tikal's old nemesis, Balaj Kaan K'awil.

But unknown to the Dos Pilas and Calakmul lords, secure in their triumphant dance, the tables had already begun to turn.

NOTES

1. As in the case of Stela 40, found recently during minor operations in the Great Plaza.
2. His name remains in dispute and is used here for convenience.
3. Most scholars believe, however, that Maya cities like Tikal did not maintain permanent, "standing" armies. Warriors contributed to armies on a part-time basis as tribute quotas from lineages and other significant social groups or patron-client relationships.
4. Adams 1999: 160–161.
5. At some time in the past, mud seeped into this tomb, thoroughly burying its contents. Over time, the wooden objects disintegrated, leaving hollow impressions in the hardened mud very much like molds. Quick thinking on the part of Rudi Larrios of the University Museum's Tikal Project allowed him to recover many artifacts by injecting their cavities with plaster of paris, the same way that archaeologists at Pompeii recovered impressions of bodies buried under the eruption of Mt. Vesuvius.

6. Coggins 1975.
7. The texts refer to ko-ba-na, or *kob'an*, and HIX-il, or *hixil*. That they refer to the area of modern Coban in highland Guatemala and the territory of the Ixil Maya is speculation, but Spanish Colonial sources record raids carried out by the Lacandon from the Petexbatun region into the districts of Coban, admittedly hundreds of years later.
8. Inferred from the circumstances, but highly speculative.
9. Coggins op. cit.
10. Ibid.
11. Sometimes called coatimundis.
12. Coggins 1975.

PART 4

THE LATE CLASSIC PERIOD

(A.D. 682–909)

The original version of Structure 5D-33, North Acropolis.

CHAPTER 10

HIS FLINT, HIS SHIELD:
THE LIFE OF JASAW KAAN K'AWIL

Immense North Acropolis building projects opened the Late Classic Period at Tikal. North Terrace stelae, including those of Siyaj Kaan K'awil II, were shattered and hauled up nearby pyramids where they were buried inside summit shrines, under the construction fill of new temples. More ambitious than anything previously attempted on the acropolis, a pyramid rose over the burial of Siyaj Kaan and the late Burials 23 and 24. Packed under huge quantities of rubble, the ancestral shrines gave way to an entirely new structure, rising sheer over the Great Plaza to a height unequaled for the next two decades. Jasaw Kaan K'awil, twenty-sixth of the successors of Yax Eb' Xook, thus publicly proclaimed his restoration of the venerable Sky Dynasty that had been initiated under the Mexican "strangers."

a   b

Name Glyphs of Jasaw Kaan K'awil.

Under Jasaw Kaan, or "Sky Banner," aspects of ceremonialism absent since the days of Teotihuacan reemerged, effectively ending any trace of Calakmul influence. Descended from Siyaj Kaan, Jasaw Kaan accomplished the same synthesis of indigenous and foreign traits as his predecessor, balancing the local necessities of aristocratic power and shoring up Tikal trade networks long left to languish.

The advent of Jasaw Kaan began in turbulence. Unwilling to gamble with the new ruler's fealty, Balaj Kaan K'awil, the ruler's old uncle, sent his daughter to Naranjo to cement a marriage alliance within months of his nephew's accession. Lady Wak Kaanal of Dos Pilas and her marriage into the local dynasty represented a new approach to Calakmul control, offered in the hope that it would bind Naranjo's recalcitrant dynasty through deeper ties. When Lady Wak Kaanal gave birth to the Naranjo heir, K'ak' Tiliw, the royal line would be bound to Calakmul forever. Hopefully, so would K'ak' Tiliw's political allegiance.

THE DEATH OF JANAAB' PAKAL

The early years of the reign of Jasaw Kaan K'awil witnessed one of the most important moments in Classic history when Tikal's old ally, Janaab' Pakal the Great, "entered the road" at Lakam Ja', the ancient western capital at Palenque. Pakal had grown rich off the westward expansion of his secondary center at Tortuguero and the maximum expansion of the Classic Maya world towards the frontiers of Mesoamerica. Trade had increased his wealth, with Palenque ideally situated to monitor goods passing up and down the Usumacinta River.

Now, at more than eighty years of age, Pakal was no more. Mourners bore his body down the interior staircase of his funeral pyramid to seal him inside his specially-made sarcophagus—among the most spectacular monuments ever conceived in Precolumbian America. Laid to rest with stucco portrait busts, a mosaic funeral mask, and jade necklaces, rings, and effigy figures, Pakal was given an astounding send-off. The sarcophagus cover alone, an enormous slab carved with an image of Pakal descending into the Underworld, weighed several tons, unequaled as a *tour de force* of sculptural expertise that included the death dates of all of Pakal's important ancestors around the edge. Nine figures molded in stucco range around the tomb walls, Lords of the Underworld wearing capes and feathered head-dresses and holding Manikin Scepters of the god K'awil.

Named after three hieroglyphic wall panels located inside the summit shrine, the Temple of the Inscriptions was probably conceived and executed during Pakal's lifetime, the vaulted stairwell left open until the final moment. Nine terraces rose in courses of ashlar masonry, actually veneer stones that held back a core of rough masonry and cement, while frontal stairs provided access to the multi-roomed summit temple. Over the three doorways reared a mansard or "battered" roof, originally capped by the latticelike stone-work of a towering roofcomb. Finished under the son of Pakal, who com-missioned the hieroglyphic panels, the Temple of Inscriptions stood roughly one-hundred feet high, one of the hallmark Precolumbian icons.

During Pakal's lifetime, Palenque had suffered defeat alongside Yaxchilán at the hands of Piedras Negras, and thus at the hands of Calakmul. Cer-tainly Pakal would have heard tales of the daring raids Calakmul had waged against Palenque in the darker days of the Middle Classic, when armies had crossed the Usumacinta in the longest-ranging raids ever recorded. Staunchly opposed to Calakmul, Pakal had laid the groundwork for Palenque's florescence, maintaining his city's independence in the face of the continuing Petén wars.

Perhaps Palenque lay too far westward for Calakmul to effectively con-trol. Whatever the reason, Pakal's kingdom remained secure on its hillside niche when he entered his tomb. His son took the throne without opposi-tion seven months later, acceding on 9.12.11.12.10 (January 10, A.D. 684) as Kaan B'alam—the "Snake Jaguar." Under the sons of Pakal the Great, Palenque would flower and bloom, becoming the most graceful and ele-gant of the Maya cities.

CELEBRATIONS FOR THE THIRTEENTH K'ATUN

Carved in very low relief and badly eroded, Tikal Stela 30 stands far from the Great Plaza off the western flank of the Maudslay Causeway, erected as part of a public architectural precinct only recently established in the

Maya lowlands. Twin Pyramid Groups were built every twenty years, specially-arranged structures that commemorate successive k'atuns of the Maya calendar. As their name implies, Twin Pyramid Groups included dual pyramids, radial platforms built with stepped terraces and equipped with stairways on all four sides. They included mandatory paired monuments consisting of an altar and stela that were usually sculpted, portraying the current ruler of Tikal in appropriate k'atun ceremonies. Stela 30 and Altar 14 in Twin Pyramid Group M were the first made for Jasaw Kaan K'awil, but the last monuments carved from the compact limestone used during the duration of the Early and Middle Classic periods. Hereafter, all monuments would be carved from dolomitic limestone.

For the first time the subject of the royal portrait stands entirely in profile, facing left as on K'an Chitam's early "staff" monuments but now with one leg almost entirely hidden behind the other. Perhaps significantly, Jasaw Kaan appears diminutive and smaller than life-size, maybe in deference to his relatively low status at this time. Adorned with huge beaded necklace strands—probably among his personal possessions and possibly worn as heirlooms—Jasaw Kaan wears the K'awil headdress of his namesake and an elaborate backshield and mask. One hand cradles his ceremonial bar, while he "scatters" with the other, the ritual of throwing his own drops of blood. Although no drops survive on Stela 30, they became mainstays of auto-bloodletting scenes rendered on Period Ending stelae common to later Twin Pyramid groups. The hand gesture alone came to denote sacrifice, in particular mutilation of the ruler's genitals.

Glyphs from the rim inscription on Altar 14 bear the Period Ending 9.13.0.0.0 (July 12, A.D. 692) and the name Jasaw Kaan K'awil, confirming the date of Group M and the ruler who commissioned it. In the center of the stone the Tz'olk'in position 8 Ajaw links Altar 14 with the Giant Ajaw stones common at Caracol, the titular administrative center that no doubt still ruled Tikal. The altar and pose on Stela 30 link the site to continuing influence from the southeastern zone, an influx of ideas feeding back into the former capital of Petén just as, years ago, Tikal style had reached outward to Belize. Thus, in the opening years of the Late Classic Period, it seems likely that Tikal remained subject to the Calakmul alliance block.

THE COURT OF CREATION

During his initial years, Jasaw Kaan built Tikal's principal downtown ball court in the middle of the East Plaza, adjacent to the so-called "Market Place." Consisting of parallel battered slopes that form between them the ball court's "playing alley"—the paved surfaces where the game took place—the court supported additional galleries on each half that served as "box seats" for the king and other prestigious spectators. Each of these galleries included round columns found nowhere else at Tikal, exotic features more "foreign" than local. More unusual still, Jasaw Kaan directed the installation of a "reviewing stand" against the northeastern end of the Central Acropolis, near Chak Tok Ich'aak I's Early Classic palace and overlooking the ball court's southern end. Architects completed the bizarre radial pyramid by equipping it with *talud-tablero* facades, giving it upper and lower battered slopes and adding pairs of Tlaloc goggle eyes and so-called "butterflies," both emblematic of central Mexico.

No one knows exactly how the game was played, but narrative pottery vessels and sculptural scenes depict the game in action, showing an oversized ball, probably of rubber, and teams of multiple players. Among the Classic Maya, the object was evidently to hit the ball solely with the hip, and to maneuver it past opposing players into an end zone. Ball court markers may have functioned to divide the court in thirds, or as goals that, when hit with the ball, gave the teams their points.

The Mesoamerican ballgame evoked sacred myths, particularly the birth of the Maize God at the moment of Creation.[1] In this crucial event, the Maize God sprang from a crack in a turtle shell, as depicted on innumerable Maya pottery vessels. Analogous to the crack in the carapace, the ball court with its battered slopes served as one of the primary conduits to the Other World, a sacred portal where communications with ancestors and deities took place. Human sacrifice took place here, the execution of prisoners taken in war and pitted against the king in unequal contests.

But Tikal also expressed in the East Plaza Ball Court its continuing affiliations with Mexico, an acknowledgment of its past relationship with Teotihuacan. By adding Mexican symbolism to the "reviewing stand," the

The "Reviewing Stand" (Structure 5D–43).

Maya equated this area with Teotihuacan, the city that had brought Tikal to the summit of its Early Classic grandeur.

What immediate impact the demise of Teotihuacan had on the Maya world during the seventh and eighth centuries remains uncertain. But the fact that Mexican symbolism reappears on the eve of the Late Classic Period suggests Tikal was reaffirming its Teotihuacan legacy, proclaiming that Teotihuacan—the Tollan of Classic Period Mesoamerica—had not truly fallen after all. Here, at Tikal, among the direct descendants of the great Teotihuacan lords of the past, much of that other Tollan continued to live, prospering as always. But within years the Maya, too, would begin wallowing, following Mexico into oblivion.

EVENTS OUTSIDE PETÉN

Trade relations must have preoccupied the Calakmul alliance block, for its special state emblems entrenched themselves for a while at Quirigua, an upstart center located near the jade mines of the lower Motágua River Valley. Among the Maya's most important commercial items, tough, lustrous jade was sought after for use in earflares, necklaces, wristlets, anklets, masks, plaques, and sundry utilitarian and decorative items. The Maya laboriously eroded forms and holes and arabesque lines with grist and wooden drills and grist-coated string saws, fashioning masterpieces unprecedented in Precolumbian art.

Quirigua rose on the political scene as an administrative center of Copán, claiming the same dynastic founder and frequently referring to the more powerful site. As such, it stood to control the retrieval and distribution of raw jade, the only known major Mesoamerican source of which extended along the Motágua River in the modern Guatemalan department of Zacapa.[2] More importantly, the Motágua itself served to channel the bulk of trade items from highland Guatemala to the Caribbean Sea. Jade, obsidian, minerals, cacao, tobacco, and cotton textiles all flowed north from here to Caribbean ports of the eastern Yucatan, and then inland along Petén river systems for the long overland portage. Many items filtered out to lowland Maya cities now firmly under the control of the Calakmul alliance block, but at least as many continued overland to the Laguna del Terminos and thence to Mexico.

By Jasaw Kaan's first k'atun-ending in A.D. 702, Quirigua Monument 12 had adopted Caracol's "Giant Ajaw" motif, signaling ties to Petén's central authority. Some controversy surrounds the nature of the Quirigua Emblem Glyph, and various authors have argued that its appearance at Pusiljá in southwestern Belize indicates dynastic control of the one site over the other. More recently, examination of Pusiljá monuments suggests the two sites may have used different emblems.

Control over Quirigua gave the Calakmul alliance block direct access to highland products. Monopolization of the basis of the Classic economy may have driven this expansion, the striving of Calakmul to take its place as head of the commercial world. Conversely, among the western river districts, the situation developed quite possibly out of control. With Tikal surrounded and subservient to Calakmul, with trade by-passing the lower Usumacinta, Pakal's successors in Palenque may have found it more difficult to compete with the new economy of the east.

The tradition of depicting women as primary portraits had extended to Calakmul and Cobá by this time, and Altar de Sacrificios, Naachtun, and Naranjo were following suit. At Cobá, a woman accompanies the date 9.12.10.5.12 (August 30, A.D. 682), the same day that Lady Wak Kaanal arrived at Naranjo and married the local king. Located among extensive lakes near the coastal districts of northeast Yucatan, the towns collectively referred to as Cobá were connected with each other by elevated causeways that radiated outward from the central district. An off-shoot of central Petén in sculptural style, Cobá's relationship with Naranjo and Lady Kaanal remains unclarified, but the possibility that the Tikal cadet line at Dos Pilas sent two women to establish the primacy of the Calakmul alliance remains quite viable, with these women instrumental in furthering Petén's political ambitions.

In addition to these events at the time of his first k'atun-ending, Jasaw Kaan was also preoccupied by the birth of his son. In middle age, this son would accede over Tikal as the twenty-seventh successor of Yax Eb' Xook.

U TOK' PAKAL

After completion of the thirteenth k'atun (9.13.0.0.0), Jasaw Kaan K'awil deemed it time to reassert the primacy of Yax Mutul, the ancient kingdom of Tikal. With the accession of five-year-old K'ak' Tiliw of Naranjo, the progeny of Lady Wak Kaanal and the old Naranjo king, Jasaw Kaan must have realized that a better opportunity would never arise. Although K'ak' Tiliw's mother, her backers, and her dead husband's factions represented the real power behind the throne, Naranjo's nominal figurehead offered a vulnerable target.

Naranjo put up stiff resistance, however, and Calakmul and Caracol may have contributed troops to repulse the armies of Jasaw Kaan. Over the next eight months Naranjo repeatedly lashed out and finally succeeded in downing Tikal's war captain and in capturing the warrior Siyaj K'awil on 9.13.2.16.0 (January 22, A.D. 695). Tikal's initial foray ended badly, crippling its armies and holding its ambitious king in check.

Jasaw Kaan must have realized it was useless to take on the giant Calakmul alliance piecemeal, as his father had done. Unlike the Dos Pilas wars, when Nuun U Jol Chaak had gone down in flames, no details survive, no victory monuments of the type commissioned among the Petexbatun kingdoms. Yet Jasaw must have amassed every resource he could command, mobilizing every cadre, every possible warrior to ready his attack. Moving out from Tikal on 9.13.3.7.18 (August 8, A.D. 695), at the height of the rainy season when warfare was usually suspended, Jasaw Kaan K'awil struck at the heart of Calakmul itself, driving towards its downtown plazas in revenge for the defeat of his father sixteen years earlier. In the most decisive conflict waged during the Late Classic Period, Jasaw Kaan captured the war palanquin of his enemy, downing the "Flint-Shield" banner of Ich'aak K'ak' and ending the hegemony of Calakmul forever.

They must have presented an extraordinary spectacle, the armies of Jasaw Kaan as they returned victorious. Jasaw's record of the war describes the sequence of celebrations two months later. After displaying his prisoner Aj B'olon Ja', "He of Many Waters," Jasaw humiliated and tortured him and then probably dispatched the luckless aristocrat during ritual ballgames in the East Plaza court. In commemoration of these rituals, he commissioned architectural roof displays on Structure 5D–57, modeled on a palace of the

Central Acropolis in stucco reliefs that depict himself in Teotihuacan war imagery restraining his nearby captive.

Servants bore Jasaw Kaan K'awil on the palanquin captured from Calakmul, straining under the weight of the massive float as it moved along the causeways of downtown Tikal. Arrayed under enormous jade necklace strands, and rigidly pontifical under his Sun God bonnet of iridescent quetzal plumes, Jasaw presented the kind of majesty unseen at Tikal since the days of Siyaj Kaan. On Lintel 3 from Temple I, the monument that depicts this scene, Jasaw rides behind the flap-staff *jasaw* banner that served as his namesake, enthroned on his cushioned seat while he bears his shield and K'awil Scepter. Behind him rears the patron jaguar god of Calakmul, seized along with the palanquin in the defeat of Ich'aak K'ak'.

Another carved lintel, only one of two original wooden lintels still in place at Tikal, depicts Jasaw Kaan seated on a palanquin wearing the scaled serpent headdress introduced from Teotihuacan. Over the ruler additional scaled serpents rear like protectors, replete with Tlaloc eyes and disks, and in his hands Jasaw wields Mexican spearthrower darts and his round shield. As on Lintel 3 from the same temple, Lintel 2 shows Jasaw Kaan riding behind his flapstaff namesake, and hieroglyphs before him give the name of the war serpent—Mexico's Waxaklajun U B'a.

Most extraordinary of all, the three tiers of the palanquin that Jasaw Kaan rides bear the signs for "barrel cactus" and "reed," the latter read *pu* and indicative of "Tollan." The signs thus recreate the territory of central Mexico, equating the king with "Place of the Cattail Reeds" and the great Mexican metropolis only just then being eclipsed. Like his ancestor Siyaj Kaan 260 years earlier, Jasaw Kaan "remembered" his illustrious past, the true power that had made Tikal great.

Celebrations for his victory over Calakmul continued with Jasaw Kaan's bloodletting, the piercing of his tongue with an obsidian lancet. Meant to invoke spiritual visions through pain and loss of blood, autosacrifice sanctified the ruler as it induced hallucinations of gods and illustrious ancestors. Stupefied and reeling, Jasaw Kaan invoked Teotihuacan.

Freed from Calakmul, Jasaw Kaan embarked on an ambitious campaign to secure his borders. Rio Azul along the northeastern approach from the Caribbean Sea, reemerged as an important if lesser town, now subordinate

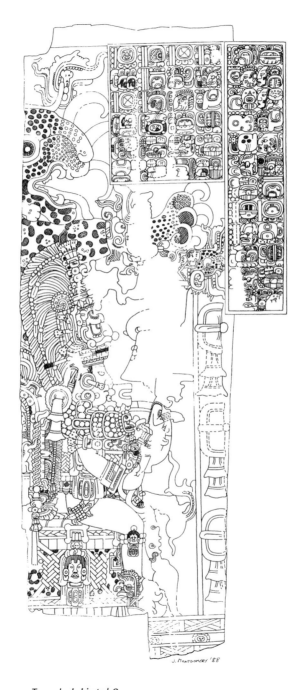

Temple I, Lintel 3.

to a three-tiered hierarchy extending up through Kinal and northern Belize. Jasaw moved against members of the Calakmul alliance as far away as Kob'an of the Guatemalan highlands, penetrating distant Ixil country conquered earlier under Dos Pilas. Dos Pilas itself knuckled under the might of Jasaw Kaan, and on 9.13.6.0.0 (February 15, A.D. 698) a new ruler rose to power over the Petexbatun, ensuring loyalty from that sector.

THE DEATH OF LADY TUN KAYWAK

Still pending was the security of Tikal's eastern border, the only direct route to the Belize Valley and the Caribbean Sea, down which bulked trade goods had to pass. Naranjo had remained recalcitrant, refusing allegiance despite Calakmul's apparent unwillingness to provide support. Nor would Dos Pilas offer aid, as it was now under the rulership of Tikal's ally.

Things came to a head when Jasaw Kaan K'awil married a woman from Yaxhá, the formerly independent kingdom absorbed by Teotihuacan during the days of Siyaj K'ak'. Herself related to Kaan Sak Wayas of Masul, Calakmul's onetime ally at Naachtun, she had emerged from a union sanctified at Yaxhá only miles west of Naranjo's border.

Lady Tun Kaywak, Jasaw Kaan's "precious flower" who was meant to solidify Tikal's defeat over Calakmul, apparently died at a very young age. Related to the Calakmul dynasty, and possibly one of Ich'aak K'ak''s daughters or some other high-placed princess, she was extraordinarily honored when she passed away.

It was an amazing stroke of statesmanship, a marriage between two superpowers like none before or afterwards. In one stroke Jasaw Kaan united key families of the alliance block with Tikal's ancient line, "refounding" as it were the old lineages of the past. Possibly the subject of a wooden lintel installed over the middle doorway of Temple II—the only definite portrait of a woman within the central precincts of Tikal—Lady Tun Kaywak wears embroidered stoles and an elaborate Sun God bonnet, her image now badly eroded and worm-eaten.

Temple II rears 125 feet over the western margin of the Great Plaza, built during what were probably the middle years of Jasaw Kaan. Dedicated in the spirit of a mausoleum probably to Lady Tun Kaywak,[3] it features

Temple II.

stepped terraces three levels high, battered and faceted with corner insets and with narrow stairways that climb the sides. Reached by monumental frontal stairs, the summit shrine includes two narrow rooms lifted still higher on their own plinth, the whole capped by a battered mansard roof and billboard-like roofcomb. Masks flank the plinth stairway, and line the frieze above the doorway, originally plastered and painted with colorful trim. With its brilliantly painted roof displays, the pyramid—literally a "sky mountain"—was the first of the Great Pyramids, and only the beginning of the city's unparalleled transformation under Jasaw Kaan.

WINDS OF CHANGE

Far in the west, Palenque's second great ruler "entered his road," the powerful Kaan B'alam or Snake Jaguar, son of Pakal the Great and the city's "architect king." Responsible for the three-pyramid Group of the Cross—the Temple of the Cross proper, the Temple of the Foliated Cross, and the Temple of the Sun—Kaan B'alam also commissioned some of the Maya's most spectacular relief sculptures, including his own father's historical record, and many buildings of the Palace. Under Kaan B'alam, Palenque architects had developed more open and wider corbelled vaults, allowing more light to penetrate inside and opening them up to large relief wall panels and other innovative forms of art.

On Kaan Balam's heels came his brother, K'an Joy Chitam, who took office under auspicious circumstances on 9.13.10.6.8 (June 3, A.D. 702). Nevertheless, K'an Joy Chitam would flounder almost immediately. Under this ruler, Palenque began to totter and started the long downward slide towards disaster, along with much of the western rivers region.

Within ten years of his accession, K'an Joy Chitam stumbled onto the battlefield unprepared to adequately challenge Toniná. Whether by an accident of fate or through poor judgment, K'an Joy was captured and dragged back to the capital of Chiapas to be humiliated and tortured by K'inich B'aknal Chaak. It was a fateful moment. For the next several years no ruler emerged to replace Palenque's king; no one was willing to take control while K'an Joy remained alive in captivity.[4] Akul Anaab' replaced him in the end, but it was already too late. Other ineffectual kings would accede, while Palenque would begin to break apart.

Yaxchilán, in contrast, prospered. Giving birth to the son of Itz'amnáj B'alam on 9.13.17.12.10 (August 27, A.D. 709), the king's Calakmul wife tied Yaxchilán to the Petén alliance sphere that was still reeling from its disastrous defeat. Yaxchilán's control of the western trade route would ensure that Calakmul would remain a continuing threat.

Naranjo also prospered under Calakmul rule. Apparently still smoldering over the marriage of Jasaw Kaan to Lady Tun Kaywak, Naranjo struck at Topoxte' Island and nearby dependent centers with its own campaign of scorched earth tactics. Scattering the bones of Topoxté's Yaxhá lord all over the island, in the midst of a spectacular four-planet astronomical conjunction, K'ak' Tiliw of Naranjo drove out the "companions of the wife of the Mutul lord," seeking vengeance against Jasaw Kaan's in-laws.

In the final days before the completion of the fourteenth k'atun (December A.D. 711), some unknown alliance managed to still the raging waters of revenge and retribution. Eight years after Lady Tun Kaywak's death, her bones and skull were exhumed, retrieved for their veneration in a tomb-opening ceremony. The events took place at Calakmul itself, where Jasaw Kaan journeyed in the company of his wife's countryman, Kaan Sak Wayas, a lord of Masul. Depicted on Tikal Altar 5, one of the most extraordinary carvings of Jasaw Kaan's career, the events surrounding her exhumation involved both men in unknown rituals before Jasaw's return to Tikal, possibly for the dedication of Temple II.

TWIN PYRAMID COMPLEX N

For completion of the fourteenth k'atun (9.14.0.0.0, or December 5, A.D. 711), Jasaw Kaan K'awil commissioned the second of his Twin Pyramid Groups, Complex N. Pairing Altar 5, the monument celebrating his wife's exhumation, with his own portrait on Stela 16, he grouped his most important public monuments together in an area of the site one-eighth of a mile west of the ancestral Great Plaza. On Stela 16, Jasaw Kaan chose to depict himself much more regally than his earlier Stela 30, commissioned over twenty years ago at the beginning of his reign. Jasaw Kaan stands majestically in

Altar 5.

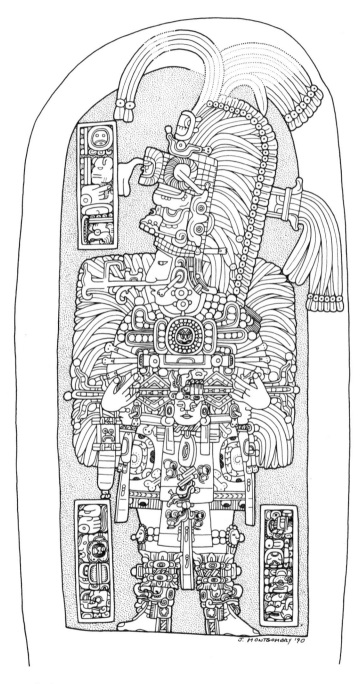

Stela 16.

Late Classic style: his feet splayed sideways, his torso in frontal view, and his face turned left. He holds delicately on his wrists his jeweled ceremonial bar, and from his right wrist dangles an incense bag emblazoned with the ringed eyes of Mexico's Tlaloc.

Arrayed with sprays of quetzal plumes, Jasaw's great backrack and saurian bonnet sweep behind him to increase his girth and mass. Tremendous jade necklaces—the same worn on Stela 30 and on his wooden lintels—and beaded breast plaques, encumber his chest and shoulders. Trophy heads of patron deities, literally "heads of power," lend girth to the loincloth. The skirt, probably of textile, includes crossed bones, jaguar pelt details, and "death eyes"; the broad, frontal loincloth flaps retain their delicate incised hieroglyphs. Beaded legbands with medallions, and high gaiters over elements of sandals, complete the costume.

The face suffered slight damage in ancient times, but the head of Jasaw Kaan indicates skull-deformation, induced in infancy by binding the forehead with cradle boards. His brow reflects the Maya's characteristic flattened or sloped forehead, indicating the "ideal" of Maya nobility. Glyphs give the date of the Twin Pyramid Group, naming Jasaw Kaan K'awil and his special titles. Tikal's Emblem Glyph follows the ruler's age: for three k'atun-endings, or between forty and sixty years, Jasaw Kaan K'awil had lived and ruled, the chief Kalomte' of Tikal.

THE FINAL YEARS OF JASAW KAAN

Cities all over the Maya world celebrated the k'atun-end 9.14.0.0.0—a momentous date associated in astronomical lore with the heliacal rising of Venus as Evening Star and viewed as a period of calm. Another of the tremendous calendrical milestones, K'atun 14 would witness unparalleled prosperity everywhere across the Classic lowlands.

Though no monuments definitely attributable to Jasaw Kaan survive after Stela 16 and Altar 5, he probably lived another twenty-two years. He may have overseen construction of Twin Pyramid Complex O (Group 4D–1), an area a few hundred yards north of the Great Plaza that was unusual for its plain stone monuments. Probably commemorating completion of K'atun 15 (9.15.0.0.0, or August 22, A.D. 731), shortly before Jasaw's reign ended,

Complex O may reflect the venerable ruler's withdrawal from public life. Conceivably he languished near death, unavailable to "sit" for his portrait.[5]

Building projects under Jasaw Kaan had exceeded any begun during the Middle or Early Classic Period. Major architectural works were consistently being built away from the ancient center, detached from the huge complex of the North Acropolis and Great Plaza. Giant causeways joined these areas for processions of state, for victory parades, and for simple foot traffic, unifying the city's physical layout.

Jasaw Kaan's lifetime coincided with a remarkable uniformity seen throughout the Classic Maya zone, a period when polychrome designs on pottery, sculptural styles, hieroglyphic writing, techniques of architecture, and political organization attained an unprecedented standardization. Maya culture and its outward manifestations became integrated, widely shared among many different towns, and thoroughly refined, resulting in the crystallization of a shared inspiration, the unification of the far reaches of the Maya world. While these years represented a return to normalcy, if "normalcy" had ever truly prevailed during Classic times, Jasaw Kaan's Sky Dynasty prospered, predicated on the revival of the old Sky Dynasty of Siyaj Kaan. United by marriage, military alliance, and trade, four main capitals had emerged as the dominant political contenders for supreme political control—all named on Copán's Stela A in the context of state visits. Achieved by Tikal's Jasaw Kaan K'awil, Copán's Waxaklajun U B'a, an unknown individual of Calakmul, and Palenque's Kaan B'alam, an uneasy truce prevailed that seemingly united all of the disparate dynasties under one sovereign at Tikal.[6] Restriction of marriage to within royal houses had perhaps led to inbreeding—a situation not necessarily detrimental to the genetic stock[7]—but it had also united ruling classes of diverse provinces at the peak of the Classic Period. Under this custom, hierarchies extended from the capital center of the province down through lesser secondary, tertiary, and even quartenary sites, all bound by ties of marriage and exchange.

As restorer of the old dynasty, legitimately descended from the great kings of the past, Jasaw Kaan's titles retained Siyaj Kaan's K'awil and "sky" elements. Miraculously, his first building projects coincided with the thirteenth k'atun anniversary (precisely 260 years) of Siyaj Kaan's Stela 31—a fantastic coincidence or clever propaganda that associated Jasaw Kaan with that ruler and a revival of the Mexican "golden age." Jasaw Kaan K'awil reintroduced emblems of his Mexican ancestors, establishing *talud-tablero* architecture, once the state architectural style of Teotihuacan, and emblazoning much of the city's downtown with Tlaloc eyes and "butterfly" symbolism and other Mexican emblems.

During some fifty-three years in power, Jasaw Kaan restored Tikal's legitimate sovereignty and returned control over the distribution of trade to Siyaj Kaan's line, temporarily reviving trade along the Tikal portage across the Yucatan. Alliances with Copán in the southeast and riverine countries of the west would largely assure authority over Tikal's dominions during his lifetime.

But as Jasaw Kaan grew old, profound changes must have anticipated his death. Factions of every ilk and motive no doubt waited to grab pieces of the weakening Tikal alliance block. For a while, Jasaw Kaan's sons would hold back the unseen and unknown forces that steadily inundated lowland civilization. But even the gods and the venerated Siyaj Kaan could not ultimately prevent the disintegration and catastrophe that would climax Late Classic Tikal.

THE BURIAL OF JASAW KAAN K'AWIL

Jasaw Kaan K'awil must have been close to eighty years old when he died. Stela 16 mentions his third k'atun or third period of twenty years, and Lintel 3 of Temple I makes note of his fourth k'atun. Possibly the ruler constructed his own tomb and the overlying pyramid, as Pakal had done at Palenque. The tomb may have remained open during his final years with access maintained through tunnels dug through the massive pyramidal base, allowing his body to be carried inside when the time arrived.

Whoever organized the tomb's construction chose an area where no funeral shrine had stood before, bringing the construction of a royal tomb and temple down off the North Acropolis for the first time. Workers dug the chamber through bedrock on the eastern lip of the Great Plaza, due east of where Jasaw had constructed Temple II for his wife, excavating through centuries of earlier plaza floors an area 14.5-feet long, eight feet wide, and thirteen feet high. Against the east, a low platform or dais was installed the length of the vault, while a narrow aisle was left on the west. Walled with masonry in horizontal coursework and stuccoed with lime plaster, the chamber formed in essence a palace room, with the platform functioning as the ruler's throne and bed.

Once finished, attendants climbed down inside to cover the dais with plaited mats woven from palm fronds and fringed with jade beads. Over the mats they arranged jaguar or ocelot pelts, leaving the paws of the great cats still attached. Assistants lowered the body, and upon the jaguar skins the funeral entourage extended Jasaw Kaan, carefully laying him to rest in the splendor of his brilliant robes.

By Maya standards, Jasaw Kaan K'awil was very tall—about five-feet, five-inches. He was an elderly man consistent with glyphic evidence of great age. Stains and residue indicated apparel of textiles, leather, and feathers, the remains of splendid costume features no doubt similar to ones he wore on his several sculptured portraits. Sixteen and one-half pounds of jade adorned and surrounded his body, including great cylindrical earplugs, numerous headdress plaques, tubular necklace beads, bracelets, anklets, and fabulous heavy collars. His personal "heirloom" necklace consisted of 114 spheres of jade ranging from one-half inch to two inches in diameter—by itself, eight and one-half pounds in weight. Pea-shaped and baroque pearls, thorny oysters scraped to reveal their interior orange-red, and stingray spines for bloodletting originated from sea coasts scores of miles from Petén. Thirty-three pottery vessels, some with food for sustenance in the Hereafter, were crammed inside the aisle and arranged around the corpse, among them vessels of jade, alabaster, massive polychrome plates, and legless cylinders painted with traditional narrative scenes.

The cylinders closely resemble each other, painted with repetitive scenes that feature enthroned lords. Four vessels include attendants who kneel in homage, while the rest depict the lord alone. Typically, the painted thrones include canopies, while the attendants kneel with their arms folded to receive some discourse offered by the seated lord. In one example, both figures were executed in light tan, with their shoulders colored reddish brown. Representing some stiff black material, the lord's headdress wraps round itself to form a conical shape, while fish nibble at crosshatched orange-red water lilies inserted into the front of the headband. From the headgear angles a single feather from the mythical Muwan Bird and quetzal plumes that cascade in typical Late Classic flamboyance. Glyphs surrounding the rim incorporate the Primary Standard

Sequence, dedicating the painted surface and explaining the vessel was used to consume *kakaw*, or fermented chocolate.

Entirely decorated with jade mosaic plaques, the most impressive cylinder carries Jasaw Kaan's bust as a handle for the lid. Incised around the edge of the cover in delicate lines, its inscriptions refer to Jasaw Kaan K'awil.

Most extraordinary of all the grave contents, more than three dozen animal and human bones were piled in the southern end of the aisle, many modified as useful and decorative items, including awls, long needles, tweezers, and bloodletting instruments. Scribes incised thirty-seven of the bones with delicate masterpieces of art, rubbed red with powdered cinnabar to color the lines.

The bones include pairs that "mirror" each other. Others were executed in sets of up to six separate pieces. One pair depicts marvelously real prisoners, stripped naked in humiliation. Bound and resigned to certain death, the captives evoke the misery of defeated enemies with harrowing realism. Other sets include canoe scenes, one with the canoes loaded with a lively iguana, a bashful monkey, a realistic parrot, and a shaggy "K'ank'in" dog, all squawking and howling as the old Paddler Gods convey the archetypal young Lord of Maize rapidly into the Underworld. Related images include almost comical fishing scenes in which the Maya Rain God stands knee-deep in water with a creel strapped to his back and a fish in his hand, gesturing angrily towards his cohort standing in the rear of their canoe. Almost one thousand years earlier, Izapa in coastal Chiapas had originated a similar scene, portraying the Rain God's counterpart in his watery world.

Information about Jasaw Kaan and his numerous relatives dominate the bones, among them statements about his mother and father. Jasaw Kaan was the son of Lady "Jaguar Cushion" and Nuun U Jol Chaak, the Middle Classic ruler defeated by Dos Pilas. Long slender needles provide information about the early dynasties of Tikal, featuring Siyaj K'ak', Nuun Yax Ayin, and Jatz'am Ku.

Once the many funeral gifts were assembled, masons roofed the vault with the renowned Maya corbelled arch, first covering the aperture to shield the body and grave contents from falling debris. Priests or other specialists kindled a small fire over the location for one final ceremony. Then workers buried the tomb under thousands of flint and obsidian chips before building the shrine.

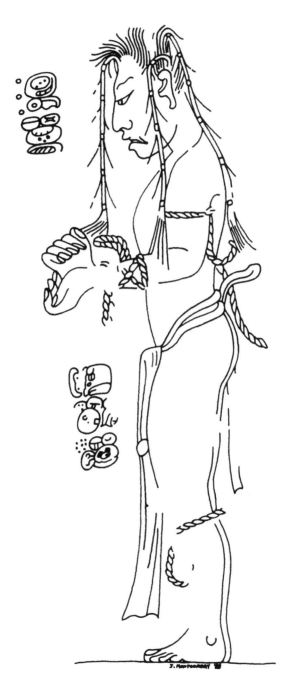

Bound Prisoner (MT39b).

Canoe Scene (MT38a).

Chaaks Fishing (MT51b).

Jasaw Kaan probably succumbed during the important *tun* that corresponds to 9.15.3.0.0.0 (August 6, A.D. 734). But the temple may have been finished as late as 9.15.5.0.0 under Jasaw's son and successor, Yik'in Kaan K'awil, and possibly not until 9.15.10.0.0, five to ten years after the project began.[8] Cores of rough masonry retaining walls packed with rubble were laid down to form the terraces, with the workers extending these higher in diminishing size. Nine terraces were added to correspond to the number of Maya Underworlds, each faced outside with neat ashlar masonry in coursework, and battered and recessed to create a sheer, forced-perspective facade. Like Temple II across the plaza, corners included double insets and aprons, with string moldings detailing each elevation. While construction proceeded, temporary stairways provided access to levels of building activity, increasing in depth and height as the pyramid rose. A final, permanent staircase was added over the original as one of the finishing touches.

Crowning the pyramid's summit, temple walls were added with double coursework that sandwiched an inner core of rubble. Out of walls like these, three rooms were built almost too narrow to be useful, organized in stages where the rear one steps up slightly higher than the stage in front. Great beams of *sapote*, among the world's hardest tropical woods, were elevated by laborers hauling on ropes draped over an A-frame scaffold above the walls. The beams were nudged into special niches over the doors to serve as lintels, nearly a hundred feet above the plaza floor. Wrapped with palm fronds and plaited mats for protection, the elevated lintels were exposed when work ended, the padding cut away to reveal portraits of Jasaw Kaan K'awil, the giant jaguar and serpent images, and records of the ruler's deeds.

Outside, work continued as masons capped the rooms with steep corbelled arches and added stonework high over the roof, a "roofcomb" sculpted with Jasaw Kaan holding his Sun Shield and Scepter. Plasterers covered the entire pyramid with white lime stucco, painting the crests and molding, the frieze and trim in brilliant red and blue, green and black, and shades of red. The pyramid itself was probably painted entirely red. Its stunning crest would have blazed above the city for miles. Slightly higher upon its completion, Temple I now stands 145 feet over the Great Plaza, delicately balanced with flanged highlights and baffled shadows.

His pyramid, his sundry grave gifts, and his symbols of power were to serve Jasaw Kaan K'awil during his journey into the Underworld and his

Temple I.

eternal afterlife. If the much later Quiché Maya *Book of Council*, or *Popol Vuh*, shares the Classic Period conception of life after death—and evidence suggests that it does—then the passage into the realm of the dead involved Herculean travels across bodies of water and ingenious ordeals devised by the gods of death and pestilence. Triumph over adversity inevitably resulted in rebirth and apotheosis, when the ruler danced his way through the jaws of death and mortal defeat to assume his place among deified kings and great heroes of the Creation Myth. Through preoccupation with physical needs beyond the grave, Jasaw Kaan was to live forever.

In furtherance of this goal, architects raised one of the most spectacular pyramids ever conceived by the Maya or any other Precolumbian people. Not at all encumbered by its own material mass, Temple I soars as a compact, streamlined turret, an aerie for priests and privileged nobility. Across the roof, the ruler's portrait, now eroded and nearly illegible, rears above the city's walls *in memoriam* and in perpetuity to this mightiest of kings. To judge from the temple, the tomb hidden beneath, and the sculptured monuments still scattered across Tikal, Jasaw Kaan K'awil will indeed live forever.

NOTES

1. Schele and Mathews 1998: 70–74.
2. The source of blue-green jade has never been found, but the Motágua Valley probably supplied Mesoamerica with the bulk of common green jade and other varieties.
3. However, no tomb was located either inside or underneath the pyramid.
4. Inferred from the inscriptional record.
5. Coggins, 1975.
6. The nature of this "unification" remains speculative, in particular whether it was the result of Tikal's political or ideological dominance.
7. Haviland 1967.
8. Coggins op. cit.

CHAPTER 11

THE SUCCESSORS OF YAX EB' XOOK

I f the seeds of Tikal's collapse and abandonment had been sown before this early date, architectural projects and ceremonialism offer no hint. Relatively new precincts at Tikal were remodeled, the broad paved causeways that criss-crossed the site were expanded from earlier ones, and populations in the surrounding residential districts were beginning to reach their maximum density. Tikal had begun its final burst of building activity, its peak construction period, set in motion by the renewed energy of its kings.

Within a year of his father's death, Yik'in Kaan K'awil acceded over Tikal as the twenty-seventh successor of Yax Eb' Xook, acquiring the throne at the age of forty-three. The new ruler eagerly commemorated his good fortune. Within two years he erected his first monument on the vast plaza of the Temple of the Inscriptions—Stela 21. Located in an ancient area of Tikal that may have functioned as the city's southeast entrance, over three-quarters of a mile from the downtown precinct, Stela 21 commemorates the date 9.15.5.0.0 (July 26, A.D. 736), Tikal's only known monument dedicated to a *hotun* or five-year period. Later broken intentionally, only the lower half survives, along with fragments of the ruler's headdress and upper inscription.

Shown in full profile, Yik'in Kaan K'awil poses in typically Late Classic style, his feet placed side by side, his right leg slightly visible behind the left. In his arm he cradles his ceremonial bar, while with his free hand he scatters drops of blood, the "harvest" of self-inflicted mutilation of his genitals. Although

Name Glyph of Yik'in Kaan K'awil.

barefoot, he wears an extraordinarily well-preserved "Perforator God" as an anklet, the deity of bloodletting paraphernalia. He is further adorned in brocaded textile skirts, shell "tinklers" that dangle beneath his belt, and shell-and-bead pendants that overlie his loincloth flaps and that hang past his knees. The backshield remains visible, together with a pendant bead and "bone" elements, woven "mat" symbols, dragon profiles, and quetzal plumes that swerve outside the border to lightly touch the ruler's heels.

Period glyphs calculate back from the monument's now lost dedicatory date, originally located at the head of the upper panel, to reach the ruler's inauguration (9.15.3.6.8, or December 12, A.D. 734). His titles end the text, plus the verb mirroring the scene portrayed—a hand scattering blood.

FISSIONING OF THE TIKAL STATE

Despite Yik'in''s peaceful inauguration, political events were again sweeping the more important districts under his control into the limelight. The Petexbatun state had once again begun to expand militarily, probably under the aegis of Yik'in''s relatives who ruled Dos Pilas. Moving first against Seibal, upstream on the Pasión River, Ruler 3 of the Petexbatun federation subjugated the local king Ich'aak B'alam, humiliating and torturing him before restoring his throne. Under the watchful eye of Ruler 3, Seibal served as an important outpost, monitoring trade flowing down the Pasión River and out of the highlands. Again, the focus of Petén expansion centered around a waterway, one that was an especially important crossroads that restricted access not only to highland goods but that was dangerously close to the Usumacinta. Seibal lay particularly close to the extensive raised field complexes on the opposite bank of the Pasión, built to drain swamps and intensify an agricultural production that could easily have helped sustain an increasingly burdensome population in the heartland districts.

Independence farther from Tikal was also being sought. Gradually at first, but gaining momentum, secondary centers began to drop from the political influence of the great regional states. Victories over larger capital districts recorded by lesser centers may have been wars of liberation, assisted by Calakmul in its bid to surround Tikal with hostile factions. Unwittingly these smaller centers were then lured into other, less obvious forms of subservience.

Among the first, and probably the greatest in impact, was the defection of Quirigua in the southeast quadrant of the Maya world. Suddenly and violently turning on his overlord, the Quirigua ruler K'ak' Tiliw[1] "pierced" the gods of Waxaklajun U B'a, the Copán ruler who took for his name the Vision Serpent of Teotihuacan. Capturing U B'a's floatlike battle palanquin around which the Copán armies had rallied, K'ak' Tiliw also seized the king himself, dragging him back to Quirigua where he removed his head.

Originally subject to Copán, the prize of the lower Motágua jade mines must have proved too tempting for K'ak' Tiliw to resist. Out of the fog of defeat, twenty years of obscurity ensued at Copán, the city's own dark ages before it was stabilized under other rulers.

Suddenly Quirigua had gained full independence. Within years its own emblem was adorning some of the largest and most impressive Maya monuments ever made. Under Quirigua's new authority, ambitious building projects were undertaken, transforming the original, relatively small residential administrative center into a monumental, dynamic seat of government. Able for the first time to harness large quantities of manpower and to widen its control over ever-larger areas of the lower Motágua Valley, Quirigua soon exploited resources much farther away, while exhausting its local building materials.

Copán had dominated products leaving the highlands for the last 250 years, cooperating with Petén in organizing and maintaining key distribution networks. These had focused on, and were probably centered at, Tikal. Once freed from Copán, Quirigua gained sole control of the Motágua route, and access to Caribbean ports became increasingly more important. With the rise of trade by sea towards the end of the Late Classic Period, when new centers of political power eroded Petén's hegemony, Tikal was inexorably cut off from vital trade items and eclipsed by the newer economic institutions of the Post Classic decline. At the heart of it all was Tikal's old nemesis, Calakmul, still viable after its defeat under Jasaw Kaan.

Thus, the severing of ties with Copán began that city's inexorable decline and, ultimately, the decline of the entire Classic world.

Quirigua was never deeply involved with lowland centers to the north. Petén sites or the surrounding districts never mention Quirigua on their monuments, with the possible exception of Pusilhá.[2] Quirigua's rulers seemingly shunned external contacts such as elite intermarriage or military alliance, never importing or manufacturing the rich polychrome pottery vessels that characterized Petén.[3] Self-sufficient within the fertile lower Motágua Valley, fiercely independent with its hard-won monopoly over highland-to-Caribbean trade, Quirigua now imposed on itself a harsh isolation that left it precluded from Classic interaction-spheres.

THE RISE OF YAXUN B'ALAM

Rebellion spread westward to Yaxchilán, but now the stakes rose much higher, encompassing the trade networks of the western rivers region and the wealth and power invested in these. By the time of Yik'in Kaan's accession at Tikal, Itz'amnáj B'alam had passed away, leaving Yaxchilán's throne to his son. But more than a decade would pass before the legitimate heir could claim his birth right, and then only after intense and desperate struggles against enemies still loyal to the status quo.

Yaxchilán's position astride the Usumacinta maintained the critical transportation of goods to the Gulf of Mexico, and ultimately to foreign markets. As the key to Petén's southern trade route, which funneled items from Caribbean Belíze and highland Guatemala, the Usumacinta depended upon the gateway cities of Yaxchilán and Piedras Negras to control the natural bulk transportation systems of the forest rivers. In this way trade entering or leaving the highlands avoided the long ocean voyage around the Yucatan, the vague political machinations of the poorly organized coastal districts, and the rise of hostile state governments just now looming on the Classic horizon. Anyone who controlled Yaxchilán controlled this flow of goods.

Yaxun B'alam, the son of old Shield Jaguar, had been born of his father's union with a woman of Calakmul, and it was this superpower that must have championed his inheritance with force. Tottering on the wave cresting over the Classic world, Yaxchilán ultimately would be carried away, and cut off from highland commerce.

THE "PALANQUIN WARS"

The eye of the storm remained anything but calm. Tikal's Yik'in Kaan hastily commissioned his second monument, Stela 5, thereby breaking tradition by not waiting for the end of the k'atun. Depicting Yik'in trampling one of his bound prisoners, and thereby emphasizing his military prowess, Stela 5 portrays the ruler in Late Classic style with legs side by side, grasping his K'awil Scepter and incense bag. Over brocaded undergarments he wears skirts of spotted jaguar pelt, replete with tail. His backrack of quetzal plumes clings to his belt, heavy with pendants and masks, while the belt sports shell "tinklers" as fringe. Stela 5 commemorates the conquest of Yax May, the late king of Naranjo, identified by name glyphs as the bound prisoner.

Continuing his father's subjugation of the kingdoms surrounding Tikal, Yik'in embarked upon new wars of extirpation, attacking first an old enemy long kept hostile by Calakmul. Seizing the downtown zones of El Peru's ally, possibly Laguna Perdida, on 9.15.12.2.2 (August 1, A.D. 743), Yik'in captured the El Peru war palanquin and then sacked and destroyed Laguna Perdida. Nine months later he ravaged Naranjo, still contentious after all these years, putting down its new ruler and capturing its palanquin.

Numerous monuments throughout downtown Tikal relate these events, boldly displaying Yik'in''s captured booty and prisoners. Shown trussed and humiliated, Chak Toj Waybi of Naranjo adorns Tikal Altar 8, Column Altar 1, and the great rock sculpture carved in billboard-fashion near the head of the Maler Causeway. The Calakmul king also came within Yik'in''s reach, shown trussed and ready for sacrifice on Altar 9.

Among the most extraordinary Maya monuments ever carved, huge wooden lintels installed over the inner doorways of Yik'in''s Temple IV depict the war palanquins taken from El Peru and Naranjo. Four of the seven carved lintels at Tikal include depictions of these objects, including those taken during the reign of Yik'in Kaan. Each shows the ruler enthroned on pyramid-like stepped or terraced platforms with frontal stairways, mounted with multi-component banners. That the platforms represent the bases of palanquins can be seen in Yik'in''s Temple IV, where the inner-most lintel depicts lashed poles at both ends, which were used to carry the palanquin on the shoulders of bearers.

Just such scenes were depicted by restless spectators of the colorful parades and ceremonial processions that must have made their way along the causeways and concourse-plazas. Perhaps years of relentless ceremony had left members of the privileged elite jaded, and watching from Temple II they scratched on one of the inner walls of the shrine a palanquin replete with its bearers. Graffiti adorns the crumbling and lichen-covered walls of numerous Tikal buildings—crude, unskilled etchings not unlike modern scribbles on the cover of a telephone book. Genuine Maya "art," the graffiti of Tikal offers subtle, often unappreciated windows into a lost world once every bit as alive as our own.

Central to the Tikal palanquins, the huge "protectors" rear in wildly monstrous shapes. Like his father's, the lintels of Yik'in portray both serpent and jaguar figures, the latter now cloaked as the very human God of Number Seven, the so-called Jaguar God of the Underworld. Identified by his "cruller" eye and feline ear, he symbolizes the Sun God in his nighttime aspect, reigning over the evening hours. Yik'in sits within a bower formed by the god and his extended arm, and by the totem battle standard erected before the platform's edge.

Lintel 3 of Temple IV portrays Yik'in enthroned beneath an overarching Vision Serpent, its body marked with belly scales and double disks. Sprays of quetzal plumes identify the creature as the famous Feathered Serpent, later the totem of Quetzalcoatl and the Toltecs. Over the scene extends the Principal Bird Deity, a composite mythical bird with bearded, out-stretched serpent-wings. The Feathered Serpent's left head, long-nosed and bearded, yawns wide to disgorge another god marked with maize curls; while the right head, skeletal and marked as "sacred," spews scrolls of blood.

Both lintels from Temple IV bear locative "place names" along their bases, identifying the region from which they originated. The one bears the main sign of the Emblem Glyph of Naranjo, the other an emblematic device common to the El Peru sphere. Probably carried into battle by non-combatant slaves or other lowly bearers, the palanquins' giant "protectors" depict what was probably the enemy's patron god, an extremely visible icon around which the king's troops could rally. On the battlefield, capture of the palanquin and consequently the patron god signaled victory, and may have formally ended the conflict. Once one's patron god was "downed," nothing remained except flight.

© 2000 J. MONTGOMERY

Temple IV, Lintel 2.

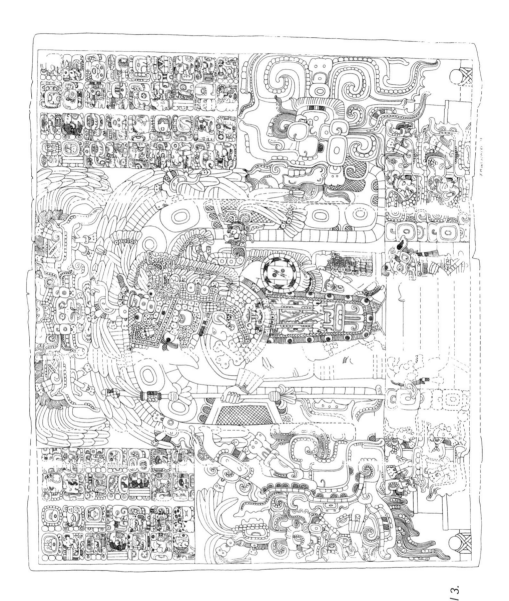

Temple IV, Lintel 3.

Capture of the enemy standards and gods of El Peru and Naranjo put an end to years of strife between these sites and Tikal. With Calakmul defeated twice—first by Jasaw Kaan in the opening years of the Late Classic Period and then by Yik'in Kaan—the remaining key towns now entirely capitulated. Probably northwestern Petén's preeminent district, and administrator of the western approach to Tikal along the Río San Pedro, El Peru had long enjoyed close ties to Calakmul, bound to its alliance block by marriage at the highest levels. Likewise, Naranjo had controlled access to the Belize Valley, the only direct route linking Petén with the Caribbean Sea. Naranjo, too, had bound itself to Calakmul, marrying its kings to members of the dominant alliance block.

With the final conquest of these zones, Yik'in won for himself a respite, a well-deserved rest from which he was prepared to prosper. After 9.15.17.10.4 (December 14, A.D. 748), references to warfare dramatically but temporarily fall off in central Petén. Other than wars of succession fought by Yaxun B'alam, erstwhile heir to the throne of Yaxchilán, comparative quiet settled over the region. For a while Yik'in would maintain his father's dominance.

The "wars of the palanquins" for El Peru and Naranjo were the last known major conflicts between the alliance blocks of Calakmul and Tikal.

EXPANSION OF THE CENTRAL ACROPOLIS

At the heart of Tikal, the Central Acropolis had increased tenfold in scale and complexity over its original structures of wood and thatch. Six private courtyards formed the core of this largest elite residential compound, four and one-half acres that sprawled along the southern margin of the East and Great Plazas. From Court 6, palaces rose two and more stories towards the west in range upon range of apartment-like compounds. By the time of Yik'in, multi-ranged galleries, monumental stairways, and elevated terraces bordered the Great Plaza itself, suitable for observing pageants unfolding on the pavements below. Within its depths, narrow, sometimes hidden stairways gave access to the various levels, while the facades of the surrounding buildings concealed more discrete residences and courtyards.

North Facade of the Central Acropolis.

Maler's Palace (Structure 5D–65), with Temple V in background.

In this warren, this labyrinth of masonry chambers, Yik'in and his closest family members resided in comparative luxury. Although the great kings of the city originally occupied the eastern end and the residential palace of Chak Tok Ich'aak I, expansion of the size of the royal family no doubt necessitated a removal to more spacious quarters. Eventually, members of the royal family must have occupied the majority of the Central Acropolis structures, with individual palaces and their outlying buildings serving as the residences of specific wives and their nuclear families.

While the majority of structures functioned as residences for the king and his extended families, others functioned as kitchen compounds and storage chambers. Still others housed administrative personnel and important members of the government, as well as attendants, teachers, consultants, and servants under the king.

Facing north onto Court 2, the building called Maler's Palace—named after the nineteenth-century German explorer who lived and worked there—probably functioned as Yik'in''s primary "throne room" or audience hall, built for the reception of official visitors and dignitaries. The building typifies "range structures" or palaces in general, laid out in capital "I" ground plan with longitudinal midsection and transverse end rooms.[4]

Key to Maya architectural technology was the celebrated corbelled arch. Maler's Palace was roofed with these throughout its several rooms, built with specialized vault stones that overlap and "lock" in place. In their monumental public architecture, the Maya failed to exploit the concept of the keystone, the primary mechanism of the true arch. They built instead "pseudo-arches," or "imbricated arches," by cantilevering or balancing each course of masonry above the next. The resulting upside-down "V" shape— the corbelled arch—mimics the shape of common thatched-roof houses, which were steeply pitched and presented a "battered" or sloped profile. Corbelled arches could be modified under skillful architects so that their slope varied from inverted step-shape, to both convex and concave slopes.

Large holes just inside the doorways, sometimes inserted with wooden or ceramic dowels, indicate that occupants closed off Maler's Palace with curtains for shade and privacy. Interiors were equipped with stone benches used as seats and for "sleeping platforms," the significantly harder equivalent of beds. Open niches in end walls provided space for storage of the king's personal belongings or for ceremonial paraphernalia. When in use, the actual throne located in Maler's Palace, and other platforms inside its

Interior of Maler's Palace (Structure 5D-65).

multiple rooms, included coverings of plaited mats, jaguar and ocelot pelts, stuffed cushions, and textiles for the comfort of the ruler.

Outside, Maya architects left the lower walls plain, but added stucco friezes over the entablature zone between the cornice and lintel, including "guardian" masks above all three doorways. Workers painted the frieze in blue and red, occasionally adding green, yellow, and black. Small holes over the doorways and below the medial molding once held doweling to support canopies that ran all along the facade to provide shade for the upper terrace.

Several works of art give clues to the function of structures like Maler's Palace. Sculptured monuments and painted pottery depict royal receptions where the king sits on a dais accepting gifts or war captives from subordinate lords, occasionally with figures seated on an exterior terrace just outside the chamber. The bench or "throne" in Room 1 of Maler's Palace, replete with armrests, occupies a position where the ruler could gaze out the central doorway down into Court 2. Together with the courtyard, the staircase, and the landing outside the palace doorways, the structure fits in every way the architectural settings of royal reception scenes.

Yik'in Kaan K'awil built the final version of another palace on the Central Acropolis that functioned perhaps as a specialized reception hall for particularly renowned guests. Rising in multiple galleries up the steep slope of the ravine holding the Palace Reservoir, the Five-Story Palace imparted a terraced, pyramidal effect to the southern facade of the Central Acropolis. Outside stairs led from one floor to another, and originally two great staircases descended from the lower range to a terrace in the ravine, convenient for collecting potable water.

At least one carved wooden lintel adorned an interior doorway of the Five Story Palace. Carved out of exceptionally durable *sapote* wood, like every other sculptured example at Tikal, the lintel was badly eroded and worm-eaten. But enough of it survives to recognize Yik'in K'awil facing left, elevating in his hand the K'awil Scepter of royal blood lines. He carries his Sun God shield emblazoned with the cruller-eyed Jaguar God of the Underworld, indicative of the sun in its nighttime aspect, and an incense bag marked with the head of the Teotihuacan War Serpent, Waxaklajun U B'a. Although more than half the lintel has been destroyed, the lower corner preserves an image of a dwarf: a tiny, turban-spangled figure carrying musical shakers or feathered wands. Around him, two long-necked

Five-Story Palace (Structure 5D-52).

waterbirds, probably composite heron-egrets, make lively additions to what survives. Glyphs identify the date 9.15.10.0.0 (June 30, A.D. 741), the same dedicatory Period Ending of Yik'in''s lintels from Temple IV.

THE COMPLETION OF K'ATUN 16

Whether Yik'in Kaan survived to see completion of K'atun 16 remains debatable, for no death dates survive for the later rulers. If he did live that long, then he also oversaw completion of Twin Pyramid Complex P in the North Zone, and the erection of Stela 20 with its paired Altar 8.

By the latter days of Yik'in, major architectural agglomerations had transformed the extreme northern perimeter of the downtown zone into a major ceremonial district, bristling with "sky-mountains" that were impressive in their own right. Located at the juncture of the Maler and Maudslay Causeways, great elevated avenues that link Group H with the downtown shrines, the North Zone effectively tripled the radius of monumental architectural groups at the heart of the civic center. The Maler and Maudslay Causeways themselves include "safety" parapets and intermittent exits, functioning as the main downtown arteries and concourse thoroughfares for the thousands of people residing at Tikal. From the central districts, causeways angled north and east, joining at the multi-plaza complex of the North Zone.

Stela 20 and Altar 8 form the center-piece of Complex P, the Twin Pyramid arrangement built at the heart of the North Group. Dedicated to the Period Ending 9.16.0.0.0 (May 9, A.D. 751), Stela 20 portrays the current ruler bearing a three-bladed halberd and standing before an altar supporting the decapitated head of a jaguar. Significantly innovative, Stela 20 introduces specialized paraphernalia not seen before, while the usual bound prisoner, the Naranjo ruler Yax May, has been transposed to Altar 8. Ball court markers from this period, removed from their original location, also depict Yik'in''s prisoners from Naranjo.

K'atun 16 saw celebrations and the dedication of monuments throughout the Maya world: at Uaxactun, Piedras Negras, Itzimté, El Chorro, Pomoná, and a host of lesser sites. Some possibility remains that Yik'in had already died by this ending, replaced by the twenty-eighth but nevertheless

unidentified successor. Records of conquests and the people involved suggest Yik'in survived considerably longer, and that the monuments of Complex P were the work of this still viable lord.

Soon after the erection of Stela 20, Yaxun B'alam's struggle over Yaxchilán
resolved in his favor. In the decade when no clear ruler emerged to govern
his city, Yaxun B'alam's mother evidently filled this capacity, bound to the
dynasty at Calakmul and associated with nobility who functioned perhaps
as regents or pretenders to the throne. Yaxchilán Stela 11 probably depicts
his final succession arrangements, showing his reception of the last great
aristocrats barring his way to power. Appropriately, all three submit humbly
on their knees.

For the next several years Yaxun B'alam would wage continual war, a
constant struggle to shore up his tottering kingdom.

BURIAL 196

At about 9.16.4.0.0 (April 18, A.D. 755), a lord succumbed who was probably the son of Jasaw Kaan K'awil and one of Yik'in Kaan's younger
brothers.[5] In many ways his tomb resembled that of his father, who had
died twenty years earlier. Built against the northwest facade of the Central
Acropolis, across from the funeral shrine of the woman who may have been
his mother (Temple II), the tomb lay beneath an unimpressive mound of
rubble faced with terraced masonry and either without a summit shrine or
with one of perishable material, long ago eroded away. Inside, workers
installed a bench to support the body, covering it with requisite mats and
jaguar pelt. The head of the man pointed west, with the torso covered in
textile robes or shrouds, studded with thorny-oyster shell, with the interiors scraped to reveal their precious red-orange. Among the nearly fifty
ceramics were wide plates, simple bowls, cylinders, and a domestic cooking
jar with residue of food inside. Stingray spines were arranged at the
pelvis, the paraphernalia of penis mutilation, together with additional
objects of shell, pearls, and tremendous quantities of jade jewelry. One
object, lightly carved in low relief, portrays a crouching baby jaguar with
a water lily over its brow, three and one-half pounds of translucent
apple jade.

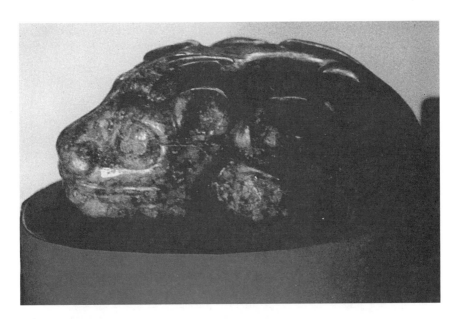

Jade Jaguar, Burial 196.

Among the polychrome cylinders present, one ranks among the most beautiful ever painted in the Maya lowlands. Smaller than typical vases, and executed in "codex style," the cream field and hieroglyphic writing resemble a page from a Maya book. The dual enthroned lords and their attendants are outlined in black, while costume details, the rulers' bodies, and the more important hieroglyphs are tinted in shades of red. Both attendants represent hummingbirds, and their long beaks pierce the hieroglyph for "flower." Another sign, written on the vase between them, reads *sa*, identifying the vessel's contents as alcoholic maize gruel. The little hummingbirds salute, giving the sign of one arm over their breast in token of "submission."

Although most likely someone who never acceded, the deceased entombed in Burial 196 may have been the hypothetical twenty-eighth successor of Yax Eb' Xook. Alternatively he may have been Yik'in Kaan himself.

Hummingbird Vase, Burial 196.

THE DESCENDANTS OF YAX EB' XOOK

The final dated monument probably from the reign of Yik'in Kaan K'awil, Temple VI—the Temple of the Inscriptions—soars over the huge walled plaza at the end of the Mendez Causeway far from the center of Tikal. Smaller than the great pyramids of the downtown zone, but impressive in its own right, the Temple of the Inscriptions dominates what was perhaps the southeastern approach to the city. Its roofcomb towers more than eighty feet over the perimeter of an enormous plaza the size of the West, Great, and East Plazas combined. Huge hieroglyphic panels adorn the sides and back, carved in relief on the lateral friezes and roofcomb.

Nearly two thousand years of "history" dominate the text, an account that goes back to a time before the first archaeological evidence of village life, when Tikal was little more than a hill in the vast reaches of the jungle. Date A falls during the late second millennium B.C.,[6] when Olmec sites to the northwest were carving Mesoamerica's oldest stone monuments. No archaeological evidence of people at Tikal survives from this early date, but conceivably settlements of farmers already existed.

Date B moves forward to the Middle Preclassic (457 B.C.), when Tikal was definitely making pottery vessels and laying down plastered floors, and just before it would begin to build masonry platforms. By Date C (156 B.C.), Tikal was erecting formal temples and building vaulted tombs for increasingly powerful rulers. It bordered on the verge of commissioning pyramids with rich, polychrome stucco work and monumental masks. Most importantly, it would soon carve stone monuments. With Date D, the inscription jumps forward into the ninth b'aktun (9.4.0.0.0, A.D. 514), to the era of Lady Kalomte' and her usurper-consort, Kalomte' B'alam. A period of prolonged instability, it was a time that saw the loss of power formerly monopolized by Tikal's Sky Dynasty. By the days of Yik'in Kaan, the Middle Classic probably remained well-documented on stela still standing in the Great Plaza and could easily have formed the basis of this "middle" history.[7]

The remainder of the text refers to Yik'in Kaan, mentioning his mother, Lady Twelve Macaw, and his age of four k'atuns. He was between sixty and eighty years old at the time the inscription was carved. Falling less than three years before inauguration of the twenty-ninth successor, the latest dates may relate Yik'in"s death, the date of his interment, or the date on which he fell critically ill.

Culminating with the reign of Yik'in Kaan K'awil, the Temple of the Inscriptions panels link Tikal's dynastic history to legendary and semi-mythological epochs of the past and the founder Yax Eb' Xook. Although its purpose was to glorify the man evidently responsible for construction of the summit shrine, the protagonist was perhaps Yik'in"s successor, Ruler 28, who could have completed the temple when he added the roofcomb and hieroglyphic text. Conceivably the same ruler erected Stela 20 in the North Zone.

There seems something nostalgic about the Temple of the Inscriptions, something melancholy in the way it carefully outlines the highlights of Tikal's past. In many ways a "remembrance," the text reviews important events as though in the last moments before death, a final passing before the eyes of everything great and noble. Tikal would build numerous monuments and much higher pyramids, but the city and all it controlled was balancing over a precipice.

BEGINNING OF THE END

Yik'in Kaan K'awil consolidated the Late Classic revival of Tikal begun by his father Jasaw Kaan K'awil, making headway against seemingly impossible odds. Wresting control decisively from the Calakmul alliance block, Yik'in Kaan had furthered the goals of peace and trade that his father had championed through persistence, shoring up an uneasy trade alliance and maintaining the hegemony of Tikal. Yik'in Kaan continued a process in which military success overcame Tikal's disastrous conquest twice during the Middle Classic Period, and broke free of an encirclement orchestrated by Calakmul that had severed Tikal from long-distance trade. Capitalizing on these successes, Yik'in adapted his father's artistic programs to proclaim his victories and the renewed wealth of Tikal.

But underlying the glory and the grandeur, there were more subtle influences at work. The monuments of Yik'in contrast subtly with those of Jasaw Kaan. Yik'in erected his first monument only two years after his accession; his second eight years later; and his third seven years thereafter—each in relatively quick succession. The ruler then ceased to erect monuments altogether.

Monuments attributable to Yik'in emphasize bound prisoners, their inscriptions nearly an endless saga of battles. Altars, columns, stelae, even a natural rock outcrop, bear prisoners bound and trussed, ready to meet their gods. Stela 5 evokes an especially self-centered preoccupation, erected hastily with the bound prisoner floundering directly under Yik'in''s feet and the ruler's inaugural date highlighted in the inscription along with his parents.[8] Just as other unstable rulers had emphasized themselves in the past, so his right to rule became a campaign to proclaim legitimacy. The massive hieroglyphs of the Temple of the Inscriptions reflect these visions of grandeur, tracing Yik'in''s decent not just from the founder, Yax Eb' Xook, but as far back as the Maya's Olmec antecedents. Yik'in was as legendary, so the image proclaimed, as all the glorified ancestors of the past.

Yet Yik'in''s monuments offer surprising originality. Each differs slightly from the one before, adding new paraphernalia, presenting newer and more dynamic compositions, or altering earlier styles to present fresh ideas. Preoccupied with power, but masterful, Yik'in would soar ever higher with construction of his funeral monument, the massive pyramid of Temple IV— an enormous building taller than any structure ever built at Tikal.

In the years before the next clearly identifiable king, possibly in the latter days of Yik'in K'awil, new wars broke out in Petexbatun that would have devastating consequences. Beginning around 9.16.9.14.3 (December 30, A.D. 760), the Petexbatun regional center of Tamarindito attacked Dos Pilas in a furious series of raids that culminated in the city's collapse. The ruler K'awil Kaan was driven out, along with the royal family, and downtown Dos Pilas was destroyed over the next seven days. Victory monuments at Tamarindito proclaimed the "driving out" of the *itz'at winik,* "the knowledgeable people," alluding to the collapse and destruction of the city's governing nobles.

More than likely, no one at Tikal saw cause for alarm. Wars had raged for more than an entire b'aktun, for more than four hundred years. Since the time of Chak Tok Ich'aak I and the Early Classic, wars had been fought and won—and lost. The besieged towns had always recovered.

But the events at Dos Pilas would be different. Unlike other regimes, the Dos Pilas lords—the king, his wives, his children, and his officials and government functionaries—would fail to recoup their losses.

Dos Pilas must have been thoroughly sacked, its vaults torn down, its foundations left exposed, and its walls scattered in ruins. Years later nothing of its glory remained, nothing of its private courtyards, its grand stairways all carved in hieroglyphs, nor its proud legacy of sculptured stelae. This time the royalty of Dos Pilas was "going down" for the last count.

The Maya collapse had begun.

TEMPLE IV

The crowning achievement of Yik'in Kaan, indeed of Tikal's one-thousand year sequence of architecture, was Temple IV—250,000 cubic yards of construction material perched high over a ridge on the downtown's western fringe. Temple IV soars in ponderous but majestic scale as no other building in Precolumbian America. Nearly vertical and blade-like, its broad roof crest depicts an enthroned Yik'in facing his father Jasaw Kaan K'awil on Temple I, a quarter of a mile to the east. Restored only in its upper facade, this greatest of Tikal pyramids reaches twenty-two stories over its base, 212 feet high, the second highest ancient structure in the Americas.[9] Its massive bulk probably covers the tomb of Yik'in Kaan K'awil.[10]

Few vistas anywhere in the world equaled what the priests must have seen from the doorway of Temple IV. All of Tikal would have sprawled at their feet. To the east, the broad, paved Tozzer Causeway extended past Jasaw Kaan's Twin Pyramid Group, or Complex N, ending in the sacred heart of Tikal and the backside of Temple II. Beyond, Temple I dominated the skyline; and, far to the southeast, Temple VI soared over the farthest perimeter of the downtown. To the north, the Maudslay Causeway angled away to intersect with Complex P, Group H, and the North Zone, itself connected through the Maler Causeway to Tikal's downtown at the backside of the North Acropolis. Altogether, Tikal's causeways resembled an enormous "Y" closed across the top, packed inside and outside with hundreds of additional buildings. All along the high ridge to the south, enormous additional paved plazas and their clustered architecture ran east-to-west—the massive South Acropolis, the Plaza of the Seven Temples, and the Lost World Pyramid.

Temple IV.

The view east from Temple IV.

For 180 degrees, the panoramic downtown precincts would have sprawled unbroken, reaching east and west to where the land sinks into broad basins of seasonal swamps. Thousands of residential sites extended around the monumental downtown core, housing at least thirty thousand people. Houses ranged from simple thatch-roof huts to more elaborate ones made of cut stone and with multiple rooms and courtyards. Among the latter were stuccoed and painted walls and occasional sculptured ornaments, with both simple and elaborate houses clustering in groups around private court-yards, where much of the daily activity occurred.

Little, if any, true jungle remained by the death of Yik'in Kaan. Never-theless, attached to and probably concealing any number of residential groups from sight were carefully managed groves and orchards of useful trees that provided food and craft and construction materials. Radiating outward from Temple IV and the Great Plaza zone, this patterned alterna-tion of artificial forest and architecture probably ranged as far as the eye could see, merging with less elaborate pyramid and plaza districts and other major towns.

From the doorway, priests would have seen not only residential dis-tricts, crammed around the hilltop setting of downtown Tikal, but much larger ceremonial districts with their own massive pyramids. Satellite towns surrounded Tikal: Uolantun, Avila, Bobal, and Navajuelal to the south and southeast; Canmul and Chikin Tikal to the west; Jimbal and El Encanto on the north and northeast; and Corozal on the east, tucked into arms of the Bajo de Santa Fe.

Most of the Maya world would have resembled this view by the last years of Yik'in Kaan. Largely denuded of original forest, the Maya lowlands bustled with urban sprawl, market places, and ritual concourse precincts massive in scale. Everything lay under cultivation or residential and cere-monial districts, packed with some five to fifteen million Maya.

Little suggested this ancient world of venerable cities and dynasties had any cause for alarm. Yet within decades, all would be swept away.

NOTES

1. No relationship to K'ak' Tiliw of Naranjo.
2. But doubtful.

3. Coggins 1975.

4. Its second story survives only as end walls.

5. Alternatively, he was a son of Yik'in's.

6. Jones 1977: 53.

7. Ibid.

8. Coggins 1975.

9. Temple IV was probably superceded in height by Teotihuacan's Pyramid of the Sun, although discrepancies in the measured height of the two buildings leaves this assertion uncertain.

10. To date, no excavations have penetrated inside or underneath the pyramidal base.

CHAPTER 12

ENTER THE SUN:
THE LAST DAYS OF TIKAL

Shortly after the death of Yik'in Kaan K'awil, succession passed to his son, Nuun Yax Ayin II, on 9.16.17.16.4 (December 29, A.D. 769). Continuing in the line established by Jasaw Kaan K'awil at the opening of the Late Classic Period, Nuun Yax Ayin II took his name from the first Mexican ruler of Tikal. In all, he was the twenty-ninth successor to Yax Eb' Xook, a fact that was carefully stated on his commissioned monuments.

Name Glyph of Nuun Yax Ayin II.

But even as the new ruler took charge of this greatest of lowland cities, turmoil seethed and overtook many of the lesser kingdoms around Tikal. Erecting monuments and pyramids regularly and methodically, Tikal remained oblivious to the decline that encroached on the fringe areas of the Classic world. Perhaps cushioned by its densely-settled buffer zones, Tikal seemingly plodded along in blissful ignorance.

Perhaps, however, drafts of the turbulent winds *had* arrived. While the last known tomb for a ruler was Jasaw Kaan's, later secondary tombs for the wealthier aristocrats reflected a total decline in polychrome pictorial ceramics. Once the mainstay of the Late Classic repertoire, lavishly decorated with enthroned lords, palace "reception" scenes, and sundry narrative motifs, little evidence of this grand medium survives after 9.16.10.0.0. Eventually, polychrome designs diminished until only a few of the most standardized features prevailed, among them the Muwan Feather, the K'an Cross, and the four-petaled flower.

TWIN PYRAMID COMPLEX Q

K'atun celebrations occupied the new ruler, as they did many of the king-doms that recorded dynastic histories. Dedicating his accession monument to the seventeenth k'atun, or 9.17.0.0.0 (January 24, A.D. 771), Nuun Yax Ayin II erected Stela 22 to serve as the "center piece" of his Twin Pyramid Group, Complex Q. The overall size of the group was to dwarf all previous Twin Pyramids, an enormous terraced platform with a total surface area of about five acres.

Entrenched at Tikal for generations, Twin Pyramids embodied the same organizational principles as the Great Plaza—the dual pyramids oriented east and west correspond to Temples I and II, while the palace and stela chambers on the south and north correspond to the Central and North Acropolis. The arrangement served to diagram the Maya cosmos, the "shape" of the universe which, in Maya lore, corresponded to the path of the sun. East was sunrise, north the sun's highest point during the solar cycle or longest day of the year (the zenith-solstice), west the sun's entrance into the Underworld, and south its lowest position or shortest day (the nadir-solstice). Similarly, the pyramid-terraces symbolized "cosmic geography," where the twelve backside terraces, together with the space above the plaza, corresponded to the thirteen levels of paradise, and the eight front terraces and plaza floor represented the nine levels of the Underworld. Excluding the Great Plaza, seven Twin Pyramids have been found at Tikal. Each corresponds to a k'atun-ending.

Stela 22 portrays Nuun Yax Ayin II in a fashion similar to that of his father on Stela 21 thirty-five years earlier: standing barefoot in profile, with feet side by side, and wearing a jaguar kilt and anklet of the Perfo-rator God. He also cradles his ceremonial bar with one hand and scatters blood with the other, indicating mutilation of his penis meant to induce visions. Emblems and long-nosed faces fall in pendants from an over-sized back-shield mounted with skeletal long-nosed heads. Quetzal plumes radiate in crests and penaches above the central headdress element, great heaping masses of costume features. Over Nuun Yax Ayin II, just visible above the hieroglyphic text, the old jaguar Paddler God "floats" where "ancestor-protectors" once filled the "sky" position, a venerable motif absent on stelae since Early Classic times.

Twin Pyramid Complex Q.

Stela 22.

Even the hieroglyphic texts of Stela 22 duplicate their predecessors. Opening on the dedicatory date of the entire complex, the two glyphic panels repeat the formulaic sequence established by Nuun Yax Ayin II's father, offering the ruler's names, his title "twenty-ninth successor," the names of his parents, and his accession date.

BURIAL 77

Within the decade after Nuun Yax Ayin II's inaugural stela, a woman died who was buried on the western fringe of the West Plaza, beneath an unfaced pyramidal mound. A crypt roofed with logs and woven palm mats, and secured under thousands of flint and obsidian chips, Burial 77 was an anomaly in many respects. The woman wore magnificent jade jewelry, including an exquisite Sun God pendant about three and one-half inches tall, as well as thorny oyster shell, pearls, and other worked shell. Her robes included jaguar skins befitting her royal status. The tomb's contents had been dusted with powdered cinnabar.

But despite indications of elite status, Burial 77 contained a mere six ceramics. Although polychromes, they were extremely simplified ones, diminished from the fine pictorial tradition to mere geometric motifs. Of the designs, "butterfly" motifs predominated, along with flowers, simple bands, and the "Muwan Feather." Clearly, artistic expression at Tikal was concentrated in monumental sculpture and architectural programs, with the diminished importance of ceramic production reflecting the demise of that medium.

Probably the daughter of Jasaw Kaan K'awil and an aunt of Nuun Yax Ayin II, she was buried between 9.17.0.0.0 and 9.17.10.0.0 (A.D. 771–781). Her burial was the last known tomb at the center of Tikal.

THE GATHERING STORM

The period after the erection of Stela 22 (A.D. 771) saw small centers emerge all over Petén, a hurried spate of activity in honor of the new "decade." Both Naranjo and El Peru experienced a construction flurry after their defeat thirty years before at the hands of Yax Ayin's father. Minor sites prospered along the Pasión and Usumacinta Rivers, spreading into every tributary and valley and documenting the swift and sudden rise of parvenu royalty. These rulers commissioned their own portraits, filling the sites of La Mar, El Cayo, Seibal, El Chorro, and hosts of others with often brilliantly executed stelae.

Whether a reflection of the breakdown in central control or the lapsing influence of Tikal as regional capital of Petén, the martial themes of the newer monuments reflect increased dynastic instability. Dominated by militarism and increased competition, the petty kings of these towns seemingly herald events that would increase as the Maya drew closer to B'aktun 10 (10.0.0.0.0). Machaquilá, Ixtutz, La Amelia, Aguas Calientes, and still other late sites portray formidably-arrayed warriors with shields and spears—what would appear to be an adaptation of ideas seeping downstream via the Pasión River.

Wars flared again along the eastern fringes of Petén, waged among the long-standing enemies of Tikal and other districts. More troublesome, the city of Piedras Negras, recently consolidated under a new ruler, conducted the first of multiple raids carried beyond the confines of the Usumacinta canyon country and down into the Tabasco Plains. Over the next several years it would continuously raid in that direction, as if obsessively and compulsively turning northward to check some impending threat.

In the last of the Twin Pyramids at Tikal, built for the k'atun-ending 9.18.0.0.0 (A.D. 791), Nuun Yax Ayin II erected Stela 19 and Altar 6. Once more, Yax Ayin stands in profile with his ceremonial bar lovingly embraced, scattering blood from his hand in standard Period Ending regalia. Down to the costume, the arrangement of the glyph panels, and even the glyphs themselves, the monument consciously imitates his predecessors. Still focused on Yax Ayin's accession, the formulaic discourse "remembers" the first twenty-year k'atun anniversary of the ruler's inauguration, self-consciously promoting something that must have already been well-documented at Tikal. Stela 19 reflects an increasing obsession with ceremonialism and architectural dedications, rituals conducted throughout the lowlands that related to the making and forming of objects. As far away as Edzná near the northwest coast of Yucatan, towns celebrated the close of K'atun 18. It was as if the calendar and its impending change to B'aktun 10 presented an uncertain future, one that only rituals could placate. Perhaps Tikal and its dependent towns already knew something threatened to strip the southern lowlands of its vitality, some impending doom inherent to the end of the b'aktun cycle.

With completion of 9.18.0.0.0, an obscure district under the control of Yaxchilán went out of its way to construct another of its several modest temple-shrines, a three-room affair with doorways spanned by carved stone lintels, typical of this area of the Usumacinta zone. But Bonampak went on to add an extraordinary series of murals to the inside walls, covering every surface—walls, sides of benches, and vault slopes—with spectacular polychrome images of sumptuously bedecked kings and other nobility.

The Bonampak murals, probably dedicated around 9.18.1.2.0 (November 15, A.D. 791), portray an exceptionally dramatic battle that rages between two groups of monstrously adorned warriors. Wild and unstoppable, the victorious armies carry away prisoners no doubt intended for sacrifice; others lance their victims or seize them by the hair. Days later, the triumphant chiefs of Bonampak and their Yaxchilán allies presented their captured enemies before Chel Te Chan, Yaxchilán's successor to Yaxun B'alam. Arrayed across the terraces of one of Yaxchilán's pyramids, the prisoners cower and hunker down, badly beaten and tortured and dripping blood from their fingers.[1] One already has had his head chopped off, lying cushioned on one of the terraces on blood-stained leaves.

Other scenes relate spectacular dance ceremonies, processions of feather-bedecked participants with towering backshields and headgear, of musicians blowing wooden trumpets and beating drums and playing shakers. One of the lesser-known images even portrays a market place or trade fair where traveler-merchants barter over jaguar hides and strings of jade beads.

Executed at the same time that Piedras Negras waged its own wars, the Bonampak murals depict events in the Middle Usumacinta Valley that would soon reach a horrendous peak. One of the most extraordinary artistic finds known from Precolumbian America, they offer an exceptionally valuable glimpse of warfare on the verge of the Maya collapse, a matchless artistic legacy that accurately reflects the genius of the Precolumbian past. Together with contemporary monuments at Piedras Negras, these innovative tableaus were among the most beautiful ever conceived in the New World. With Bonampak and Piedras Negras, Classic

Maya art reached its pinnacle, a lofty summit few contemporary American cultures would attain. They were among the last monuments ever produced at either site.

Much of the turbulence may have arisen out of the loss of one of the most powerful cities of the Usumacinta region. Among the western quadrant's premier gems, Palenque's fall opened the region's floodgates to an approach by people of marginal Classic culture. Crowned in majestic architecture and sculptural traditions the equal of Egypt or Sumeria, the city had helped cement Classic civilization by its alliance with Tikal during the days of Nuun U Jol Chaak, offering refuge to Tikal's exiled ruler. By the half-k'atun position 9.18.10.0.0 (August 19, A.D. 800), Palenque's power had faded irrevocably, gone with its kings and aristocrats. With their loss, the abandonment of the great city began.

THE LAST DAYS OF NUUN YAX AYIN II

The monuments of Nuun Yax Ayin II lack innovation and excessively imitate those of his father, although the latter commissioned original variations on the prevailing style. Yax Ayin imitated his father in every way, implying that local sculptors had become inhibited, that they lacked direction and purpose after the accomplishments of Jasaw Kaan and Yik'in Kaan K'awil. True, Tikal had always chosen exceptionally conservative sculptural programs, with the exception of the massive wooden lintels of the Great Pyramids, exhibiting a remarkable uniformity confined only to a handful of different poses. Compared to the great art styles of the Usumacinta River Valley, Petén sculpture itself remained rigidly bound by traditional motifs. Yet in contrast, circumscribed by dozens of traditional portraits, the two known monuments of Yax Ayin lack any innovation whatsoever.

Most noticeable of the changes seen during the reign of Nuun Yax Ayin II was the quantum leap in the size of building projects, especially the Twin Pyramid Groups. But even these seem a stopgap measure initiated under a lackluster dynasty, a hasty act of defiance in the face of diminishing resources and the evaporation of Tikal hegemony. If it can be said that Yax Ayin's architects lacked creativity—content to make things larger, but not different—perhaps the ruler met the crises enveloping his realm with blunt force, rather than with creative statesmanship. Perhaps, he met Tikal's troubles with escalating force, unable to handle the rearrangement of power that had signaled the downfall of Palenque.

Preoccupation with self image and uncertainty characterized the reign of Nuun Yax Ayin II, along with subtle changes that began during his middle years and soon gathered strength. These changes appeared in the decreased production of pottery vessels, a decline in decorative motifs in that medium, the static imitation of previous art styles, and the end of k'atun-celebrations and the construction of Twin Pyramid Groups. No tombs or clearly datable burials have been found after Burial 77, leaving more than a century of Late Classic Tikal without datable funeral pottery so crucial to identifying the "flavor" of the times. Already by the middle of Yax Ayin's reign, populations in the surrounding districts were declining, possibly migrating in response to the emergence of smaller cities all over the Maya lowlands. By the death of Yax Ayin, these subtle changes were overcoming the ruling elite, and they would finally shake the city to the ground.

INTO THE FIRE

Slowly at first, but gathering force, cities dropped from the roll call of towns that were commissioning monuments with carved dates. Period Endings were measured at ten year intervals now, whereas previously twenty-year intervals had sufficed. With the destruction of the three greatest regional capitals of the western rivers—Piedras Negras, Palenque, and Yaxchilán—bulk trading expeditions had fallen off alarmingly. These activities would collapse completely with the loss of the southeastern Motágua Valley.

At 9.19.0.0.0 (June 28, A.D. 810), Quirigua commissioned its last dated inscriptions, thereafter vanishing from the historical record. With the two main river arteries lost, not only the Maya but many of their distant patron-clients would be caught in the spiraling collapse of power.

Nor had the situation along the middle network of rivers stabilized. Faced with the expulsion of its ruling elite, the commoners who had comprised the bulk of the population were still living at Dos Pilas, struggling to maintain an equilibrium among their city's decay. Farmers and other commoners had concentrated amid the downtown rubble, building simple "bush-huts" of sticks and thatch and occasionally of wattle and daub. Well-shaped cut-stones for house platforms were available readily enough, and survivors began stripping the ruined temples and palaces of fine masonry, using it to construct platforms for their simple houses.

But something happened to disrupt this hand-to-mouth subsistence. As the collapse of the Usumacinta districts progressed, new trouble appeared in the form of unidentified marauders, raiding parties that were traveling far up the Usumacinta. Possibly the destroyers of both Piedras Negras and Yaxchilán,[2] these groups descended upon the hapless commoners clinging to their settlement at Dos Pilas.

Dos Pilas hastily accelerated its pace of stripping masonry from the walls. First, stones and other rubble were piled in irregular lines to form an inner perimeter of footing-walls capped by log palisades. Faced with increasing desperation, they established still another palisade to form an outer wall, intent on holding back the invaders. Not only Dos Pilas, but many other settlements of the Petexbatun hastily built their own perimeter walls, while others withdrew to hilltop positions, ensuring a first line of defense.

Exactly when the first wave came remains uncertain. At nearby El Duende, enemy invaders found themselves trapped inside a cleverly arranged "killing alley," two parallel walls designed to snare anyone attempting to force the defenses. Projectiles from the defenders rained down to impede the first assault, warding away the raiding armies. But burned wattle and impressions of burnt logs indicate that the invaders prevailed, capturing Dos Pilas and El Duende and doubtlessly slaughtering the populations inside.

There were those who escaped, and these people made their way eastward to the last redoubt of civilization in Petexbatun. During the earlier troubles that had seen the Dos Pilas dynasty destroyed, its shattered ruling family had withdrawn to Aguateca, maintaining itself at this still vigorous site and even managing to erect a few monuments. Aguateca spans the great escarpment that runs from north to south along the western edge of Lake Petexbatun, a sixty-foot sheer cliff that forms a natural defense. Running along the top at depths of up to 180 feet and up to forty-five feet wide, an enormous chasm divides the site in two, further augmenting its already impressive natural defenses.

As refugees from Dos Pilas streamed into the city, Aguateca hastily erected its own stone walls and palisades, ringing the site and subdividing it with more than three miles of defensive works. But the enemy attacked nonetheless, investing the town both from the east and west. As warriors scaled the cliffs, the defenders hurled stones and javelins from above, raining down missiles of every sort to stem the tide. Enemy warriors clawed their way up the cliff-side gullies and ravines, clinging to maintain their hold. At first, those who gained the summit were easily dispatched, but as wave upon wave of wildly arrayed attackers advanced, the Aguatecans retreated inside the first line of plazas behind their defensive palisades, and then across the natural bridge beyond the chasm.

The enemy forces were determined. Bringing up logs, they began to cross over and span the chasm, with some falling wounded into the ravine below. Others successfully gained the farther side to penetrate the last defenses. Already thatched roofs were in flames, and much of the precinct had been sacked, the temples destroyed, the palaces overrun. Enemies carried the outer defenses now, rushing to join their comrades at the battle over the chasm.

The end must have come quickly as more enemy warriors scaled Aguateca's defenses. Unable to resist, the defenders surrendered or fled, finding refuge in the surrounding jungle. Women were taken as concubines or slaves, the men seized and dragged off for sacrifice. Within hours, the Petexbatun had ended all resistance to the invading troops.

Still there were those who escaped. Fleeing to nearby districts, some to Seibal on the Pasión, others north to Tikal and in between, they were absorbed by populations already preoccupied with escalating disasters of their own. Last of all, remnants of an elite family withdrew onto Punto de Chimino, a narrow peninsula jutting into Lake Petexbatun from the west. As a last ditch measure, they dug three separate moats across the land, flooding these with water from the lake and reinforcing them with sturdy defensive palisades, making their town a virtual island.

It was here, years later, that the final Petexbatun drama would play out, the last desperate acts of a once proud aristocracy.

THE LAST K'ATUN OF B'AKTUN 9

Rulers must have continued succeeding at Tikal, however, for after Nuun Yax Ayin II at least two Great Pyramids were commissioned and at least two stelae erected. Some doubt remains about the date of the construction of Temple V, built near the southern perimeter of the downtown zone just east of the South Acropolis. The second tallest pyramid at Tikal at a height of 190 feet, its massive bulk has never been explored or repaired, and virtually nothing has been determined about its relationship to Tikal history.

Probably the last Great Pyramid, Temple III soars over the center of the downtown precincts at the head of the Tozzer Causeway, roughly midway between Temple I and Temple IV. Essentially identical in all of its basic features to the other major pyramids, it consists of a massive, terraced base with frontal staircase, and an aerie summit temple of two rooms capped by an almost vertical roofcomb. The frieze and roofcomb both included stucco sculpture over stone armatures, only traces of which remain.

Lintel 2 from the summit shrine, installed over the central doorway, depicts the ruler identified only as "Dark Sun," the man named and portrayed

Name Glyph of Dark Sun.

on Stela 24 at the bottom of the temple staircase. Tikal's latest surviving wooden monument, Lintel 2 shows an unusually complex scene where Dark Sun and two companions dance with staffs and tri-lobed obsidian knives. Dark Sun wears the costume of an exceptionally corpulent jaguar replete with patterned spots, his head encased within the great beast's yawning maw. Triple-tiered backrack elements sweep over the skeletal head of a long-nosed deity and over the head of the rear companion, flamboyantly arrayed with sprays of quetzal feathers waving and swishing as Dark Sun dances. The ruler stands in revived Middle Classic style—the profile stance where one foot advances before the other—a formal convention not seen since the days of K'an Chitam and Chak Tok Ich'aak II (ca. 9.2.0.0.0, or A.D. 475). Badly eroded glyphs along the lower right name Dark Sun's father, Nuun U Jol K'inich, or "Great Headed Sun Face," presumably the ruler who succeeded Nuun

Name Glyphs of Nuun U Jol K'inich.

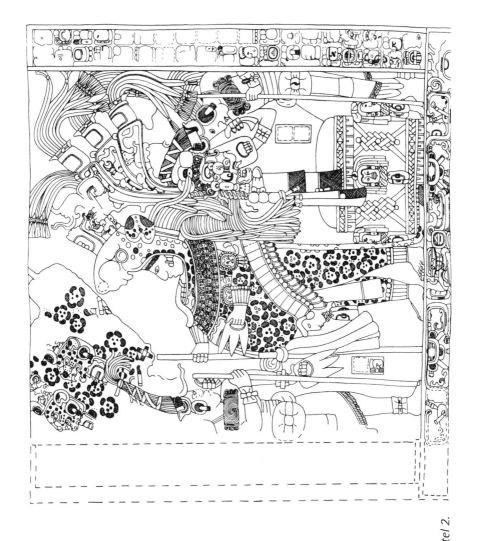

Temple III, Lintel 2.

Yax Ayin as the thirtieth successor of Yax Eb' Xook. No other references to Nuun U Jol survive.

At the base of the staircase surmounting Temple III, Stela 24 celebrates the k'atun-ending 9.19.0.0.0 (June 28, A.D. 810), but its portrait was destroyed and most of its hieroglyphic text was shattered, the pieces scattered around the location by remnant populations in the latter days of Tikal. Archaeological reconnaissance of the temple staircase uncovered fragments with bits and pieces of text, enough to reconstruct the name Dark Sun, his title *aj kalajun ab'ta*—a numbered sequence of unknown meaning but related to rulers at Seibal and the Petexbatun—and the Tikal Emblem "divine Mutul lord."

Temple III was probably completed during the final half-k'atun of B'aktun 9 (after 9.19.10.0.0, A.D. 820), but perhaps as late as the beginning of B'aktun 10 (10.0.0.0.0, March 15, A.D. 830). With this monument, Tikal completed its grand design for the downtown precincts initiated with Jasaw Kaan's construction of Temple I. Tikal's downtown organization suggests very deliberate, very ordered plans that required generations to execute, grafted over an east-west layout that had characterized Tikal since Middle Preclassic times, more than a thousand years in the past.

Temples I and V form the north-south arm of an enormous right-angle, completed by the roughly east-west line-of-sight between the doorways of Temples I and IV. But rather than an alignment exactly oriented to the cardinal directions, the deployment skews about seventeen degrees east of north, so that Temples I and IV form a line-of-sight oriented 285 degrees towards the horizon. There can be no coincidence that this same alignment characterizes the grid pattern at Teotihuacan, as well as the axial coordinate of the Street of the Dead, thought to correspond to the rising of the Pleiades on Teotihuacan's local horizon.

And yet Tikal's Late Classic layout goes well beyond anything conceptualized at the greater city of the Mexican highlands. At first glance, Temple I's westward line-of-sight connects with the doorway of Temple II, the three-tiered shrine located on the western margin of the Great Plaza; however, the true east-west axis from Temple I connects with Temple III, the last Great Pyramid at Tikal and probably the funeral shrine of Dark Sun. In this way, Temples I and III form axial markers for both the spring and fall equinox.[3] Not content merely with these simple manifestations of

The view west from Temple I.

astronomical proficiency, the architects of Temple III positioned its roof-comb so that, as seen from the doorway of Temple IV, the highest pyramid at Tikal, the sun rises over its central block on the winter solstice. Tikal's Great Pyramids thus form one of the most grandiose observatories ever created, a project that took some sixty years to complete, where the pyramids signal one another across space and shape the void between them.

Temple III towers to a height of 180 feet, the third tallest pyramid at Tikal. No excavations have yet explored its massive pyramidal base.

COLLAPSE OF THE PERIPHERY

Perhaps the final years of B'aktun 9 were "dangerous" ones, seen by Maya populations as something to be feared. Shortly after 9.19.3.13.12 (March 11, A.D. 814) at Comalcalco, a city renowned for its hieroglyphic bricks, the last known date signaled the collapse of the farthest western zone. At the opposite end of the Maya world, in highland Honduras, Copán celebrated its last Period Ending on Stela 11 at 9.19.10.0.0 (May 6, A.D. 820), explicitly proclaiming the "toppling of the Founder's House," or the fall of the lineage of Yax K'uk' Mo'. That it should refer so candidly to its own demise reflected perhaps an awareness of what was happening to its more northerly allies.

Copán's last dated monument, Altar L, features a dynast face to face with Yax Pasaj, the immediately preceding king, with the accession date of the newly-elevated king featured prominently between them. Not an ambitious sculpture as Copán monuments go, the four-sided altar was interrupted midway through the process of carving, its sculptors managing to begin only one other side before abruptly abandoning the project. There was simply no successor left to carve.

For years Copán had shown signs of stress within its ruling cabal, the fissioning of power at its highest levels. Lesser nobility usurped some of the privileges traditionally restricted to the ruler, including ever more grandiose and ornate houses sumptuously decorated with costly sculpture. But there were other, more immediate problems facing those who occupied the Copán Valley. Since populations had peaked more than a century before, the valley had been denuded of tree cover, including its pine-forested higher slopes.[4] The need for wood to produce lime stucco and for firewood, had left the region bare, contributing to heavy erosion of already fragile soils. Farming further damaged the valley and probably every surrounding district, leading to the underproduction of agricultural fields and concomitant malnutrition. Trade was in disarray, and the material wealth of Copán no longer resembled the splendor of its once great kingdom.

After the k'atun-ending 9.19.10.0.0, Naranjo's elite on the eastern periphery of Tikal also had disappeared. Waxaklajun U B'a, Naranjo's last known ruler, "set the stone" for the k'atun, then vanished.

The k'atun ending also saw Caracol wage war against an unknown upstart at Witznal, now the site of Ucanal, near the border of modern Belize. Who it was that Caracol battled here remains of some importance, for Ucanal came under the influence of invaders who briefly resurrected the site with distinctly "foreign" traits. At this time, dynasts there erected Stela 4, "Maya" in every outward appearance but harboring subtle oddities not readily explained by the simple revival of Mexican motifs.

Ucanal Stela 4 carries an invading warrior "floating" over the principal scene, an *atlatl*-and-dart-wielding militant wrapped in the coils of scaled blood-scrolls that represent a bloody serpent. Square hieroglyphs, not seen in Petén since Early Classic times, hint at new messages conveyed—perhaps Maya rulers were importing mercenaries to fight their battles for them, in particular the Mexicanized Maya of the north. On the other hand, the weakened condition of Petén may have attracted military regimes who were less impacted by the troubles of the central zone, or who were driven by their own crises to raid southward into the Petén heartland.

Whatever his meaning, the "floater warrior" replaces conventional "ancestor-protector" motifs, located in the "sky" position on Petén stelae since the earliest monuments. This "foreign" influence quickly spread further south, seeping onto stelae in more subtle ways at Machaquilá, then to other areas of the Pasión proper.

Few towns celebrated the Period Ending of B'aktun 10 (March 15, A.D. 830)—an event rather like our own modern culture failing to note the year 2000. A handful of east-central sites in Petén and Belíze erected stelae, but nothing that compared to earlier k'atun celebrations. Uaxactun still commissioned monuments, as did Xultun, both venerable sites that had thrived since late B'aktun 8 in the Early Classic Period. Calakmul still prospered, in a manner of speaking, though few intact monuments survive from these late times. Xunantunich and Machaquilá retained enough resources to declare themselves members of the stela cult. However, districts commemorating dynastic histories were shrinking in size, the overall extent of the stela cult inexorably withdrawing back to its original area.

THE ARRIVAL OF AJ B'OLON AB'TA

Of all the manifestations of these new "strangers," none equaled those at Seibal. Seibal has long attracted attention for its exceptional stelae, packed into only two or three k'atuns of activity on the verge of the Maya collapse. An elevated, defensible site perched above the bluffs of the Pasión River where it makes an enormous westward sweep, Seibal first came to the attention of the German explorer Teobert Maler. Since excavated by the Peabody Museum of Harvard University, the site was found to function as an outpost of river-traveling foreigners who moved upstream from the Gulf of Mexico to enter the Pasión drainage, just as the Maya were declining and abandoning their major towns. These foreigners, the Peabody archaeologists argued, either precipitated collapse or exploited the resulting anarchy. According to this view, foreigners invading the river systems brought non-Maya architectural and sculptural styles, pottery vessels, and political institutions, briefly reviving Seibal until they themselves were eclipsed.

In recent years, scholars have rejected this position, taking up a very different argument. Those who challenge the theory point to "foreign" motifs during earlier Classic times, identifying later motifs as merely rare indigenous variations of the same themes. Most recently, excavations in the Petexbatun region discovered pottery that, earlier opinion believed, were importations. Here, the collapse seems to have resulted from internecine warfare, an escalation of hostilities arising out of the destruction of the local elite, rather than from an invasion or the effects of environmental breakdown.

For the k'atun ending 10.1.0.0.0 (November 30, A.D. 849), Seibal dedicated an unusual radial pyramid with stairways located around its four sides, decorated across its roof frieze with polychrome sculptures modeled in stucco. Before each stairway the local ruler of the site erected magnificent stelae, plus additional portraits over each doorway, portraying lords who participated in local k'atun ceremonies involving the usual self-sacrifice.

Stela 11, positioned before the temple's southern stair, portrays the "floater" type warrior seen on Ucanal Stela 4, regal over his bound prisoner and carrying a club or other weapon. Overhead, inscriptions relate Aj B'olon Ab'ta's "arrival" at Seibal "under the authority of" Kan Ek' of Ucanal one day before the k'atun-end. He arrived with four "palanquin lords" and "eight palanquins," a contingent of nobles who came from all over the Maya world.

Where they arrived, of course, was Seibal, the site of evidently grand ceremonies or of a political alliance, gathered together in celebration of the first k'atun of Cycle 10. To further elaborate, another monument, Stela 10, depicts one of the lords who arrived in typical Maya costume and holding his traditional double-serpent bar. Tall, overloaded with quetzal plumes, the portrait includes odd features missing in run-of-the-mill Maya art. He wears a prominent mustache and just the faintest goatee, very much in keeping with the companion Stela 11.

Nothing could be further from the portraits on Stelae 8 and 9. The latter reflects typically Late Classic features, depicting a purely Maya lord with sloped forehead indicative of cranial deformation, who stands barefoot in traditional costume while embracing his ceremonial bar. Stela 8 portrays a "jaguar lord," a ruler with spotted mittens and booties and a looping cruller over his nose, identifying him as the Maya Jaguar God of the Underworld.

Stela 10 offers important clues to the identity of the Seibal figures. Inscribed panels relate that the k'atun ceremonies were "witnessed"—that is, they were "overseen"—by Jewel K'awil, a ruler of Tikal; Kan Pet, a ruler of Calakmul; and Kan Ek' of Nal, possibly San José de Motul on the northern shore of Lake Petén Itzá. Stela 11 depicted Aj B'olon Ab'ta, while each "palanquin lord" became the subject of his own monument, with Stela 10 possibly depicting Jewel K'awil, the "Mutul lord" who ruled Tikal.

Name Glyph of Jewel K'awil.

Slightly later stelae at Seibal changed even more drastically than those of Aj B'olon Ab'ta. Stela 13 depicts someone with exceptionally long hair wearing belts and loincloth flaps made of serpents. One hand ends in blood scrolls, and an exceptionally rare "speech scroll" curls from his mouth, indicating sound or language in a convention much more common to central Mexico. Glyphs call him the "West Kalomte'," in the same way that inscriptions referred to Mexican intruders hundreds of years in the past. Above all, they similarly identify his place of origin, the city of Pu—or Tollan, the legendary capital of Toltec fame. A rare hieroglyph with a square cartouche completes the "foreign" look.

Even stranger motifs prevailed—portraits of the Mexican Wind God, called Ehécatl, identified by his diagnostic bird mask, and "Mexican" style warriors with *atlatls* and unidentified "curved sticks." Claims to the contrary notwithstanding, the overall impression of Seibal at this time resembles a foreign outpost, an elaborate town capable of commanding attention from such magnets as lords of Calakmul and Tikal. Not inconceivably, these or related warriors helped sack Yaxchilán and other towns along the Usumacinta. It was perhaps against these marauders that the Petexbatun threw up its defensive walls and stockades in an attempt to stem the tide of invading warriors. Launched from two directions at once, down the eastern perimeter of Petén and along the western rivers region, invaders of a number of different groups were probably making their way deeper into Petén, profiting from poor conditions and encountering little resistance.[5]

THE LANGUAGE OF ZUYUA

What happened next would change Mesoamerica forever, not just the Maya world or its immediate contacts, but societies as far north, perhaps, as the American Southwest. Hardly accidental or coincidental, at precisely the same moment that hieroglyphic dates and inscriptions declined in Petén's southern districts—the "core" of Classic Maya civilization—newer, very different inscriptions began to document events much farther north, almost as far north on the Yucatan Peninsula as the Maya existed.

Much drier and very different from the southern lowlands, northern Yucatan gives way to low scrub brush and thickets, a rugged district with low hills—called the Puuc—bordering along the west. Populations in this region have always depended upon natural sinkholes or *cenotes*, in addition to extensive caverns, for their primary source of water. Ancient settlements founded here in Preclassic and Classic times centered around these "wells." Life-sustaining oases, *cenotes* played prominent religious roles, becoming the focus of legends and pilgrimages.

Of all the *cenotes* none equaled the "Well of the Itzá," or Chichén Itzá, the focus of the most grandiose town ever built in the Yucatan. Here, beginning no later than 10.1.15.3.6 (November 17, A.D. 864), a violent military regime took hold, centered around joint rule and founded under ephemeral "foreigners" called the Itzá Maya.

Chichén Itzá arose precisely at the time Seibal did, or soon thereafter, conquering the Yucatan Peninsula and doubtlessly sending raids into the Classic heartland. Establishing itself at Ucanal, then Seibal—after a possible stint at Machaquilá—invaders related to Chichén's founding regime[6] dragged back to the north tremendous numbers of sacrificial captives, slaves and other resources. Centuries later, dredged by modern underwater equipment, the Chichén *cenote* yielded quantities of Classic Period jade inscribed with dates and emblems, brought from as far as Palenque and Piedras Negras. Gold made an appearance at this time, imported from lower Central America, Columbia, and almost every part of Mexico, suggesting Chichén controlled the distribution of this metal. Into the well went modeled disks of gold and objects of copper-gold alloy, including marvelous narrative scenes in relief. Significantly, quantities of obsidian reached Chichén from nearly every representative source in Mexico—except traditional sources of highland Guatemala—suggesting Chichén's commercial ties extended to the north and east, not south to the ancient trade routes of the Classic period. Most telling of all were objects of turquoise, imported from the distant American Southwest and the well-known turquoise mines of New Mexico. More impressive than Teotihuacan's, the trade networks of Chichén retrieved objects from a much wider area, indicating a new "world economy" considerably expanded in breadth.

Sculptures and painted murals portray the military exploits of Chichén Itzá, showing warriors subduing populations conceivably as far south as the Chixoy River, one of the Usumacinta's highland tributaries. Amidst energetic scenes of battle—nearly as ferocious as those of Bonampak—Itzá warriors attack in uniforms imbued with Mexican symbols, features usually associated with the legendary Toltecs. Warriors wear Toltec "pillbox" hats, arm guards, slippers, and other wildly non-Maya elements that are very closely associated with features at Seibal. Above all, they brandish spearthrowers and darts, their accouterments decked-out with Tlaloc eyes.

As the Classic world came crashing down, elements of Chichén style extended well beyond the immediate area. From the same period, fabulous scenes of warfare appear in highland Mexico, depicting at the site of Cacaxtla an affray between clearly jaguar-like people and warriors in costumes of birds, the latter rendered in almost "pure" Maya style. Similarly, Xochicalco portrayed seated Maya lords within Feathered Serpent friezes, embraced in the coils of rattlesnakes, unequivocally indicating the presence of Maya in highland Mexico, just as Mexicans had appeared in the Maya lands over the last several hundred years.

From all over Mesoamerica, dynasties evidently arrived at Chichén Itzá to receive the "proper" tokens of rulership, indicating that kings in many areas of Mesoamerica acceded by the grace and goodwill of Chichén's leadership. Chronicles written at the time of the Spanish conquest, not only in the Maya world but in Mexico as well, speak of the special, cryptic "language" that only legitimate lords could fathom, and of a series of symbols required to show this legitimacy that only the lord of Tollan could bestow. Posed as a series of questions, the "language of Zuyua" belonged to those who could claim official descent from Tollan, the city the Maya called pu. Those who were pretenders knew nothing of this code, and were exposed as such, their false pretensions subjecting them to oblivion. Obliquely, these references were perhaps to Chichén Itzá and its warrior kings.

THE RISE OF WUK AB'NAL

Over what must have been an exceptionally brief period, Chichén Itzá rose on the plains of northern Yucatan after its founding by a federation of Itzá Maya and others who were associated with foreign descent. Traditionally from the west, and associated with the arrival of Kukulcán, or the Feathered Serpent of Toltec fame, the Itzá were among the most illusive people in Mesoamerican history. Possibly an amalgamation of many disparate Maya-related people who also possessed strong Mexican characteristics, and probably arriving at Chichén Itzá from the Usumacinta Delta region of the Mexican Gulf Coast, the Itzá were one of numerous loosely-related people that included the Putun Maya, the Olmeca-Xicalanca, Tapku Oliman, Kokom, Tutul Xiu, Zuyuans, and Nonoalcans.[7]

The period from 10.1.15.3.6 to 10.2.13.13.1 (November 17, A.D. 864 to February 26, A.D. 883) represents the "Great Period" of Chichén inscriptions, when most of the site was built and its rulers reached their height of power. While scholars tend to no longer divide Chichén into separate "old" Maya and "newer" Toltec sections, the site was invaded numerous times by similar or identical people, and "Toltec" Chichén may date to one of these later episodes. In any case, it remains clear that Chichén Itzá served as the seat of one of Mesoamerica's most potent governments. A "new" Tollan established after the fall of Teotihuacan, and possibly more influential than even that city, Chichén commanded allegiance from an enormous area that few civilizations had equaled at any time in the Precolumbian past. While many of its exotic trade items were obtained through complex networks of exchange, Chichén traders possibly ranged as far as New Mexico and Columbia. That Chichén controlled areas around Santa Lucia Cotzumalhuapa suggests one of its key interests was chocolate, the currency of Mesoamerica and the primary alcoholic beverage of Mesoamerican elites.[8]

The legacy of Chichén reached well beyond its own districts after its brief rise. During sojourns of its warrior cadres or those of other related people, Chichén inspired or perhaps founded the town of Tula, Hidalgo, identified by archaeologists as the Toltec's central Mexican capital in early Post Classic times. An "outpost" featuring similar artistic elements— reclining Chak Mol sculptures, massive feathered serpent columns, and early Maya-style stelae—Tula dominated central Mexico from about A.D. 1000 to 1150, inspiring claims by Mesoamerican royalty to a Toltec heritage. Even the Aztecs, on the verge of the Spanish conquest, adapted Toltec, and by extension, "Itzá Maya" style—an unbroken lineal descent at the heart of Aztec dynastic art.

THE LAST OF THE MUTUL KINGS

Tikal outlived the "great period" at Chichén Itzá and the short but furious local dynasty at Seibal. Elsewhere in the Maya lowlands inscriptions referred to the Emblem of Mutul—in other words, Tikal—as long as a k'atun after Stela 24 and the massive complex of Temple III, indicating continued social and political survival. But while occupation of house-sites and other residential districts surrounding the site-core persisted into the first k'atuns of B'aktun 10, Tikal's record of succession passed irrevocably into oblivion.

Tikal Stela 11 helps clarify the late sequence of rulers. Depicting the second Jasaw Kaan K'awil to rule, the monument portrays him in frontal view with feet splayed, imperious before the usual bound prisoner and embracing the traditional ceremonial bar. The monument continues traditions established by Yik'in K'awil but varies considerably in detail and style, especially in the rare carved border around the rim. Stylistically linked to contemporaneous monuments of the Pasión drainage system, and incorporating traditional overhead Paddler Gods floating amid blood scrolls, Stela 11 records the Period Ending 10.2.0.0.0 (August 17, A.D. 869), the last record of a ruler from the downtown districts of Tikal.

Among Stela 11's few recognizable glyphs, the Tikal Emblem remains relatively clear and distinct, representing the back of someone's hair bound and tied with a headband. Probably identifying the political district or "polity" of Mutul, it signifies in full form an individual lord, a "divine ruler" when accompanied by appropriate auxiliary signs. The Mutul Emblem made its first appearance on Stela 29 at the opening of the Early Classic Period, around A.D. 292 (8.12.14.8.15), the earliest stela at Tikal and the earliest securely-dated monument from the Maya lowlands. Thus, from first to last, the Tikal Emblem reflected an unbroken tradition of dynastic influence that spanned exactly 585 years—far longer than any other tradition in the Maya lowlands.[9] This in itself was a tremendous accomplishment, one that no other Classic city could boast. If for no other reason, Tikal must have held very special importance among the Classic Period elite, the political hub of a Precolumbian world that saw many "Tollans" and many preeminent districts rise and fall.

That the ruling elite commanded importance as late as 10.3.0.0.0 finds acknowledgment from several sites that mentioned Tikal's Emblem long after Tikal itself had ceased carving inscriptions. Elsewhere the situation remained very different. Revived after one or two k'atuns of neglect, Quirigua erected a Chac Mol in the tradition of Chichén Itzá, which may indicate control by that city. Unquestionably Chichén and its allies sought to reestablish trade in these districts, seeking to return commerce to its former pace. Seibal itself may represent an attempt to reestablish this

Stela 11.

trade, a move to secure the Pasión drainage and resume long-distance exchange. Commemorating the tun-ending at 10.2.5.0.0 (July 22, A.D. 874), monuments at Comitán indicate that late dynasties were still extant in southern Chiapas; and Ixlu Altar 1, celebrating 10.2.10.0.0, refers to cere-monies attended by the "divine Mutul lord."

Tikal's status must have remained unchanged during these years. Even as Mexican-style "floater-warriors" appeared on monuments erected at Tikal's outlying satellite districts, splinter dynasties at these sites continued refer-ring to Tikal and drew status from their associations with its kings. Both Jimbal and Ixlu erected monuments with Maya Paddler Gods floating amid dotted blood-scrolls, some with the tell-tale "floater-warriors" brandishing *atlatls* and darts, nearly all with square hieroglyphs bearing unrecognizable signs. These two sites represent the final remnant of Tikal hegemony, the last shred of Tikal power after years of regional preeminence.

The Tikal artistic tradition had come full circle, confined once more to a very narrow district at the center of Petén, just as it had been at the time of the initial stela cult six hundred years earlier. Among the last centers that participated in traditional stone sculpture, Jimbal persisted as one of the tiniest of the great center's satellites. Located only a few miles north, outside of Tikal's defensive earthworks, Jimbal mentioned the Tikal Emblem Glyph on its Stela 2 at 10.3.0.0.0 (May 4, A.D. 889), the last reference to Tikal in any Maya inscription. After Jimbal, Yax Mutul passes from recorded his-tory, never to be mentioned again.

NOTES

1. The exact location of this scene remains unknown, but seems someplace other than Bonampak.
2. Recent archaeological investigations have suggested that Yaxchilán sacked and burned Piedras Negras, before suffering a similar fate. Exactly who it was in control at Yaxchilán at this time, however, remains uncertain, and could easily have included advance elements of the marauders who would later reach higher along the Pasión. The last days of the Middle Usumacinta dynasties remain to be clarified.

3. As seen from the doorway of Temple III the sun rises directly over Temple I, while from the doorway of Temple I the sun sets directly behind Temple III (Malmström 1997).

4. Martin and Grube 2000: 213, and Fash 1991.

5. A similar hypothesis was advanced by Arlen Chase (1985).

6. "Founding" in the sense of its hieroglyphic-producing dynasties.

7. New hieroglyphic evidence suggests that the Itzá could claim an ancestral homeland in Petén, specifically the area of Lake Petén Itzá just south of Tikal, and that they migrated north during the Late Classic Petén wars to found dynasties at Chichén Itzá and elsewhere. In light of the exceptionally strong visual evidence that Chichén-related peoples invaded the southern Petén lowlands, I would argue that at this time there were movements of people both north *and* south in succession. It seems reasonable that the "founders" of Chichén returned to Petén to reassert control over what was in essence a "natural birthright" to political preeminence.

8. Monuments from Santa Lucia Cotzumalhuapa incorporate costume and other motifs similar to those at Chichén, while concentrating like Chichén on ballgame scenes. Although placed much earlier by Parsons, they were more likely contemporaneous with Chichén Itzá, or roughly 10.1.15.3.6 to 10.2.13.13.1 (November 17, A.D. 864 to February 26, A.D. 883).

9. A second leading contender for this distinction is Uaxactum.

CHAPTER 13

COLLAPSE AND ABANDONMENT

Almost every conceivable theory has been offered to explain the Maya collapse. Natural disaster, agricultural failure, environmental degradation, warfare, lower-class revolution, and overpopulation—all have played important roles in shaping the public's view of the last years of the Classic Period. Of devastating proportions perhaps unequaled in human history, the collapse of the Classic Maya evokes real and imagined dangers of civilization gone awry, an apocalyptic scenario chilling in what it tells us about our own potential for disaster. But it remains true that, for all the explanations advanced up to the present time, none have entirely convinced a skeptical world.

The final century of the Classic Period saw unprecedented numbers of monuments erected at dozens of major and minor settlements. Architectural schemes engendered great pyramid-plaza groups and palatial compounds. Populations climbed into the millions. On the surface, Maya civilization thrived with little outward sign that it verged on total collapse or permanent abandonment.

Overall, the picture of decline at Tikal itself comes across in the archaeological record as especially harsh and chilling, alluding to sudden chaos, a breakdown in political and social organization, and an inability to command labor and carry out repairs. From an eighty percent occupation of residential dwellings, populations at Tikal plummeted to a low of ten percent, a loss of 27,000 to 70,000 people.[1] Tikal's ruling elite somehow disappeared from the scene, leaving the survivors to fend for themselves.

Almost any scenario fits these grim facts. Tikal lacks any mass burials, the essential evidence to prove plague, warfare, or other destructive agents. The jungle nevertheless rapidly decomposes organic material, and skeletons in direct interments or left exposed to the elements stand little chance of surviving archaeologically. Lacking burials, witnesses, documentation, or other facts, scholars must turn to theory and "educated guesses." No scenario has universally convinced scholars, and the question of collapse remains unsettled and open to serious argument.

Evidence from the Petexbatun region, just south of Tikal, suggests a world torn apart by endemic warfare, where settlements sought to defend themselves against seemingly anarchistic conditions. Sites in the Petexbatun region—Dos Pilas, Aguateca, and elsewhere—show eleventh-hour fortifications and palisades, thrown up hastily to defend against outside attacks as Classic Maya civilization collapsed around them. Fortresses were established for the same purpose, incorporating moats and natural chasms.

Still more recently, new evidence has come forward in support of environmental degradation as the chief cause, specifically drought conditions that scholars surmise were impossible to overcome. A long-standing question has focused around the role of over-cultivation of soil, the resultant deforestation, and the concomitant collapse of agricultural systems.

One of the more recent ideas about the Maya involves the breakdown of managerial organization. Overall, there seems something significant in the proliferation of small-scale ceremonial zones throughout the general Maya region. The prosperity of splinter dynastic groups suggests a fissioning of aristocratic power, the rise of competition both within the major capitals and among their dependents. At Copán, monuments gradually moved from the exclusive domain of the king to feature an array of lesser noblemen, hinting at shared influence and power. The weakening of the royal lineages and the loss of political monopoly indicates a complication of decision-making processes, a movement towards decentralization that perhaps ignited insurmountable crises or that left the lowlands incapable of combating already extant problems.

Little evidence survives for the rise of a lesser nobility at Tikal. Moreover, Tikal itself reflects little evidence of any primary cause or combination of causes. Nevertheless, beyond Tikal's facade of grandeur and material spectacle, a few clues from the perspective of art history point toward imminent disaster and collapse. In the medium of stone sculpture, motifs acquired a decidedly decadent turn, copying earlier ones verbatim. Certain conventions "discarded" long ago in Tikal history reappeared at the final hour, especially early profile poses and the so-called "ancestor-protector" themes.

Architecture, especially the Twin Pyramid Groups, increased in size during the Late Classic, as if engineers saw no end to the material resources at their disposal or quantities of manpower. Sheer mass and physical height were hallmarks of the times, unstinting and ever-increasing, with little indication that anything would change.

Late Classic artistic ideas were particularly uniform and unexceptional, as though some thing or some motivation had inhibited inspiration. This absolute repetition of artistic and architectural programs implies adherence to tradition at any cost, a rigidity and persistence in the face of, or in reaction to, some threat or challenge either physical or ideological. It suggests that, whatever problems plagued their civilization, the Maya confronted them with an ill-prepared and singularly inflexible stance, unable to adapt new strategies or to carry out adequate solutions.

Certainly, other factors figure in theories of the collapse and, generally speaking, scholars tend to accept that the Maya collapse resulted not from single events but multiple ones—a sort of snowball effect where crises accumulated to the point that recovery became impossible. Favored scenarios vary according to the weight placed on the lines of evidence, with not everyone agreeing that events unfolded in a particular sequence or involved the same combination of crises.

RECONSTRUCTING THE MAYA COLLAPSE

Tikal's location astride a major overland trade route, at virtually the geographical center of the Maya world, gave it an ability to control raw materials and craft-goods crossing Petén. Moreover, Tikal maintained intimate ties to key transportation routes along the Pasión and Usumacinta Rivers, as well as to the distant Motágua Valley, influencing these regions at a dynastic level and perpetuating a commercially profitable interrelationship. Petén maintained ties to key "international" centers known for bulking and distributing raw and finished goods, and these materials turn up at Tikal in conspicuous, if limited, amounts.

It seems probable that Tikal's balanced yet fluctuating exchange system broke down precisely at its peak moment. One factor was that warfare had steadily increased in Late Classic times among major regional capitals, as dynasts augmented their dominions and sought to control ever-larger areas and their natural resources. Regional competition saw an aggrandizement of contiguous areas, plunging Petén into almost continuous warfare—especially along the river systems that were the avenues of trade.

At the same time, political fragmentation increasingly complicated Tikal's organizational matrix, leaving an encumbered decision-making process. Tikal's *k'ul ajaw*, his councils, and whatever additional political or economic interests existed at the time failed either to fully perceive an imminent crisis or a series of crises, or lacked the ability to cope with them.

Ultimately, the development by the Maya of new ocean-going canoes resulted in changes in international trade, which saw a shift from a trans-Petén route by land to a route mostly by sea. Avoiding the long portage across the Yucatan, heavily-manned cargo canoes carried trade goods around the peninsula along the Caribbean and Gulf Coasts, giving rise in northern Yucatan to parvenu political centers at Chichén Itzá, at Uxmal and, later, at Mayapán. In concert with these events, the demise of Teotihuacan, central Mexico's most potent and far-reaching "empire," drove groups of raiders and other military organizations across the Maya area, seeking to reestablish the glory of "Tollan."

But apart from problems in regional and international commerce, Petén and the Classic Maya cities no doubt suffered other, less obvious crises. Warfare may have led to the increased conscription of farmers, leaving shortages of manpower to tend fields and repair public agricultural works. The frequency and pitch of battle may have laid waste to crops and stores, precipitating food shortages. Whatever the cause, it seems likely that crop yields declined as ever-larger numbers of commoners strained the local resource base. As crises compounded one by one, further aggravated by drought conditions, and as chain reactions touched off related problems, agriculture failed completely and malnutrition followed. Skeletal studies indicate that members of elite-level families, who controlled access to higher-quality foods and protein, reached significantly higher physical statures than commoners. Conceivably, stress reached an intensity where commoners revolted, as archaeologists once believed; although modern research discounts "proletariat revolution," despite the fact that the problem remains largely one of failed elite culture. However, the proliferation of lesser towns and works of art that depict non-royal individuals suggest there were regional districts that revolted against larger zones, reflecting the fissioning of Classic Maya political structure at levels well above those of the commoners themselves.

As if not enough, one final blow shook the Tikal district and its Classic world. Stone sculptures and the presence of non-Classic pottery vessels at sites along the Pasión River suggest the arrival of foreigners to this region. The very latest Classic monuments depict elite warriors belonging to these armies, who were affiliated with Chichén Itzá and its "founders." Perhaps drawn by Petén's exhausted and demoralized condition, it was the descendants of these canoe-traveling "Mexican-Maya," sometimes called the Putun-Ch'ontal,[2] who controlled coastal trade around Yucatan when, five hundred years later, Europeans appeared on America's shores and discovered the Precolumbian mainland.

While causes of the Maya's system-wide collapse present themselves at every opportunity, there remains the larger question of how the Maya actually "disappeared." Many believe that crisis drove populations to northern Yucatan, or to a chain of lakes a few miles south of Tikal, or to more distant areas of Mexico. The fate of these several million Maya presents a greater puzzle than the collapse itself. As a theory, highly dispersed settlements without elite control seems the preferable one. Once elite culture collapsed, the Maya simply abandoned their cities and dispersed over the land.

In fact, evidence exists of the presence of thriving and populous towns in Belize and along the Caribbean coast, where people constructed Classic-style architecture and existed in a manner similar to cities of Petén. Among these settlements, populations survived well into the period of Spanish expansion *ca.* A.D. 1519. In addition, Maya tribes survived north of Tikal, albeit in much less spectacular circumstances. As late as 1696, the Spaniards found tribes of Maya living in impressive towns south of Tikal, in Petén's central lake district. The survival of numerous populations like these has led more than one scholar to question the notion of "abandonment," a reassessment advanced in conjunction with the notion of the "collapse" of civilizations in general.[3]

Regardless of the perspective of individual scholars, it remains true that modern Tikal, and countless major and minor Classic towns, lie overgrown

and uninhabited except for modern tourists, grave robbers, and the occasional archaeologist. That towns originally supported thousands, or even millions of individuals remains incontrovertible. Tikal and its world irreversibly
ended, leaving limestone skeletons of architecture and worn and eroded
monuments of stone sculpture that the Maya of today no longer fully understand. Something brought about its demise, whether very slowly or very
rapidly. Whatever the causes, scholars will no doubt continue debating the
fate and fall of the ancient Maya for a long time to come.

THE LAST MAYA AT TIKAL

By the reign of Yik'in Kaan K'awil—the second of the great Late Classic kings
and the twenty-seventh successor of Yax Eb' Xook—Tikal's populations had
reached higher numbers than at any time in the past. Archaeological reconnaissance has shown that ceramic debris from this period covers the city,
almost everywhere in quantities that indicate occupation of some ninety-
five percent of the mapped residential structures. Most of the eight hundred
ceremonial buildings and elite residences were likewise in use. The pottery
examples from this period comprise the largest inventories collected archaeologically—a time that also saw the construction of all five of Tikal's Great
Pyramid, six Twin Pyramid Groups, and dozens of immense palaces.

Nothing contrasts more dramatically than the succeeding pottery
phase, recovered from a mere fourteen impoverished locations, not one of
which indicates occupation of a single house mound. All traces of occupation come from multi-roomed "range" buildings, mostly vaulted structures
of the "palace" type. The strongest concentrations of debris were found in
the Great Plaza area, especially the Central Acropolis generally recognized
as the residence of the ruling kings.

But the people who lived there had ceased living like nobility.[4] The
number of buildings probably housed no more than four or five hundred
people, along with an additional couple of hundred scattered along the
peripheries. Other small populations persisted in the tiny satellites on the
border of the site-center, beyond Tikal's once-thriving urban sprawl.

On the Central Acropolis, courtyards accumulated unsightly piles of
garbage, including discarded pottery, left-over kitchen products, everyday

waste normally swept away in Classic times. Buildings fell into disrepair, and living conditions grew squalid. Whole corner vaults collapsed, filling up the ends of rooms with stone and crumbled plaster. Debris lay where it fell, too much trouble to move away unless shelter remained, in which case the desperate survivors pushed the largest stones away then went on living among the rubble. Reduced, it seems, to starvation, they consumed human flesh,[5] the dead bodies of relatives or murdered friends.

A tiny platform in outer Tikal and a few simple burials were hastily made during this period, but all major construction had long stopped. Rituals were still performed in temples and around the stelae that remained, and to aid these customs broken stelae fragments were carefully reset, often in "inappropriate" locations, or with "incorrect" caches made around the butt. The strangeness of these actions resemble someone's feeble attempt to maintain the lost stela-cult, but their misplaced efforts suggest an inability to understand the images or hieroglyphs. It was as if whoever performed these actions were grossly mimicking something they had only witnessed, or remembered, but in which they had never participated. In short, they were attempting to half-heartedly resurrect the past, to recapture what was hopelessly gone.

By 10.8.0.0.0 (A.D. 987), most of this remnant population had vanished. Concentrations of pottery shards near the Tikal Reservoir, near the modern archaeological camp, suggest that the survivors here occupied an insubstantial "bush hut" of sticks and thatch. Lesser concentrations south of the Temple of the Inscriptions, far from Tikal's deserted downtown, may be the remains of another house or camp.

Shards littering the rooms and staircase of Temple I and Temple II probably indicate debris from sporadic ceremonial visits or pilgrimages from distant provinces. One or two houses scattered around the periphery maintained their tenuous hold on a wilderness suited to solitary lives, sheltering outcasts from other districts or loners craving isolation.

Eventually jungle prevailed, thoroughly inundating the zone and burying the ruins. Human voices fell quiet, leaving the once great center silent except for an occasional Maya who wandered in from Lake Petén Itzá, other travelers who accidentally stumbled upon a fallen temple, or relatives who visited the ghosts of the past to make *costumbre*, the barely-remembered rituals for some spirit or for the memory of a now nameless Maya lord.

NOTES

1. Depending on the original peak estimate.
2. Also called the Puntun Itzá or simply the Itzá.
3. For example, Rome.
4. Harrison 1999.
5. Ibid.: 197.

APOTHEOSIS

For nearly ten centuries the buildings at Tikal deteriorated. Exteriors accumulated implacable rain forest and shrubs and trees that grew up through roof crests, undermined masonry joints, and tumbled mortared walls. Gradually almost everything the great Mutul rulers had accomplished crumbled away into mounded heaps of rubble.

Over the long centuries, Tikal regularly drew local Indians who were attracted by memories of ancestors or hero-gods, as attested to by evidence from the archaeological record. Populations had persisted to the north and south, scattered throughout the forests in simple villages long after Tikal's collapse. Still other Maya, this time historically attested, immigrated from the Chichén Itzá district, founding impressive masonry towns on the lake shores and islands of central Petén. Still later, Indian refugees from the Spanish conquest fled into the forests, seeking freedom and anonymity in solitude.

From time to time members of all these groups probably visited Tikal's abandoned shrines and temples, and in a sense local Maya never really "lost" the site. Its great pyramids no doubt served as objects of pilgrimage, as indicated by surface debris left by worshipers long after the forests had staged their comeback. At one point settlers lightly recolonized nearby uplands, reusing monuments for utilitarian objects like grindstones and farming with slash-and-burn methods.

In any event, it was evidently local Maya who gave Tikal its present name, generally considered a reference to the lingering "spirits" and "forces" occupying the derelict shrines. Traditionally, the name means

"Place of the Voices," at once a reminder of Tikal's homage to the supernatural and its reverence for the dead.[1]

Subjugated late in the Colonial Period in 1696, Petén came under effective Spanish control only slowly, saved from colonization by torrential rains, horrendous mud, and deep isolation. With improved communications and outside contact, rumors circulated about the Maya's lost cities and their strange monuments. Responding to a growing European awareness of the world's antiquities, government-sponsored expeditions returned with reports of Palenque, Copán, and the great cities of northern Yucatan. For many early travelers they were the remains of Atlantis, the Lost Tribes of Israel, or refugees of the lost continent of Mu—anything but the work of the ancient Maya.

Curiously, much of Petén remained cartographically blank. When John Lloyd Stephens and Frederick Catherwood journeyed across Central America in the early 1800s, their route by-passed the central lowlands despite the fact that Stephens had heard of at least one significant ruin in this region. Stephens and Catherwood nonetheless touched off waves of local expeditions, including one that would lead to the discovery of Tikal and its first published notices.

The expedition of Colonel Modesto Mendez, government secretary of Petén, and Ambrosio Tut, the Petén's Maya governor, explored Tikal's principal buildings in 1848. An expedition member produced crude drawings of selected stelae and temples, meant to supplement a report Mendez wrote but that failed, in the end, to attract much interest.

In the spring of 1879, a young German adventurer, Teobert Maler, wandered into the ruins of Palenque about 160 miles to the west, with lots of time on his hands. Maler originally had traveled to the New World to fight for Maximilian, the ill-fated Hapsburg installed by Napoleon III as Emperor of Mexico. With Maximilian's execution, Maler found himself unemployed and, for lack of anything to do, set off along the length of the country in search of antiquities.

It was at Palenque that, quite by accident, Maler met Gustav Bernoulli, a Swiss botanist. Bernoulli talked of ruins that were located in the Guatemalan interior and called Tikal, and he described his scheme for removing great wooden sculptures that still spanned some of the temple doorways. His plan was to transport the carvings to the Pacific Coast and then ship them to Europe. He intended to sell them to a continental museum to preserve their intricately carved designs.

But Bernoulli suffered violent fits of coughing and appeared too ill for the long overland journey and the rigors of jungle life, and Maler doubted that he would accomplish the task. Maler himself lacked funds to cross the Usumacinta and penetrate Petén, finding himself unable to assist the botanist. The two parted company, with Maler off to Merida and the Yucatan.

Bernoulli, it turned out, not only reached Tikal after the meeting at Palenque, but he managed to pull down two of the great *sapote* lintels—a feat accomplished with extraordinary physical and personal stamina. Nevertheless, Maler's concerns proved all too accurate. Sailing home to Europe by way of California, with his prized lintels aboard the ship, Bernoulli died from the disease in his lungs without arranging for the sculptures' proper care. Creditors seized them, with Lintel 3 of Temple IV, the most valuable of the wooden sculptures, going to the Museum für Völkerkunde in Basel, where they currently remain—worm-eaten and deteriorated, but on public display.

Bernoulli's journey led to wider consequences when his visit to Palenque inspired Teobert Maler, the German ex-soldier-of-fortune, to devote his life to the exploration of Maya ruins. Maler not only reached Tikal some fifteen years later, he returned in 1904 on behalf of the Peabody Museum of Harvard University as one of the first to systematically photograph, map, and report the site. Traveling alone except for mule skinners and hired hands, he packed his equipment on mules and traveled the length of the peninsula, taking along large-format box cameras and glass plate negatives. For the then phenomenal period of two months, the old explorer slept on the Central Acropolis in the palace now named after him (Str. 5D-65), using an ancient chamber as his darkroom and combing the ruins for sculptured monuments.

Photographic technology at the turn of the century involved a cumbrous, painstaking affair. To produce photographic negatives, a fragile glass plate had to be coated with light-sensitive collodion solution and rushed into the camera. After exposure, it was necessary to hurry back to the darkroom before the solution dried, and then fix the negative permanently with additional chemicals. Maler accomplished all this, rushing back and forth from the various Tikal precincts both near and far with his glass plates and fast-drying chemicals, careful to maintain exact controls and masterfully achieving fine results. To bring out details, he photographed at night with artificial raking light, provided by gunpowder flashes. Once everything had been photographed, he crated the negatives on his mules and, through mud, up and down rugged slopes, over tortuous root systems, transported his work as far as Merida in northern Yucatan and eventually to Cambridge. That his photographs made it into print represents a major feat in its own right.

Maler lived a strange, reclusive life, spending years alone in the wilderness. Cantankerous and obdurately suspicious, he came to believe the Peabody Museum had somehow violated an unwritten agreement between them, secretly profiting from the materials he made available. Consequently, Maler withheld his technical description and map of Tikal. (The map ultimately disappeared). Faced with mounting another expedition, Harvard dispatched Alfred M. Tozzer, whose investigation resulted in a monograph credited to both explorers. Maler himself died alone and penniless a few years later, but his indefatigable and exacting contribution to Maya studies remains a scholarly tool indispensable to modern research.

Alfred P. Maudslay, an English contemporary of Maler, also mapped and photographed Tikal. The last of the great explorers, Sylvanus G. Morley mounted expeditions for the Carnegie Institution in the 1920s and 1930s, collecting data on hieroglyphic dates and materials for his massive compendium, *Inscriptions of Petén*. In keeping with archaeological tradition, the four early explorers—Maler, Tozzer, Maudslay, and Morley—have had ancient causeways named after them, perpetuating their memory along with the lost city that they made so famous.

THE UNIVERSITY MUSEUM
AND OTHER PROJECTS

As early as 1946, plans got underway in the United States to excavate and restore major areas of Tikal. Organized by the University Museum of the University of Pennsylvania, the first real attempt to archaeologically investigate the site was nevertheless put on hold for ten long years. It was made possible only when the Guatemalan army built a nearby airstrip, facilitating the landing of supplies and equipment.

The choice of Field Director fell to Ed Shook, veteran archaeologist of the Carnegie Institution, whose experience included excavations at Kaminaljuyu, Uaxactun, and Copán. Early in 1956 Shook flew a team of Guatemalans to the site from nearby Lake Petén Itzá, organizing them to clear forest from the downtown ruins and build paths and access roads. The crew constructed camp buildings to house field workers for the following seasons, and homes for archaeologists who would collect and process any retrievable material.

Water proved critical those first years. Ancient inhabitants at Tikal had relied almost exclusively upon large-scale reservoirs to carry them through the dry season, a period of three rainless months. Hopelessly silted-in now and clogged with forest, the reservoirs lay beyond Shook's budget to carry out repairs. But as each season advanced and the rains abated, one by one the small natural waterholes dried up, hardening into clay and cracking in the jungle heat. Shook desperately set men to digging wells by hand, working his crews twenty-four hours a day for over a month. But none reached water.

Now the Project faced a menacing truth. Modern technology seemed useless in the rain forest. Shook realized only Tikal's ancient reservoirs offered hope for year-round water and that the Maya had hit upon the only practical solution, even by modern standards. Shook ordered refurbishment of the catchment basin near field headquarters, the Tikal Reservoir, introducing a live crocodile[2] to this intra-jungle oasis to give it an exotic flare.

With the problem of water solved, excavation advanced in the Great Plaza at full scale. The Project opened a wound in the forest as it stripped back layers of construction debris, leaving exposed foundation walls and parapets flashing white under the tropical sunlight.

Workers reopened ancient quarries to replace fallen and damaged stonework, shaping new blocks with machetes and handsaws. The several specially-skilled masons employed by the Project cemented back together selected architectural features with mortar slaked in the manner of the ancient Maya, pulverizing limestone gravel over a fire of kindling and adding water to the resulting lime powder. Shook imported metal scaffolding to reach high onto temple facades to repair and clean them, and gradually his dedicated workers restored the core of the stunning archaeological park seen today.

A new Field Director took over in 1963. Under William R. Coe, Museum archaeologists dug a huge and ambitious trench through the North Acropolis, penetrating its millennium of construction phases and stratigraphically plotting the history of the Great Plaza. Coe organized exploratory side trenches and a crew that tunneled through the great pyramidal base of

Temple I, hoping to locate royal tombs or other evidence of the pyramid's function. Rich graves and crypts turned up in numerous locations, virtually season after season, swelling inventories of jade, painted vases, shell work, bone, pyrite, alabaster, and other artifacts. The accumulated material prompted officials to build an on-site museum, the first of two impressive displays of Tikal art.

Other interests occupied the Coe team. Archaeologists cut four survey strips at right angles from the Great Plaza, extending them through the jungle seven and one-half miles through the downtown zone into the surrounding hinterland. Here archaeologists sampled unobtrusive, small-scale residential structures for evidence of habitation and population density. Similarly, experiments with crop production, storage longevity in tropical climates, and botanical investigations addressed issues of subsistence, agriculture, and environmental impact. The Project inventoried, photographed, and drew the corpus of Tikal art, enlisting art historians and students of inscriptions to add to the research tools of visual symbolism and hieroglyphic writing.

By the end of the University Museum's concession in 1969, few archaeological parks anywhere in the Americas rivaled Tikal. Work continued into the 1970s and 1980s under Rudi Larrios and Miguel Orrego of Guatemala's National Institute of Anthropology and History, and then under Juan Pedro Laporte of the University of San Carlos of Guatemala City. These projects, collectively known as the Proyecto Nacional, restored dozens of additional structures—Mundo Perdido (or the Lost World Pyramid) and its environs; Los Mascarones; Groups F, G, and H; and the small peripheral complex that includes the Morley Causeway. Most recently, plans were announced for the restoration of Temple V, the second-highest Great Pyramid at 190-feet tall, which Guatemala will carry out with funds provided by the government of Spain.

In the late 1980s Coe and original project members Christopher Jones and William Haviland summarized Tikal's history of excavation by explaining:

> "Perhaps no Maya site has been investigated with such prolonged intensity and care, and conceivably none ever will."

And yet, as excavation continues, research seems barely competent to penetrate this deeply accumulated mass of architecture. That whole worlds of features await discovery remains certain, ready to perfect our understanding of the Maya and no doubt to change many of the views held by professionals and amateurs alike. Above all, the incredible monumental scale of Tikal assures the visitor that the site will hold surprises in years to come, and that a return visit—a year or even a decade from now—will prove as rewarding as that first glimpse of the towering stone relics of Tikal's exceptional past.

NOTES

1. More recent analysis suggests "Tikal" derives from *ti ak'al*, "at the water-hole," in reference to one of the city's reservoirs. See Martin and Grube 2000: 30.
2. Technically a caimen.

TIKAL'S DYNASTIC SEQUENCE

LATE PRECLASSIC PERIOD

Yax Eb' Xook

- "First Step Shark?"
- Ruled: *ca.* A.D. 150
- The dynastic founder
- Mentioned on: Numerous monuments throughout Tikal
- Burial 125?

Jaguar Paw

- "Great Fire Claw"; "Great Jaguar Paw"
- Ruled: *ca.* A.D. 275
- 7th or 8th successor
- Depicted on: Stela 29 in the "sky" position

EARLY CLASSIC PERIOD

Foliated Ajaw
* Ruled: *ca.* A.D. 292
* 8th or 9th successor
* Monuments: Stela 29

Animal Headdress
* Ruled: *ca.* A.D. 295
* 10th successor
* Wife: "Lady Skull"
* Son: Siyaj Kaan K'awil I
* Mentioned on: El Encanto Stela 1

Siyaj Kaan K'awil I
* "Sky Born Ancestor God"; "Sky Born K'awil"; "Stormy Sky"
* Ruled: *ca.* A.D. 300
* 11th successor
* Father: "Animal Headdress"
* Mother: "Lady Skull"
* Monuments: El Encanto Stela 1
* Mentioned on: The "Dynastic Pot"

Lady Une B'alam
* "Lady Jaguar Tail"; "Lady Baby Jaguar"
* Ruled: *ca.* A.D. 317
* 12th successor?
* Mentioned On: Stela 26 and Stela 31, and shard from Problematic Deposit PNT–21

Muwan Jol
* "Hawk Head"; "Bird Skull"; "Feather Skull"
* Ruled: *ca.* A.D. 355?
* 13th successor
* Death: 8.16.2.6.0 11 Ajaw 13 Pop (May 24, A.D. 359?)
* Mentioned on: The "Dynastic Pot"
* Son: Chak Tok' Ich'aak I

Chak Tok Ich'aak I
- "Great Fire Claw"; "Great Jaguar Paw"; "Toj Chak Ich'ak"; "Jaguar Paw I"
- Ruled: *ca.* A.D. 375?
- 14th successor
- Acceded: 8.16.3.10.2 11 Ik' 10 Sek (August 8, A.D. 360?)
- Died: 8.17.1.4.12 11 Eb' 15 Mak (January 16, A.D. 378)
- Monuments: Stela 39?
- Father: Muwan Jol
- Mother: Lady B'alam Way
- Burial 22? (Temple 5D–26)

Nuun Yax Ayin I
- "First Great Crocodile"; "Curl Nose"; "Curl Snout"
- Ruled: *ca.* A.D. 400?
- 15th successor
- Acceded: 8.17.2.16.17, 5 Kab'an 10 Yaxk'in (September 13, A.D. 379)
- Death: 8.18.8.1.2, 2 Ik' 10 Sip, June 18 (A.D. 404?)
- Father: Jatz'am Ku ("Spearthrower Owl"), ruler of Teotihuacan
- Wife: Lady K'inich
- Son: Siyaj Kaan K'awil II
- Monuments: Stelae 4 and 18
- Burial 10 (Temple 5D–34)

Siyaj Kaan K'awil II
- "Sky Born Ancestor God"; "Sky Born K'awil"; "Stormy Sky"
- Ruled: A.D. 411–448
- 16th successor
- Acceded: 8.18.15.11.0 3 Ajaw 13 Sak (November 27, A.D. 411)
- Death: 9.1.0.8.0 10 Ajaw 13 Muwan (February 4, A.D. 456)
- Father: Nuun Yax Ayin I
- Mother: Lady K'inich
- Wife: Lady Ayin
- Sons: K'an Chitam, Río Azul ruler
- Monuments: Stelae 1, 2, 28?, and 31
- Burial 48 (Temple 5D–33)

MIDDLE CLASSIC PERIOD

K'an Chitam
* "Yellow Peccary"; "K'an Ak"; "Kan Boar"
* 17th successor
* Birth: 8.18.19.12.1 (November 26, A.D. 415?)
* Acceded: 9.1.2.17.17 4 Kab'an 15 Xul (August 9, A.D. 458)
* Father: Siyaj Kaan K'awil II
* Mother: Lady Ayin
* Wife: Lady Tzutz Nik
* Sons: Chak Tok Ich'aak, "Quetzal"
* Monuments: 2, 9, 13, and 40

Chak Tok Ich'aak II
* "Great Fire Claw"; "Great Jaguar Paw"; "Toj Chak Ich'ak"; "Jaguar Paw II"
* Ruled: *ca.* A.D. 508
* 18th successor
* Death: 9.2.13.12.5 13 Chikchan 13 Xul (July 25, A.D. 508)
* Father: K'an Chitam
* Mother: Lady Tzutz Nik
* Son: Wak Kaan K'awil
* Daughter: Lady Kalomte'
* Monuments: 3, 7, 15, 26?, and 27

Lady Kalomte'
* "Lady Ruler"; "Lady of Tikal"; "Woman of Tikal"
* Co-ruler with Kalomte' B'alam?
* Birth: 9.3.9.13.3 (September 2, A.D. 504)
* Acceded: 9.3.16.8.4 11 K'an 17 Pop (April 21, A.D. 511)
* Monuments: Stelae 6, 12, and 23

Kalomte' B'alam
* "Jaguar Ruler"; "Curl Head"
* Ruling: *ca.* A.D. 515
* 19th successor

- Brother: Wak Kaan K'awil
- Monuments: Stelae 10, 12, and 25?

Unknown
- "Bird Claw"; "Feather Skull"; "Animal Skull I"; "E Te' I"
- Ruled *ca.* A.D. 530?
- 20th successor
- Monuments: Stelae 25? and 8?

Wak Kaan K'awil
- "Stood-Up Sky Ancestor"; "Stood-Up Sky K'awil"; "Double Bird"
- 21st successor
- Acceded: 9.5.3.9.15 12 Men 18 K'ank'in (December 30, A.D. 537?)
- Father: Chak Tok Ich'aak II
- Mother: Lady Hand
- Monuments: Stela 17

E Te'
- "Animal Skull"; "Lizard Head"; "E Te' II"
- Ruling: *ca.* A.D. 562
- 22nd successor
- Father: Black Fire Cross
- Mother: Lady Hand Sky
- Mentioned on: Numerous provenanced and unprovenanced polychrome plates
- Burial 195 (Temple 5D–32)

Unknown
- 23rd successor

Unknown
- 24th successor

Nuun U Jol Chaak
- "Great His Head Rain God"; "Shield Skull"; "Nun Bak Chak"
- Ruling: *ca.* A.D. 657
- 25th successor?

- Father: E Te'?, Vulture Head?
- Wife: Lady Jaguar Seat
- Son: Jasaw Kaan K'awil I
- Mentioned on: Temple I, Lintel 3; MT 25 and MT 44; and numerous monuments at Dos Pilas and Palenque

LATE CLASSIC PERIOD

Jasaw Kaan K'awil I

- "Sky Banner K'awil"; "K'awil Who Clears the Sky"; "Ah Cacau"; "Ah Cacaw"; "Ah Kakaw"; "Ruler A"
- 26th successor
- Accession: 9.12.9.17.16 5 Kib' 14 Sotz' (May 4, A.D. 682)
- Father: Nuun U Jol Chaak
- Mother: Lady Jaguar Seat
- Wife: Lady Kalajun Une' Mo'
- Wife: Lady Tun Kaywak?
- Sons: Yik'in Kaan K'awil, and Successor 28?
- Monuments: Stelae 16 and 30; Altars 5 and 14; Temple I, Lintels 2 and 3
- Burial 116 (Temple I)

Yik'in Kaan K'awil

- "Dark Sky K'awil"; "K'awil Who Darkens the Sky"; "Yik'in Chan Chak"; "Ruler B"
- 27th successor
- Acceded: 9.15.3.6.8 3 Lamat 6 Pax (December 8, A.D. 734)
- Father: Jasaw Kaan K'awil I
- Mother: Lady Kalajun Une' Mo'
- Son: Nuun Yax Ayin II
- Monuments: Stelae 5, 20?, and 21; Altars 2, 8?, and 9; Lintel from Str. 5D–52; Temple IV, Lintels 2 and 3; Rock Sculpture at head of Maler Causeway?
- Burial: Temple IV?

Unknown

- 28th successor
- Ruling: *ca.* A.D. 767?

Nuun Yax Ayin II

- "First Great Crocodile"; "Chitam"; "Ruler C"
- 29th successor

- Acceded: 9.16.17.16.4 11 K'an 12 K'ayab' (December 26, A.D. 768)
- Father: Yik'in Kaan K'awil
- Monuments: Stelae 19 and 22; Altars 6 and 10

Nuun U Jol K'inich

- "Great His Sun Head"?; "Great Headed Sun"?
- Ruling: *ca.* A.D. 790?
- 30th successor?
- Son: Dark Sun?
- Mentioned on: Temple III, Lintel 2

Dark Sun

- Ruling: *ca.* 820?
- 31st successor?
- Father: Nuun U Jol K'inich
- Monuments: Stela 24; Altar 7; Temple III, Lintel 2
- Burial: Temple III?

Jewel K'awil

- Ruling: *ca.* A.D. 849?
- 32nd successor?
- Mentioned on: Seibal Stela 10

Jasaw Chaan K'awil II

- "Sky Banner K'awil"; "K'awil Who Clears the Sky"
- 33rd or 34th successor?
- Ruling: *ca.* A.D. 869 until A.D. 889?
- Monuments: Stela 11
- Mentioned on: Waxaktun Stela 12?

APPENDIX 2

CHRONOLOGY

*Indicates an approximate date.

600 B.C.	*6.7.0.0.0	Earliest archaeological evidence of the Maya at Tikal
150 A.D.	*8.5.10.0.0	Burial 125, the tomb of the founder of the Tikal dynasty, Yax Eb' Xook?
250	*8.10.10.0.0	Approximate reign of the ruler Jaguar Paw
292	8.12.14.8.15	Earliest surviving Long Count from Tikal and the Maya lowlands; Stela 29, during the reign of Foliated Jaguar
295	*8.12.17.0.0	Approximate time of Animal Headdress?
298	*8.13.?.8.4?	Reference to Siyaj Kaan K'awil I on El Encanto Stela 1?
359	8.16.2.6.0	Death of Muwan Jol, the 12th successor and consort of Lady Une B'alam, Corozal Stela
360	8.16.3.10.2	Accession of Chak Tok Ich'aak I, the 14th successor

374	8.16.17.9.0	Accession of Jatz'am Ku (Spearthrower Owl), the ruler of Teotihuacan
378	8.17.1.4.12	Arrival of strangers at Tikal (Siyaj K'ak') and the death of Chak Tok Ich'aak I
379	8.17.2.16.17	Accession of Nuun Yax Ayin I, the fifteenth successor
393	8.17.16.12.2	Mention of Siyaj K'ak' on Río Azul Stela 1
396	*8.18.0.0.0	Mention of Siyaj K'ak' on Copán Xukpi Stone
404	8.18.8.1.2	Death of Nuun Yax Ayin I
411	8.18.15.11.0	Accession of Siyaj Kaan K'awil II, the 16th successor; Stela 31
415	8.18.19.12.1	Birth of K'an Chitam, the 17th successor; Stela 40
417	8.19.1.11.9	Mention of Jatz'am Ku (Spearthrower Owl), the ruler of Teotihuacan, on El Zapote Stela 1
439	9.0.3.9.18	Death of Jatz'am Ku (Spearthrower Owl), the ruler of Teotihuacan; Stela 31
458	9.1.2.17.17	Accession of K'an Chitam, the 17th successor; Stela 40
486	9.2.11.7.8	Raid against Masul by Kalomte' B'alam, the military leader of Tikal, under K'an Chitam, the 17th successor; first major military conflict mentioned in Classic Maya inscriptions
495	9.3.0.0.0	Period Ending celebrated by Chak Tok Ich'aak II, the 18th successor; Stelae 7, 15, and 27

504	9.3.9.13.3	Birth of Lady Kalomte'
508	9.3.13.2.10	Birth of Wak Kaan K'awil, the 21st successor
508	9.3.13.12.6	Death of Chak Tok Ich'aak II, the 18th successor?; Toniná monument
508	9.3.13.12.19	Capture of an underlord of Chak Tok Ich'aak II by Yaxchilán, under the auspices of Calakmul; Yaxchilán Lintel 37
511	9.3.16.8.4	Accession of Lady Kalomte', co-ruler (?) with Kalomte' Balam, the 19th successor and Tikal's war chief during the reign of K'an Chitam; Stela 23
520	9.4.5.6.16	Ceremony performed by the wife of a Calakmul king at El Peru; El Peru Altar 1
527	9.4.13.0.0	Period Ending celebrated by Lady Kalomte' and Kalomte' B'alam, the 19th successor and Tikal's war chief during the reign of K'an Chitam
546	9.5.12.0.4	Installation of Aj Wosa as ruler of Naranjo by Caracol; Naranjo Stela 25
553	9.5.19.1.2	Yajawte' K'inich installed as ruler of Caracol by Tikal; Caracol Altar 21
556	9.6.2.1.11	Raid against Caracol by Tikal; Caracol Altar 21
557	9.6.3.9.15	Last date before Tikal's hiatus, recorded by Wak Kaan K'awil, the 21st successor; Stela 17
562	9.6.8.4.2	Conquest of Tikal by Calakmul; Caracol Altar 21

584	9.7.10.16.8	Marriage of Lady Batz' Ek' of Calakmul to the ruler of Caracol; Caracol Stela 3
599	9.8.5.13.8	Palenque attacked by Calakmul; longest-distance raid recorded in Maya inscriptions; Palenque Hieroglyphic Stairway
615	9.9.2.4.8	Accession of Janaab' Pakal the Great of Palenque
625	9.9.12.11.2	Accession at Dos Pilas in the Petexbatun of Balaj Kaan K'awil, son of E Te', the 22nd successor of Tikal; cadet lineage founds its own dynasty at Dos Pilas
628	9.9.15.0.0	Mention of E Te', the 22nd successor, at Altar De Sacrificios at the juncture of the Pasión and Usumacinta Rivers; Altar de Sacrificios Stela 8
631	9.9.18.16.3	Conquest of Naranjo by Caracol under the authority of Calakmul, after repeated wars; Caracol Stela 3 and Stucco Text; Naranjo Hieroglyphic Stairs
657	9.11.4.5.14	Tikal attacked by Calakmul; Nuun U Jol Chaak, the 25th successor (?) driven out and pursued; Dos Pilas Hieroglyphic Stairs II, East, Step 1
659	9.11.6.16.11	Capture of the prisoners of Nuun U Jol Chaak; Palenque Hieroglyphic Stairs
672	9.12.0.8.3	Dos Pilas attacked by Nuun U Jol Chaak of Tikal; Balaj Kaan K'awil of Dos Pilas driven out; Dos Pilas Hieroglyphic Stairs II, West, Step 1, and IV, Step 3

677	9.12.5.9.14	Conquest of Nuun U Jol Chaak of Tikal by Dos Pilas, under the authority of Calakmul; Dos Pilas Hieroglyphic Stairs II, West, Step 1
677	9.12.5.10.1	Continuing conquest of Nuun U Jol Chaak of Tikal by Dos Pilas; Dos Pilas Hieroglyphic Stairs IV, Step 3, and II, West, Step 1
679	9.12.6.16.17	Final conquest of Nuun U Jol of Tikal by Dos Pilas and Calakmul; Dos Pilas Hieroglyphic Stairs IV, Step 5, and II, West, Step 2; El Peru Altar 1
681	9.12.9.8.1	Accession of Itz'am B'alam (Shield Jaguar the Great) of Yaxchilán; Yaxchilán Hieroglyphic Stairs III
682	9.12.9.17.16	Accession of Jasaw Kaan K'awil I, the 26th successor at Tikal
682	9.12.10.5.12	Arrival of Lady Wak Kaanil of Dos Pilas at Naranjo, as bride to the Naranjo king; Naranjo Stelae 24 and 29; arrival of a woman (from Dos Pilas) at Cobá
683	9.12.11.5.18	Death of Janaab' Pakal of Palenque
686	9.12.13.17.7	Accession of Ich'aak K'ak' of Calakmul; Dos Pilas Panel 7; El Peru Stela 34
695	9.13.3.7.18	Conquest of Calakmul by Tikal; Temple I, Lintel 3
703	9.13.11.6.7	Death of Lady Tun Kaywak of Topoxte' Island; Altar 5
711	9.13.19.13.3	Capture of the Palenque king K'an Joy' Chitam by Toniná; Toniná Panel

711	9.13.19.16.6	Opening of the bones and skull of Lady Tun Kaywak of Topoxte' Island; Altar 5
711	9.14.0.0.0	Period Ending celebrated by Jasaw Kaan K'awil I, the 26th successor; Stela 16
734	9.15.3.6.8	Accession of Yik'in Kaan K'awil, the 27th successor; Stelae 21 and 5
738	9.15.6.14.6	Capture of Waxaklajun U B'a of Copán by Quirigua; Quirigua Stelae J, E, F, and Zoomorph G; Copan Hieroglyphic Stairs
742	9.15.10.17.14	Death of Itz'am Balam (Shield Jaguar the Great) of Yaxchilán; Yaxchilán Stela 12
743	9.15.12.2.2	Conquest of El Peru by Tikal; Temple IV, Lintel 3
744	9.15.12.12.13	Conquest of Naranjo by Tikal; Temple IV, Lintel 2
751	9.16.0.0.0	Period Ending celebrated by Yik'in K'awil; Stela 20
752	9.16.1.0.0	Accession of Yaxun B'alam of Yaxchilán after an 11-year struggle to gain the throne; Yaxchilán Stela 12
761	9.16.9.15.10	Dos Pilas sacked and destroyed, and the nobility driven out, by Tamarindito; beginning of the Classic Maya collapse; Tamarindito Hieroglyphic Stairs
763	9.16.12.5.17	Accession of Yax Pasaj, the last great king of Copán; Copan Altar U; Temple 11, Bench; Temple 11, Panel

766	9.16.14.17.17	Dedication of the Temple of the Inscriptions by the 28th successor?
768	9.16.17.16.4	Accession of Nuun Yax Ayin II, the 29th successor; Stela 19
771	9.17.0.0.0	Period Ending celebrated by Nuun Yax Ayin II, the 29th successor; Stela 22
787	9.17.16.14.19	Beginning of the Pomoná wars waged by Piedras Negras and its allies; Piedras Negras Stela 12
790	9.18.0.0.0	Period Ending celebrated by Nuun Yax Ayin II, the 29th successor; Stela 19
792	9.18.1.15.5	Date painted in Room 2 of the Bonampak Murals
799	9.18.9.4.4	Accession of the last king of Palenque; Palenque Initial Series Pot
808	9.18.17.13.14	Last date at Yaxchilán; Yaxchilán Lintel 10
810	9.19.0.0.0	Period Ending celebrated by Dark Sun(?) of Tikal; Stela 24
814	9.19.3.13.12	Last known date at Comalcalco, the western-most Classic Maya city; Comalcalco Brick
822	9.19.11.14.5	Last dated monument at Copán; Copan Altar L
830	9.19.19.17.19	Arrival of Aj B'olon Ab'ta at Seibal; Seibal Stela 11
849	10.1.0.0.0	Period Ending celebrated by Aj B'olon Ab'ta at Seibal; Seibal Stelae 8, 9, 10, 11, and 21

864	10.1.15.3.6	Beginning of the "Great Period" of hieroglyphic inscriptions at Chichén Itzá
869	10.2.0.0.0	Period Ending celebrated by Jasaw Kaan K'awil I of Tikal; last known date at Tikal; Stela 11
879	10.2.10.0.0	Period Ending celebrated by ruler of Ixlu in the company of the ruler of Tikal; Ixlu Altar 1
889	10.3.0.0.0	Period Ending celebrated at Jimbal with the ruler of Tikal; Jimbal Stela 2
901	10.3.11.15.14	Beginning of the hieroglyphic inscriptions at Uxmal
909	10.4.0.0.0	Last known date at Toniná; last known Long Count date from the Classic Period; Toniná Monument 101
910	10.4.1.0.0	Period Ending celebrated at Itzimte'; last known hieroglyphic date from the Classic Period; Itzimte' Stela 6

REFERENCES

TIKAL

Carr, R.F., and J.E. Hazard

1961   Map of the Ruins of Tikal. *Tikal Reports No. 11*, Museum Monograph 21. Philadelphia: University Museum, University of Pennsylvania.

Coe, William R.

1958   Two Carved Lintels from Tikal. *Archaeology*, 11(2): 75–80.

1959a   Stela 29, Tikal, Guatemala. *Bulletin*, 13(1): 1–3. Philadelphia: Philadelphia Anthropological Society.

1959b   Tikal 1959. *Expedition*, 1(4): 7–12.

1962   A Summary of Excavation and Research at Tikal, Guatemala: 1956–1961. *American Antiquity*, 28(3): 479–507.

1963   A Summary of Excavation and Research at Tikal, Guatemala, 1962. *Estudios de Cultura Maya*, 3: 41–64.

1965a   Tikal, Guatemala: An Emergent Civilization. *Science*, 147(3664): 1401–1419.

1965b   Tikal: Ten Years of Study of a Maya Ruin in the Lowlands of Guatemala. *Expedition*, 8(1): 5–56.

1967   *Tikal: A Handbook of the Ancient Maya Ruins.* Guatemala: Piedra Santa.

Coe, William R., and John J. McGinn

1963   Tikal: The North Acropolis and An Early Tomb. *Expedition*, 5(2): 24–32.

Coggins, Clemency C.

1975   *Painting and Drawing Styles at Tikal: An Historical and Iconographic Reconstruction.* Ph.D. dissertation. University of Pennsyvania. Ann Arbor: University Microfilms.

1979   A New Order and the Role of the Calendar: Some Characteristics of the Middle Classic Period at Tikal. *Maya Archaeology and Ethnology,* N. Hammond and G.R. Willey, eds.: 39–50. Austin: University of Texas Press.

Culbert, T. Patrick

1993   *The Ceramics of Tikal: Vessels from the Burials, Caches, and Problematical Deposits.* Monograph of the University Museum. Philadelphia: University of Pennsylvania.

Culbert, T. Patrick, Laura J. Kosakowsky, Robert E. Fry, and William A. Haviland

1990   The Population of Tikal, Guatemala. *Precolumbian Population History in the Maya Lowlands.* T.P. Culbert and D.S. Rice, eds.: 103–121. Albuquerque: University of New Mexico Press.

De Solis, Patricia

1976   *Tikal.* Guatemala: Filmtrek.

Fahsen, Federico, and Linda Schele

1991   Curl-Snout Under Scrutiny, Again. *Texas Notes on Precolumbian Art, Writing, and Culture No. 12.* Austin: Kinko's Files.

Grube, Nikolai, and Simon Martin

2000   *Notebook for the XXIVth Maya Hieroglyphic Forum at Texas.* Austin: Department of Art and Art History, University of Texas.

Grube, Nikolai, and Linda Schele

1994   Tikal Altar 5. *Texas Notes on Precolumbian Art, Writing, and Culture No. 66.* Austin: Kinko's Files.

Guenter, Stanley P.

2000   The Murder of the Queen of Tikal? *PARI Journal* 1(2): 22–24. San Francisco: The Pre-Columbian Art Research Institute.

Harrison, Peter D.

1970   *The Central Acropolis, Tikal, Guatemala: A Preliminary Study of the Functions of its Structural Components During the Late Classic Period.* Ph.D. dissertation, University of Pennsylvania. Ann Arbor: University Microfilms.

1986 Tikal: Selected Topics. In *City States of the Maya: Art and Architecture.* 45–71. E.P. Benson, ed. Denver: Rocky Mountain Institute for Pre-Columbian Studies.

1999 *The Lords of Tikal: Rulers of an Ancient Maya City.* New Yok: Thames and Hudson.

Haviland, William A.

1967 Stature at Tikal, Guatemala: Implications for Ancient Maya Demography and Social Organization. *American Antiquity,* 32(3): 316–326.

1977 Dynastic Genealogies from Tikal, Guatemala: Implications for Descent and Political Organization. *American Antiquity,* 42(1): 61–67.

1981 Dower Houses and Minor Centers at Tikal, Guatemala: An Investigation into the Identification of Valid Units In Settlement Hierarchy. In *Lowland Maya Settlement Patterns.* W. Ashmore, ed., 89–117. Albuquerque: University of New Mexico Press.

Hellmuth, Nicholas M.

1976 *Tikal-Copan Travel Guide: A Complete Guide to All of the Maya Ruins of Central America.* Guatemala: Foundation for Latin American Anthropological Research.

Jones, Christopher

1977 Inauguration Dates of Three Late Classic Rulers of Tikal, Guatemala. *American Antiquity,* 42(1): 28–60.

1988 The Life and Times of Ah Cacaw, Ruler of Tikal. In *Primer Simposio Mundial Sobre Epigraphía Maya.* 107–120. Guatemala: Asociación Tikal.

Jones, Christopher, and Linton Satterthwaite

1982 *The Monuments and Inscriptions of Tikal: The Carved Monuments.* Tikal Report No. 33A. Philadelphia: University Museum, University of Pennsylvania.

Maler, Teobert

1911 *Explorations in the Department of Peten, Guatemala: Tikal.* Memoirs of the Peabody Museum 5(1). Cambridge: Harvard University.

Malmström, Vincent H.

1997 *Cycles of the Sun, Mysteries of the Moon: The Calendar in Mesoamerican Civilization.* Austin: University of Texas Press.

Martin, Simon
 1994 Warfare and Political Organization in the Late Classic Central Southern Lowlands. Paper presented at the 10th Texas Symposium, Austin.
 1995 New Epigraphic Data of Classic Maya Warfare. Paper presented at the Primer Mesa Redonda de Palenque, Nueva Epoca, Palenque.
 1996 Tikal's "Star War" Against Naranjo. *8th Palenque Round Table*: 223–235. San Francisco: The Pre-Columbian Art Research Institute.
 1998 Middle Classic Tikal: Kings, Queens, and Consorts. Paper presented as "Lindafest." Unpublished manuscript in author's possession.
 1999a The Queen of Middle Classic Tikal. *Newsletter*, March: 4–5. San Francisco: Pre-Columbian Art Research Institute.
 1999b The Baby Jaguar: Dynastic Legitimization and Matrilineal Descent at Early Classic Tikal. Paper presented at the Palenque Round Table.
 2001 Unmasking "Double Bird," Ruler of Tikal. *PARI Journal* 2(1): 7–12. San Francisco: The Pre-Columbian Art Research Institute.

Maudslay, Alfred P.
 1889– Tikal. *Archaeology*; Vol. III of text: 44–50; Vol. III of plates: 67–82. London:
 1902 Biologia Centrali Americana.

Michel, Genevieve
 1989 *The Rulers of Tikal: A Historical Reconstruction and Field Guide to the Stelae*. Guatemala: Publicaciones Vista.

Miller, Mary
 1984 Tikal, Guatemala: A Rationale for the Placement of the Funerary Pyramids. *Expedition*, 27(3): 6–15.

Montgomery, John
 1981 *How to Reach Tikal by Tour, Plane, Helicopter, Bus, Car, Hitchhiking, and Walking*. Guatemala: Imprenta Offset Ruiz.
 1987a *Lords of Tikal: Dynastic Succession at a Lowland Maya Regional Capital*. Unpublished manuscript.
 1987b *Caracol Influence at Tikal*. Unpublished manuscript in author's possession.
 1988 *Tikal*. Weston: Pictures of Record.

Morley, Sylvanus G.
1937–ㅤ*The Inscriptions of Petén.* 1: 266–382. Publication 437.
ㅤㅤㅤWashington, D.C.:
1938ㅤㅤCarnegie Institution of Washington.

Puleston, Dennis E., and Donald W. Callender
1967ㅤㅤDefensive Earthworks at Tikal. *Expedition,* 9(3): 40–48.

Satterthwaite, Linton
1963ㅤㅤNotes on Hieroglyphic Bone from the Tomb Below Temple I,
ㅤㅤㅤTikaI. *Expedition,* 6(1): 18–19.

Schele, Linda
1991ㅤㅤSome Observations on the War Expressions at Tikal. *Texas Notes
ㅤㅤㅤon Precolumbian Art, Writing, and Culture No. 16.* Austin.

Schele, Linda, and Federico Fahsen
1991ㅤㅤA Substitution Pattern in Curl-Snout's Name. *Texas Notes on
ㅤㅤㅤPrecolumbian Art, Writing, and Culture No. 12.* Austin.

Schele, Linda, Federico Fahsen, and Nikolai Grube
1992ㅤㅤEl Zapote and the Dynasty of Tikal. *Texas Notes on
ㅤㅤㅤPrecolumbian Art, Writing, and Culture No. 34.* Austin.

Schele, Linda, and Nikolai Grube
1994ㅤㅤSome Revisions to Tikal's Dynasty of Kings. *Texas Notes on
ㅤㅤㅤPrecolumbian Art, Writing, and Culture No. 67.* Austin.

Shook, Edwin M.
1958aㅤField Director's Report: The 1956 and 1957 Seasons. *Tikal
ㅤㅤㅤReports 1.* Museum Monographs. Philadelphia: University
ㅤㅤㅤMuseum, University of Pennsylvania.
1958bㅤThe Temple of the Red Stela. *Expedition* 1(1): 26–33.
1960ㅤㅤTikal Stela 29. *Expedition,* 2(2): 28–35.

Shook, Edwin M., and Alfred Kidder
1961ㅤㅤThe Painted Tomb at Tikal. *Expedition* 4(1): 2–7.

Stuart, David
2000ㅤㅤ"The Arrival of Strangers": Teotihuacan and Tollan in Classic
ㅤㅤㅤMaya History. In *Mesoamerica's Classic Heritage: From Teoti-
ㅤㅤㅤhuacan to the Aztecs.* D. Carrasco, L. Jones, and S. Sessions,
ㅤㅤㅤeds.: 465–513.

Tozzer, Alfred M.
1911ㅤㅤ*A Preliminary Study of the Ruins of Tikal, Guatemala.*
ㅤㅤㅤMemoirs of the Peabody Museum 5(2). Cambridge: Harvard
ㅤㅤㅤUniversity.

Trik, Aubrey S.
  1963   The Splendid Tomb of Temple I at Tikal, Guatemala.
          Expedition, 6(1): 3–18.
Villela, Khristaan D.
  1993a   A New Curl-Snout Event on the Hombre de Tikal. *Texas Notes
          on Precolumbian Art, Writing, and Culture No. 39.* Austin:
          Kinko's Files.
  1993b   Parallel Throne Phrases at Tikal and Palenque. *Texas Notes on
          Precolumbian Art, Writing, and Culture No. 40.* Austin:
          Kinko's Files.
Wanyerka, Phil, ed. and trans.
  2000   *The Proceedings of the Maya Hieroglyphic Workshop: Tikal
          and Its Neighbors.* Parma.
Webster, Helen T.
  1963   Tikal Graffiti. *Expedition*, 6(1): 36–47.

THE MAYA AND MESOAMERICA

Abrams, Elliot M.
  1994   *How the Maya Built Their World: Energetics and Ancient
          Architecture.* Austin: University of Texas Press.
Adams, Richard E.W. Adams
  1999   *Río Azul: An Ancient Maya City.* Norman: University of
          Oklahoma Press.
Baudez, Claude, and Sidney Picasso
  1992   *Lost Cities of the Maya.* New York: Harry N. Abrams.
Berrin, Kathleen, and Esther Pasztory, eds.
  1993   *Teotihuacan: Art from the City of the Gods.* New York:
          Thames and Hudson.
Boot, Eric
  1999   A Maya-English Hieroglyphic Vocabulary. Austin: Kinko's Files.
Carneiro, R.
  1970   A Theory of the Origin of the State. *Science* 169:733–738.
Chase, Arlen F.
  1985   Troubled Times: The Archaeology and Iconography of the
          Terminal Classic Southern Lowland Maya. *Fifth Palenque*

Round Table, 1983, Vol. VII, 103–114. San Francisco: The Pre-Columbian Art Research Institute.

Chase, Arlen F., and Diane Z. Chase

1987 *Investigations at the Classic Maya City of Caracol, Belize: 1985–1987.* Monograph 3. San Francisco: Pre-Columbian Art Research Institute.

Clancy, Flora S.

1999 *Sculpture in the Ancient Maya Plaza: The Early Classic Period.* Albuquerque: University of New Mexico Press.

Demarest, Arthur A.

1997 The Vanderbilt Petexbatun Regional Archaeological Project: 1989–1994. *Ancient Mesoamerica,* 8(2): 209–227.

Demarest, Arthur, Matt O'Mansky, Claudia Wolley, Dirk Van Tuerenhout, Takeshi Inomata, Joel Palka, and Héctor Escobedo

1997 Classic Maya Defensive Systems and Warfare in the Petexbatun Region: Archaeological Evidence and Interpretations. *Ancient Mesoamerica,* 8(2): 229–253.

Fash, William L.

1991 *Scribes, Warriors, and Kings: The City of Copán and the Ancient Maya.* New York: Thames and Hudson.

Fash, William L., and Barbara J. Fash

2000 Teotihuacan and the Maya: A Classic Heritage. In *Mesoamerica's Classic Heritage: From Teotihuacan to the Aztecs.* D. Carrasco, L. Jones, and S. Sessions, eds.: 433–463. Boulder: University Press of Colorado.

Freidel, David, Linda Schele, and Joy Parker

1993 *Maya Cosmos: Three Thousand Years on the Shaman's Path.* New York: William Morrow.

Gallenkamp, Charles

1985 *Maya: The Riddle and Rediscovery of a Lost Civilization.* Third revised edition. New York: Viking.

Hammond, Norman

1982 *Ancient Maya Civilization.* New Brunswick: Rutgers University Press.

Henderson, John S.
1981   *The World of the Ancient Maya.* Ithaca: Cornell University Press.
Houston, Stephen D.
1989   *Hieroglyphs and History at Dos Pilas: Dynastic Politics of the Classic Maya.* Austin: University of Texas Press.
Houston, Stephen D., and Peter Mathews
1987   *The Dynastic Sequence of Dos Pilas.* Monograph 1. San Francisco: The Pre-Columbian Art Research Center.
Houston, Stephen D., Stacey Symonds, David Stuart, and Arthur Demarest
n.d.   A Civil War of the Late Classic Period: Evidence from Hieroglyphic Stairway 4. Recent Finds at Dos Pilas, Gautemala III. Unpublished manuscript.
Inomata, Takeshi
1997   The Last day of a Fortified Classic Maya Center. *Ancient Mesoamerica,* 8(2): 337–351.
Malström, Vincent H.
1997   *Cycles of the Sun, Mysteries of the Moon: The Calendar in Mesoamerican Civilization.* Austin: University of Texas Press.
Marcus, Joyce
1976   *Emblem and State in the Classic Maya Lowlands: An Epigraphic Approach to Territorial Organization.* Washington, D.C.: Dumbarton Oaks.
Martin, Simon, and Nikolai Grube
1995   Maya Superstates. *Archaeology* 48(6): 42–46.
2000   *Chronicle of the Maya Kings and Queens.* New York: Thames and Hudson.
n.d.   Evidence for Macro-Political Organization Among Classic Maya Lowland States. Unpublished manuscript.
Miller, Mary
1999   *Maya: Art and Architecture.* New York: Thames and Hudson.
Millon, René
1993   The Place Where Time Began. *Teotihuacan: Art from the City of the Gods.* K. Berrin and E. Pasztory, eds.: 17–43. New York: Thames and Hudson.
Montgomery, John
2001a   *Dictionary of Maya Hieroglyphs.* New York: Hippocrene Books.
2001b   *How to Read Maya Hieroglyphs.* New York: Hippocrene Books.

Pasztory, Esther

1998   *Pre-Columbian Art.* Cambridge: Cambridge University Press.

Proskouriakoff, Tatiana

1960   Historical Implications of a Pattern of Dates at Piedras
       Negras, Guatemala. *American Antiquity,* 25(4): 454–475.

1963   Historical Data in the Inscriptions of Yaxchilán, Part I.
       Estudios de Cultura Maya, 3: 149–167.

1964   Historical Data in the Inscriptions of Yaxchilán, Part II.
       Estudios de Cultura Maya, 4: 177–202.

1993   *Maya History.* Austin: University of Texas Press.

Sabloff, Jeremy A.

1989   *The Cities of Ancient Mexico: Reconstructing a Lost World.*
       New York: Thames and Hudson.

1990   *The New Archaeology and the Ancient Maya.* New York:
       Scientific American Library.

Scarborough, Vernon L., and David R. Wilcox, eds.

1991   *The Mesoamerican Ballgame.* Tucson: University of Arizona Press.

Schele, Linda, and David Freidel

1990   *A Forest of Kings: The Untold Story of the Ancient Maya.*
       New York: William Morrow.

Schele, Linda, and Nikolai Grube

1994   *Notebook for the XVIIIth Maya Hieroglyphic Workshop at
       Texas.* Austin: The University of Texas.

1995   *Notebook for the XIXth Maya Hieroglyphic Workshop at
       Texas.* Austin: The University of Texas.

Schele, Linda, and Peter Mathews

1998   *The Code of Kings: The Language of Seven Sacred Maya
       Temples and Tombs.* New York: Scribner.

Sharer, Robert J.

1994   *The Ancient Maya.* Fifth edition. Stanford: Stanford
       University Press.

Stuart, David, Stephen D. Houston, and John Robertson

1999   *Notebook for the 23rd Maya Hieroglyphic Workshop at Texas.*
       Austin: University of Texas.

Stuart, George, and Gene Stuart

1977   *The Mysterious Maya.* Washington, D.C.: National Geographic
       Society.

Willey, Gordon R., and Peter Mathews, eds.

1985 *A Consideration of the Early Classic Period in the Maya Lowlands.* Institute for Mesoamerican Studies, Publication 10. Albany: State University of New York at Albany.

RAIN FOREST AND WILDLIFE

Anonymous

n.d. *The Rain Forest Unfolds: Eco Guide.* New York: Van Dam.

Ayensu, Edward S.

1980 *Jungles: An Exploration of the Most Mysterious of All Natural Worlds.* New York: Crown Publishers.

Lamb, F. Bruce

1966 *Mahogany of Tropical America.* Ann Arbor: University of Michigan Press.

Leopold, A. Starker

1959 *Wildlife of Mexico: The Game Birds and Mammals.* Berkeley: University of California Press.

Moser, Don

1975 *Central American Jungles: The American Wilderness.* New York: Time-Life Books.

National Geographic Society

1990 *The Emerald Realm: Earth's Precious Rain Forests.* Washington, D.C.: National Geographic Society.

Newman, Arnold

1990 *Tropical Rainforest: A World Survey of Our Most Valuable and Endangered Habitat with a Blueprint for its Survival.* New York: Facts on File.

Peterson, Roger Tory, and Edward L. Chalif

1973 *Mexican Birds: Peterson Field Guides.* Boston: Houghton Mifflin.

Sanderson, Ivan T. And David Loth

1965 *Ivan Sanderson's Book of Great Jungles.* New York: Julian Messner.

INDEX

Acosta, Jorgé, 73–74
agriculture
    ecological damage of, 211
    preclassic, 13–15, 24
    terraces, 115, 122
Aguateca, 204–205
Aj B'olon Ab'ta, 212–214
Aj B'olon Ja', 149
Aj Nik, 136
Aj Wosa, 116–117
Akul Anaab', 154–155
Altar 1, 41
Altar 5, 155
Altar 8, 183
Altar 14, 144
Altar 21, 117–118
Animal Headdress, 43
animals, rainforest, 10–11
archaeology techniques, 94
architecture
    late classic, 159, 179, 225
    talud-tablero, 62, 159–160
    at Yaxchilán, 114
art history, 224
astronomy, 25
    organization of monuments, 208, 210

auto de fe, 93
automutilation, 169, 196
autosacrifice, 144, 150

Balaj Kaan K'awil, 123, 131–133,
    136, 142
ball court, 145–147, 149
Ball Court Marker, 66–68
Berlin, Heinrich, 55
Bernoulli, Gustav, 232–233
Bonampak murals, 123, 201
books, Maya, 93
Burial 10, 56–57, 60–61
    Teotihuacan's contribution to,
    63–64
Burial 22, 51–52
Burial 23, 133–134
Burial 24, 134–135
Burial 77, 199
Burial 160, 110–112
Burial 162, 112–113
Burial 195, 126
Burial 196, 184–185
burial gifts
    in Burial 195, 126, 136n5
    of Jasaw Kaan K'awil, 162

of Nuun Yax Ayin, 57, 77n1
of Siyaj Kaan K'awil, 86
burials of kings, 56–57

cacao beans, 13–14, 60, 217
Calakmul, 117–118, 132–133
    Caracol-Naranjo war, 125
    end of hegemony, 149
    friction with Tikal, 100–101, 107
    population, 115
    raids on Palenque, 120–121
    trade, 114, 147–148
Calendar Round, 20, 33
calendars
    Gregorian, 33
    Maya Long Count, 32–34, 42n1
    Precolumbian, 20
    solar, 25
cannibalism, 130, 132, 229
canoes, ocean-going, 226
canopy trees, 10
Caracol
    attack by Tikal, 117–118
    and Naranjo war, 125
Carnegie Institution, 234
Catherwood, Frederick, 232
cenotes, 214–216
Central Acropolis, 46
    expansion, 177–183
    late classic, 228–229
ceramic dating, 12–13
ceramic texts, 43
ceramics. See pottery
Chak Tok Ich'aak, 44, 46–49, 51–54
Chak Tok Ich'aak II, 101–102
Chichén Itzá, 215–217, 218, 221n7
chocolate, 13–14, 60, 217
chultun, 112, 118n4
classic civilization
    expansion of, 113–115

climate, 7
Cobá, 148
Coe, William R., 235–236
Coggins, Clemency, 55–56
Comalcalco, 210
commerce. See trade
construction
    late classic, 159
    preclassic, 23–24
Copán, 82–84, 210–211
costumbre, 229
Court of Creation, 145–147
currency, 60, 217

Dark Sun, 206–208
death, metaphors for, 84
death-mask, 111
defensive fortifications
    of Dos Pilas, 204
    early classic earthworks, 53
    Petexbatun region, 224
defensive tactics
    late classic, 204
dental modification, 134–135

E Te', 120–121, 126
economy
    early classic, 60
    late classic, 148
    Teotihuacan, 63
El Mirador, 23
environmental degradation
    and Maya collapse, 224
equinox, 208, 221n3

farming
    ecological damage of, 211
    middle classic, 122
    preclassic, 13–15, 24
    techniques, 123

Feathered Serpent, 18
Feathered Serpent Temple, 62
52-Year Cycle, 20, 33
First Macaw-Quetzal, 83
First Step Shark, 38, 40, 42n3
Five-Story Palace, 181–183
Foliated Jaguar, 34, 36
foreign influence
    on collapse, 227
    early classic, 60

games, 145–147, 149
graffiti, 174
Great Fiery Claw, 44, 46–49, 51–54
growth
    early classic, 83–84
    preclassic, 24–26

Haviland, William, 236
hieroglyphics
    epigraphers, 55–56
    language, 27
    late classic, 159
    mathematical, 20, 32
    scribal language, 101
    square, 211, 214
    writing, 27
hubuy Mutul, 118
huipil, 105

Itzá Maya, 215
Itz'amnáj B'alam, 132, 135–136, 155
Ixlu, 220
Ixtepeque Volcano, 83
Izapa, 21

Jaab' cycle, 33
jade, 19
jade mines, 147, 168n2, 171
Jaguar dynasty, 43–54

Jaguar Paw lineage house, 46, 48–49
Janaab' Pakal, 142–143
Jasaw Kaan K'awil, 144, 148
    attack on Narango, 149–150, 152
    burial of, 160–168
    final years, 158–160
    marriage to Lady Tun Kaywak,
        152, 154
    restoration of Sky Dynasty,
        141–142
    Twin Pyramids, 155–158
Jatz'am Ku, 71, 74, 84–85
Jimbal, 220
Jones, Christopher, 236

Kaan B'alam, 143, 154
Kaan Sak Wayas, 155
K'ak' Tiliw, 142, 149, 155, 171
Kalomte, 34
Kalomte' B'alam, 101, 105, 107, 112
Kaminaljuyu, 21, 59–60
K'an Chitam, 96–101, 103–104
K'an Joy Chitam, 154–155
K'atun 16, 183–184
kingship, 34, 36
K'inich B'aknal Chaak, 154

Lady Batz' Ek', 120
Lady Kalomte', 105, 107, 112
Lady Skull, 43
Lady Star, 107
Lady Tun Kaywak, 152–154, 155
Lady Une B'alam, 43–44
Lady Wak Kaanal, 142, 149
lakes, freshwater, 10
Landa, Diego de, 93
language
    hieroglyphic scribal, 101
    preclassic, 27
    Zuyua, 214–216

Laporte, Juan Pedro, 236
Larrios, Rudi, 136n5, 236
lintels of Yaxchilán, 114
López, Marcos, 31–32
Lost World Complex, 24–25

Maler, Teobert, 212, 232–234
marauders
    late classic, 204
Marcador, 66–68
Marcos's Stela, 31–32. See also Stela 29
masonry, preclassic, 23
Masul, 100
mathematics, 20
Maudslay, Alfred P., 234
Maya
    beginning of collapse, 188–190
    books, 93
    collapse, 223–229
    periods of development, 94
    traditional garment, 105
    warfare, 123–125, 136n3
Mendez, Modesto, 232
Mexico. See also Teotihuacan
    establishment of Copán, 82–84
    retreat from Tikal, 95–96
    symbolism, 75–76, 145–147
    Teotihuacan, 61–63
Millon, René, 95
milpas, 14
Morley, Sylvanus G., 234
Motágua River Valley, 147, 168n2, 171
mutilation, 144, 150, 169, 196
mutul, 36
Mutul Emblem. See Tikal Emblem
    Glyph
Muwan Jol, 44

Na Ek', 107
Na Kalomte', 102, 103, 105, 107, 112

Naranjo, 155
    and Caracol war, first, 125
    attack by Jasaw Kaan K'awil,
        149–150, 152
    defection from Calakmul, 130
    palanquin wars, 173
National Institute of Anthropology
    and History, 236
New Fire ceremony, 62
North Acropolis, 24, 38
Nuun U Jol Chaak, 130–133
Nuun Yax Ayin, 64–66, 69, 74–76,
        79–80
    burial of, 56–57
    death of, 76–77
Nuun Yax Ayin II, 195, 196
    last days, 202–203

Old Fire God, 57
Olmec, 7
    dragon, 57
    jade, 19
    legacy, 20–21
    trade, 18
Orrego, Miguel, 236
owl and weapon motif, 71

palanquin wars, 173–174, 177
Palenque
    beginning of decline,
        154–155
    fall of, 202
    raids by Calakmul, 120–121
    and trade route, 142–143
Pasión River, 7, 114–115
Peabody Museum, 233, 234
people
    preclassic, 8, 12–27
Petén core, 23–27
    expansion of, 74–76

Petexbatun, 204–205
  evidence of collapse, 224
Piedras Negras, 114, 120, 200
Place of the Ancient Ones, 59–60
Place of the Cattail Reeds, 73–74
Place of the Voices, 232
plants, rainforest, 10
poaching, 110
political organization, 49–51, 54n2,
    159, 168n6
  early classic, 46
  fissioning of power, 227
  and Maya collapse, 224
population, 210–211
  Calakmul, 115
  classic, 60
  early classic, 46, 49, 61
  late classic, 204, 223
  middle classic, 95, 115, 122
  proto-classic, 25–26
  theory on disappearance, 227
potable water, 7, 24, 214–215, 235
pottery
  ceramic debris, 228
  early classic, 51, 54n3
  late classic, 159, 227
  polychrome pictorial ceramics, 195
  preclassic, 12–13
  proto-classic, 26
  Teotihuacan, 63–64
  tomb of Siyaj Kaan K'awil, 86
Precolumbian civilization, 17–27
Proskouriakoff, Tatiana, 55–56
Punto de Chimino, 205
pyramids, 17
  astronomical organization, 208, 210
  Kaminaljuyu, 59
  Lost World, 25
  of the Sun, 61
  Temple I, 166–168, 208

Temple II, 152–154, 168n3, 208
Temple III, 206, 208, 210
Temple IV, 173–174, 190–193,
    208, 210
Temple V, 208
Temple VI, 187–188
Temple of the Feathered Serpent, 62
Temple of the Inscriptions, 143,
    169, 187–188
  three-pyramid Group of the
    Cross, 154
  Twin Complex N, 155–158
  Twin Complex P, 183
  Twin Complex Q, 196–199
  Twin Group M, 144

Quetzal, 110–112
quetzal bird, 110–111
Quetzalcóatl, 18
Quirigua, 147–148, 218
  independence, 171–172
Quirigua Emblem Glyph, 148

radiocarbon dating, 13
raids
  Bonampak murals, 201
  late classic, 200, 204
rain forest environment, 10–11
Real Xe complex, 12, 15n
rebellion, 172
relative dating, 12–13
revolt, 226
Río Azul, 107
ritual ballgames, 149
river systems, 113–115
Rubber People, 17

Sacred Round, 33
sacrificial mutilation, 144, 150, 169, 196
sacrificial victims, 57, 85

sarcophagus of Janaab' Pakal, 142–143
sculpture
    destruction of, 119–120
    Izapa, 42
    late classic, 159, 202, 224–225, 227
    Mexican influence, 64
    Olmec, 18
    Tikal origins, 41–42
Seibal, 212–214, 218, 220
serpents, 18, 34
    scaled feathered-serpent helmet,
        62, 66, 69
    Temple of the Feathered Serpent, 62
    War Serpent, 66
Shook, Ed, 31–32, 234–235
Siyaj Kaan K'awil, 79–82
    death of, 85–86
    legacy, 88, 90
Siyaj K'ak', 66, 68–69, 71, 74–77
Sky-Born K'awil, 81–82
Sky Dynasty, 79–90
    late classic, 159–160
    restoration of, 141–142
Snake Jaguar, 143, 154
social hierarchy
    early classic, 49–51, 54n2
    preclassic, 24, 27
    proto-classic, 25–26
solar calendar, 25
solstice, 210
Spanish missionaries, 93
sports, 145–147
Stela 4, 64, 211
Stela 5, 173, 189
Stela 13, 213–214
Stela 16, 155, 158
Stela 20, 183
Stela 21, 169–170
Stela 22, 196, 199
Stela 29, 31–32, 34–36
Stela 30, 143–144

Stela 31, 68–69, 74, 79–80
Stela 32, 75
Stela 39, 44–45
Stela 40, 97–98, 104n4
Stela 8-11, 213
stela-altar complex, 21
Stephens, John Lloyd, 232
stone-tool production, 123
successor glyph, 38
Successor Vase, 43
Sun Pyramid, 61
survey techniques, 94
symbolism
    Mexican, 75–76, 145–147
    shells and feathers, 75

talud-tablero architecture, 53, 62
Temple I, 166–168, 208
Temple II, 152–154, 168n3, 208
Temple III, 206, 208, 210
Temple IV, 173–174, 190–193,
    208, 210
Temple V, 208
Temple VI, 187–188
Temple of the Feathered Serpent, 62
Temple of the Inscriptions, 143, 169,
    187–188
Teotihuacan, 61–63, 73–74. See also
    Mexico
    contribution to Burial 10, 63–64
    fall of, 95–96
    growth, early classic, 83–84
    population, 95
    trade, 95
theories
    on May collapse, 223–229
    on population disappearance, 227
Thomas, Cyrus, 55
Thompson, J. Eric S., 55
Tikal
    attack by Caracol, 117–118

decline and collapse, 223–229
defeat of, 118
founder of, 38, 40
friction with Calakmul, 100–101, 107
growth, early classic, 83–84
last days, 195–221
late classic revival, 188–190
Mexico's retreat from, 95–96
organization of monuments, 208
revival of Maya culture, 96
trade routes, 225
Tikal dynasty. *See also* Jaguar dynasty
origins of, 36, 38
Tikal Emblem Glyph, 36, 218, 220
Tlaloc, 63, 69
Tollan, 73–74
Toltecs, 73–74
Toniná, 154
Tozzer, Alfred M., 234
trade
Chichén Itzá, 215
early classic, 50–51, 60, 83–84
international, 226
Kaminaljuyu obsidian, 59–60
late classic, 142, 147–148, 155,
160, 171–172, 172, 188, 203,
211, 218, 220
middle classic, 95, 100, 114–115
preclassic, 7–8, 23
river (middle classic), 122
river systems, 113–115
Teotihuacan, 62–63
and Tikal's location, 225
Tula, 73–74
Tut, Ambrosio, 232
Twin Pyramid Complex N, 155–158
Twin Pyramid Complex P, 183
Twin Pyramid Complex Q, 196–199
Twin Pyramid Groups, 144
Tzolk'in, 33

Uaxactun, 25
University Museum, 234
University of San Carlos, 236
unrest, 199–200
Usumacinta districts
collapse, 204
Usumacinta River, 7, 113–115

volcanoes
Ixtepeque, 83
Volcán Ilopango, 25–26

Wak Kaan K'awil, 102, 103–104, 112
return of, 115–117
War Serpent, 66
warfare, 226. *See also* raids
water, potable, 7, 24, 214–215, 235
water wells, 214–215, 235
Well of the Itzá, 215
Wuk Ab'nal, 216–217

Xukpi, 128
Xukpi Stair, 83

Yajawte' K'inich, 117
Yax Eb' Xook, 38, 40, 42n3
descendants of, 187–188
Yax K'uk' Mo', 83
Yaxchilán, 132, 155, 172, 184
architecture and lintels, 113–114
Yaxun B'alam, 172, 184
Yik'in Kaan K'awil, 183–184,
188–190
accession to power, 169–170
palanquin wars, 173–174, 177
Yoat B'alam, 113
Yuknoom the Great, 132, 136

Zapotecs, 20
Zuyua language, 214–216

Other Maya-Interest Titles from Hippocrene...

Dictionary of Maya Hieroglyphs

John Montgomery

A visual dictionary of 1,100 secured glyphs—Each entry includes the glyph, its phonetic transcription, Mayan equivalent, part of speech, and meaning. A wide range of signs, a guide to pronunciation, extensive definitions, and multiple indices for cross-referencing comprise this unique reference. Glyph illustrations are drawn by the author.

1,100 entries • 250 pages • b/w line drawings • 6 x 9 • 0-7818-0862-6 • (337) • $19.95pb

How to Read Maya Hieroglyphs

John Montgomery

This complete outline of the hieroglyphic script of the ancient Maya serves as both an introduction to the script and a convenient reference to its basic features and symbols. It presents the script's content and grammatical structure, individual signs and their meanings, and explanations of the sophisticated Maya calendrical and mathematical systems. Glyph illustrations by the author, diagrams, maps, and photographs accompany the text.

250 pages • b/w line drawings, 8-page color insert • 6 x 9 • 0-7818-0861-8 • (332) • $24.00hc

Maya-English / English-Maya (Yucatec) Dictionary and Phrasebook

John Montgomery

With a selection of common words and phrases in Yucatec Maya (the most widely spoken branch of Maya), this dictionary and phrasebook includes phonetic pronunciation and translations for each word or phrase in English and Spanish, the language of most non-Maya communication in Mexico and Central America. An introduction to grammar, a pronunciation guide, and practical cultural information make this an ideal language guide for students, travelers, and Maya enthusiasts.

1,500 entries • 180 pages • 3¾ x 7 • 0-7818-0859-6 • (244) • $12.95pb

Mayan Cooking: Recipes from the Sun Kingdoms of Mexico

Cherry Hamman

The inspiration for this cookbook is the small village of Acabchen, a remote Maya pueblo where villagers still follow the customs of their ancestors. It contains more than 150 recipes that date back several centuries, as well as contemporary creations that represent Maya ingenuity and imagination in borrowing new foods and culinary ideas.

275 pages • b/w charcoal drawings • 5½ x 8½ • 0-7818-0580-5 • (680) • $24.95hc

Other Illustrated Histories from Hippocrene...

Arizona: An Illustrated History *(Patrick Lavin)*
252 pages • 60 photos/maps/illus. • 5 x 7 • 0-7818-0852-9 • (102) • $14.95pb

The Celtic World: An Illustrated History *(Patrick Lavin)*
185 pages • 50 photos/maps/illus. • 5 x 7 • 0-7818-0731-x • (582) • $14.95hc

China: An Illustrated History *(Yong Ho)*
142 pages • 50 photos/maps/illus. • 5 x 7 • 0-7818-0821-9 • (154) • $14.95hc

Cracow: An Illustrated History *(Zdzislaw Zygulski)*
160 pages • 60 photos/maps/illus. • 5 x 7 • 0-7818-0837-5 • (542) • $12.95pb

England: An Illustrated History *(Henry Weisser)*
166 pages • 50 photos/maps/illus. • 5 x 7 • 0-7818-0751-4 • (446) • $11.95hc

France: An Illustrated History *(Lisa Neal)*
214 pages • 55 photos/maps/illus. • 5 x 7 • 0-7818-0872-3 • (340) • $12.95pb

Greece: An Illustrated History *(Tom Stone)*
181 pages • 50 photos/maps/illus. • 5 x 7 • 0-7818-0755-7 • (557) • $14.95hc

Ireland: An Illustrated History *(Henry Weisser)*
166 pages • 50 photos/maps/illus. • 5 x 7 • 0-7818-0693-3 • (782) • $11.95hc

Israel: An Illustrated History *(David C. Gross)*
160 pages • 50 photos/maps/illus. • 5 x 7 • 0-7818-0756-5 • (024) • $11.95hc

Italy: An Illustrated History *(Joseph Privitera)*
142 pages • 50 photos/maps/illus. • 5 x 7 • 0-7818-0819-7 • (436) • $14.95hc

Korea: An Illustrated History *(David Rees)*
147 pages • 50 photos/maps/illus. • 5 x 7 • 0-7818-0873-1 • (354) • $12.95pb

Mexico: An Illustrated History *(Michael Burke)*
183 pages • 50 photos/maps/illus. • 5 x 7 • 0-7818-0690-9 • (585) • $11.95hc

Paris: An Illustrated History *(Elaine Mokhtefi)*
150 pages • 50 photos/maps/illus. • 5 x 7 • 0-7818-0838-3 • (136) • $12.95pb

Poland: An Illustrated History *(Iwo C. Pogonowski)*
270 pages • 50 photos/maps/illus. • 5 x 7 • 0-7818-0757-3 • (404) • $14.95hc

Poland in WWII: An Illustrated Military History *(Andrew Hempel)*
114 pages • 50 photos/maps/illus. • 5 x 7 • 0-7818-0758-1 • (541) • $11.95hc

Russia: An Illustrated History *(Joel Carmichael)*
252 pages • 50 photos/maps/illus. • 5 x 7 • 0-7818-0689-5 • (154) • $14.95hc

Spain: An Illustrated History *(Fred James Hill)*
175 pages • 50 photos/maps/illus. • 5 x 7 • 0-7818-0874-X • (339) • $12.95pb

Prices subject to change without notice. **To purchase Hippocrene Books** contact your local bookstore, call (718) 454-2366, or write to: HIPPOCRENE BOOKS, 171 Madison Avenue, New York, NY 10016. Please enclose check or money order, adding $5.00 shipping (UPS) for the first book and $.50 for each additional book.